WITHDRAWN

FROM

DMH STAFF LIBRARY

Accepting Voices

Prof. Marius Romme and Sandra Escher

DATE DUE FOR RETURN	
19 SEP 2001	
5 NOV 2002	
15 MAR 2004	
01 OCT 2004	
14 DEC 2004	
17 NOV 2006	
2 8 OCT 2011	
1 3 DEC 2012	
2 0 MAY 2014	
1 2 SEP 2017	

This book may be recalled before the above date

90014

M

Pu

MEDICAL LIBRARY
QUEEN'S MEDICAL CENTRE

First Published in Great Britain 1993
MIND Publications,
Kemp House, 1st Floor,
152-160 City Road,
London EC1V 2NP

from February 1994
Granta House,
15-19 Broadway
London E15

Original Dutch language edition (Stemmen Horen Accepteren) published by:

Rijksuniversiteit Limburg, Vakgroep Sociale Psychiatrie Siso. 86 UDC 616.89-052:editors
Prof. Dr. M.A.J. Romme; Mw. A.D.M.A.C. Escher

© Prof. Marius Romme and Sandra Escher

All rights reserved. No part of this book may be reprinted or reproduced or utilized in any
form or by electronic, mechanical, or other means, now known or hereafter invented,
including photocopying and recording, or in any information storage or retrieval system,
without permission in writing from the publishers.

ISBN 1 874690 13 8
cover design by Phil Ellington
Printed in Great Britain by Blackmore Press, Longmead Industrial Estate, Shaftesbury, Dorset.

100 2241419

CONTENTS

8. GROWING OUT OF PSYCHIATRIC CARE

9. HEARING VOICES: PSYCHIATRIC AND PSYCHOLOGICAL PERSPECTIVES

FOREWORD

The Rt. Hon. the Lord Ennals, President of MIND

If we are to believe the popular press, hearing voices is a phenomenon which almost always drives people to violent and destructive acts.

And if we are to believe orthodox psychiatry, the only way out for people who hear voices is to take drugs which may well take away the voices but can leave people feeling sluggish or restless; drugs which may even, it is said, leave the taker with permanent brain damage if taken in high doses over long periods of time.

Against this background, Accepting Voices destroys the popular press stereotype of mad people being dangerous and controlled by unseen evil forces. It also illustrates that a large number of us **do** have unusual auditory experiences; that many of us **do not** have recourse to psychiatry; and that quite a few of us **have** found ways of coping, without this interfering with our day-to-day life and activities.

The core of this book is, I believe, represented by the 13 personal accounts written by people who have come to terms, in one way or another, with their experiences and incorporated them into their lives. These accounts are interspersed with a variety of theoretical frameworks, some of which approach the phenomenon of hearing voices from outside the illness model, while others represent the frames of reference to be found within psychiatry itself.

The last section of the book will probably be the most useful to those who want to learn how to deal with their voices. This focuses on techniques designed to gain greater control of the experience and so ensure, as Professor Romme puts it, that personal growth is stimulated rather than inhibited.

Professor Marius Romme and Sandra Escher, the editors of this book, are to be congratulated not only for producing an excellent piece of original research to which many British and Dutch voice-hearers have contributed, but also for their tireless campaigning throughout Europe to overcome the social taboo surrounding the subject.

1. INTRODUCTION

Marius Romme and Sandra Escher

This book is primarily intended for those of you who hear voices. Our main objective is to enable you to relate to the experiences of other voice-hearers in a way that may help you to understand and manage your own. Voice-hearers and others interested in this phenomenon will know that it is not an easy subject to broach with those around us in everyday life; indeed, it is virtually taboo. We are therefore most grateful to those individuals who have been so willing to describe their experiences with voices, and who have put themselves at some risk in doing so. This is probably the only way to get this form of perception more widely understood and accepted.

Different people have widely different ways of coping with their voices. If you hear voices yourself, the way you cope today is not necessarily the only way. Chapters 6 and 8 tell the stories of various voice-hearers in their own words. A close reading will show that the blanket term hearing voices covers a wide range of highly divergent experiences.

A person who cannot cope with these voices usually ends up needing psychiatric help. The treatment offered has long been based on the view that the best outcome for the patient is the total eradication of the voices. This view has, however, gradually begun to change. People are starting to realize that the real problem is not so much the hearing of these voices, but rather the inability to cope with them.

Parts of this book will show that there are people who have developed a very positive relationship with the experience of hearing voices, and have managed without any psychiatric treatment or support. They have adopted a theoretical frame of reference (such as parapsychology, reincarnation, metaphysics, the collective unconscious, or the spirituality of a higher consciousness) which connects them with others rather than isolating them: they have found a perspective that offers them a language in which to share their experiences. They enjoy a feeling of acceptance; their own rights are recognized, and they develop a sense of identity which can help them to make constructive use of their experiences for the benefit of themselves and others. Some of these people describe their experiences in chapter 6.

The book also tells the stories of people who have needed psychiatric care because they have been unable to cope either with the hearing of voices or with associated problems in their daily lives. Chapter 8 gives their accounts of such experiences. We have chosen people who have managed to find their own individual ways of dealing - however painfully - with their voices and perceptions. From a psychiatric point of view, these could be described as severely ill people; they have all, at some point, been admitted to a psychiatric hospital. Should you meet them now, however, you would find that they radiate warmth, energy and strength. None, perhaps, could have come so far if they had not found partners, friends or family who were prepared to acknowledge and accept the presence of the voices and related perceptions.

It is also significant that these people continue, to some extent, to identify with their voices, but without this presenting any obstacle to normal social intercourse. The nature and extent of such identification varies greatly. A number of people who hear voices have arrived at the point where they have decided to refuse any further psychiatric assistance. This is usually because hearing voices has been considered solely as a symptom of illness, and the psychiatric intervention has paid no attention to the possible meaning of the voices within the patient's life history. This kind of treatment allows no room for identification with the voices, which is the essential first step towards effective coping; the concept of illness eclipses everything else.

In classical psychiatry, a hallucination is viewed primarily as a symptom of the severe mental illness known as schizophrenia. This was the perspective of almost all the fathers of psychiatry such as Kraepelin, Griesinger and Schneider. This interpretation has, however, been modified somewhat by subsequent eminent psychiatrists, Carl Jung being perhaps the best-known. The traditional model is also fundamentally questionable in the light of descriptions of hallucinations experienced in extreme circumstances: 80% of those who have endured torture have hallucinated during their ordeal (Amnesty International), and the phenomenon is also seen amongst long-distance yachtsmen (Bennet, 1972). In cases like these, there is no evidence of the presence of any mental illness - indeed, often quite the contrary.

Earlier research - much of which has provided the inspiration for this book - is dealt with in chapter 2, which also describes how the inability of so many people to cope with hearing voices led us to search for those who had found successful strategies. In chapter 3, Paul Baker reports on developments in Britain that were prompted by this investigation.

In chapter 4, Dr de Bruijn gives a brief historical summary which examines the perennial human search for ways of understanding and explaining unusual experiences and perceptions. This account highlights the difficulties, both for the individual and those around him or her, that make it hard to accept such phenomena.

Mutual support is of enormous importance in a situation that can be extremely difficult and painful. The enduring social taboo around the issue of hearing voices has provided much of the impetus for the formation of an organization to help voice-hearers to meet one another. The encouragement and promotion of communication amongst those who hear voices is a major priority for the British Hearing Voices Network, as well as for therapists and social workers. This kind of reciprocal communication has proved very useful for many people, as shown by Sandra Escher in chapter 5.

Chapters 6 and 8 are undoubtedly the most important parts of this book. These relate the personal experiences of those who hear or have heard voices: chapter 6 concentrates on a number of Dutch people who have never received professional psychiatric attention, while chapter 8 is devoted to the experiences of one Dutch and five British users and ex-users of the psychiatric system.

Chapter 7 examines some non-psychiatric perspectives on the subject which do not place hearing voices within the illness model. In chapter 9 we examine various approaches to be found within the psychiatric profession; these are included to acquaint the reader with the diversity of explanatory theories offered by psychiatry.

In chapter 10 we look at some strategies which may be useful in helping the voice-hearer to retain or regain some degree of control. Some of these can be put into practice by the voice-hearer him or herself, such as keeping a diary and participating in self-help groups; others, such as anxiety management techniques and medication, can be resorted to with the help of skilled professionals.

Chapter 11 offers a provisional summary of the book's scope and implications, and chapter 12 pays tribute to all our contributors, without whom this book would never have been possible.

Scientific analysis will always be of limited use in the understanding of hearing voices, because of the very nature of the phenomenon. To paraphrase Jung, when he talks about science and art, science works with concepts of averages which are far too general to do justice to the subjective variety of an individual life. The essence of hearing voices, as with art and religion, is its subjectivity. The exercising of choice and will, in situations where we can either express ourselves or lose ourselves, offers us the chance to experience our individuality. We must put our faith in the strengthening of this individuality - that which distinguishes one person from another - and in the struggle to develop it as a creative force to integrate ourselves in our daily lives.

We hope that those of you who hear voices will find a friend in this book, and that it may offer you some guidance towards a manageable relationship with your voices. We hope it will help you to use your experiences as positive, stimulating elements in your personal growth.

We hope, too, that your family, friends, therapists, and social workers will understand more clearly this important aspect of your life, be better able to accept your uniqueness, and offer whatever support you may choose to ask for.

2. THE NEW APPROACH: A DUTCH EXPERIMENT

Marius Romme and Sandra Escher

Beginnings

For some years, one of my patients, a 30-year old woman, has been hearing voices in her mind. These voices give her orders or forbid her to do things, and dominate her completely. She has been hospitalized several times and diagnosed as having schizophrenia. Neuroleptics have no effect on the voices, although they do reduce her anxiety. Unfortunately, these drugs also reduce her mental alertness; consequently, she does not take medication over long periods, nor does she remain long as an in-patient when she is hospitalized. Nevertheless, the voices have increasingly isolated her by forbidding her to do things she had always loved.

Last year she started to talk more and more frequently about suicide, and I could see her starting down a path from which there might be no return. The only positive note in our conversations at that time was provided by the theory she had developed about the nature of the voices. This theory was based on a book by the American psychologist Julian Jaynes, The Origin of Consciousness in the Breakdown of the Bicameral Mind (1976). She found it reassuring to read that the hearing of voices had been regarded as a normal way of making decisions until about 1300 BC. According to Jaynes, the experience of hearing voices has almost entirely disappeared and been replaced by what we now call consciousness.

I began to wonder whether she might prove to be a good communicator with others who also heard voices, and whether they might find her theory acceptable or useful. I thought this might have a positive effect on her isolation, her suicidal tendencies and her feelings of dependency on her voices. Together, she and I began to plan ways in which she might share some of her experiences and views.

In due course, we set up one-to-one meetings with others who heard voices. As I sat there listening to their conversations, I was struck by the eagerness with which they recognized one anothers' experiences. Initially, I found it difficult to follow these conversations: to my ears, the contents were bizarre and extraordinary, and yet all this was freely discussed as though it constituted a real world of and unto itself.

se meetings on several occasions, and every session
deal of mutual recognition. However, they also
d of powerlessness: in my experience, none of these
cope with their voices. We therefore had to think of
̄g..t bring us into contact with voice-hearers who did not
surrer this powerlessness and could even, perhaps, cope well. Television
seemed to us to offer the only way to communicate clearly about the
experience. We also wanted to reach a sufficiently large number of people
for us to stand a reasonable chance of finding someone who had
developed a good coping strategy - a way to help others achieve greater
control over their voices.

From this point, things progressed rapidly. Speaking on a popular
Dutch television programme, my patient and I invited people to contact
us, and after the broadcast, 700 people responded to our appeal. 450 were
voice-hearers: of these, 300 described themselves as unable to cope with
their voices, while 150 said they had found ways to manage theirs. The
response from this latter group was especially important in encouraging
me to organize contacts between people who heard voices and who
wanted to exchange ideas about their experiences. Because of the
practical difficulties involved in meeting with such a large number of
people, we first sent out a questionnaire; later, we organized a congress
for those who had responded to the television programme, in order to
gather more information.

The questionnaire

We were interested in a number of aspects such as: the age of onset, the
number and nature of the voices, events and experiences prior to the first
hearing, means of coping, the extent of control over the voices, medical
history, etc. Of most immediate interest, however, were the differences
between those who could cope well with their voices and those who could
not.

Comparisons between those who coped well with their voices and those who did not

The frequency of different types of response to hearing voices is
illustrated by the following tabulations of the questionnaire responses.
We organized the data according to the differences between those who

said they could cope (Group A) and those who said they could not (Group B). Table 1 shows some of the variables that appeared to distinguish the two groups.

Table 1

Differences between 'good' and 'bad' copers		
Total N=173=100%		
	A Group Coping	B Group Non-coping
	58 (34%)	115 (66%)
Which is stronger?		
self	39 (72%)	40 (38%)
voice	5 (10%)	44 (42%)
other	9 (16%)	20 (19%)
		p<0.001
	Group B voice more often the stronger	
Nature of voices		
positive	16 (30%)	10 (10%)
contradictory	14 (26%)	17 (16%)
negative	23 (43%)	75 (73%)
		p<0.001
	Group B voices more often negative	
Commanding voices		
yes	10 (20%)	26 (24%)
no	38 (74%)	41 (38%)
sometimes	3 (6%)	41 (38%)
		p<0.001
	Group A experienced fewer commands	

Many people (34%) reported that they were able to manage their voices well, but most (66%) said they could not. Those who managed well felt themselves to be stronger than the voices, while the reverse was true for the other group. Those who could not handle the voices generally experienced them as negative and aggressive, whereas those who could often experienced them as positive and friendly. Those who could cope well experienced fewer commands from their voices.

We were also interested to see what the differences were between the good and the bad copers in terms of the kinds of coping strategy used.

Table 2

Coping strategies comparing copers and non-copers			
	total	A Group Coping	B Group Non-coping
Distraction			
yes	42 (24%)	10 (26%)	32 (43%)
no	72 (42%)	29 (74%)	43 (57%)
missing	59 (34%)		p<0.05
		Group A less distraction	
Ignoring			
yes	54 (31%)	31 (56%)	23 (25%)
no	57 (33%)	21 (37%)	36 (39%)
sometimes	37 (21%)	4 (7%)	33 (36%)
missing	25 (14%)		p<0.001
		Group A more ignoring	
Selective listening			
yes	30 (17%)	19 (46%)	11 (14%)
no	87 (50%)	22 (53%)	65 (85%)
missing	56 (33%)		p<0.001
		Group A more selective listening	
Setting limits			
yes	45 (26%)	19 (48%)	26 (30%)
no	79 (46%)	20 (51%)	59 (70%)
missing	49 (28%)		p<0.001
		Group A set more limits	

Selective listening was entered for those who listened to some of their voices, eg the positive ones rather than the negative. Setting limits was entered for those who were able to say no, I will not listen to the voices any more when a voice became too strident or critical, etc. The A Group - the good copers - used more selective listening and set more limits. The A group was also better able to ignore the voices, and seldom used distraction techniques, while the reverse was true for the bad copers.

Another point of statistical interest to us was the difference between those who had been psychiatric patients and those who had not. The most relevant differences were as follows:

Table 3

Relevant differences between non-patients and patients		
	Non-patients	**Patients**
Marital status	**N=58**	**N=79**
single	11 (19%)	30 (38%)
married	35 (60%)	31 (39%)
divorced	11 (19%)	15 (19%)
widowed	1 (2%)	3 (4%)
	non-patients are more often married	
Perceived support	**N=70**	**N=96**
no	1 (2%)	47 (49%)
yes	69 (98%)	49 (51%)
	non-patients perceive more support	
Do others know about the voices?	**N=69**	**N=101**
no	2 (2%)	15 (14%)
yes	69 (98%)	86 (86%)
	non-patients communicate more about the voices	

As demonstrated by the above tables, there are considerable differences between the two groups. These are summarized in Table 4.

Table 4

Summary of differences	
Group A **People who can cope:**	**Group B** **People who cannot cope:**
– feel stronger	– feel weaker
– experience more positive voices	– experience more negative voices
– experience less commanding voices	– experience more commanding voices
– set more limits to voices	– do not dare to set limits to voices
– listen selectively to voices	– seek relief by using more distraction techniques
– experience more support from others	– experience less support
– communicate more often about their voices	– communicate less about their voices

These comparisons lead us to an important conclusion: the crucial advantage enjoyed by those who succeed in coping well is their greater strength with regard both to their voices and to their environment, and in their more favourable experience of that environment as supportive rather than threatening. We may therefore view the hearing of voices not solely as a discrete individual psychological experience, but as an interactional phenomenon reflecting the nature of the individual's relationship to his or her own environment, and indeed vice versa. In other words, it is not only a psychological but also a social phenomenon.

From those who returned the questionnaire, we selected a number of people who could cope with their voices, and invited them for an interview to discuss their ways of coping. We then selected 20 who were able to explain their experiences clearly. On 31 October 1987, these 20 became the speakers at a conference attended by 360 voice-hearers.

The conference

The conference was held in a large trade union hall with no connection, physical or otherwise, to any psychiatric or medical institution. Although members of our psychiatry department were active in organizing and facilitating the meeting, the plenary speakers were all people who heard voices and had responded to the television programme. Following the morning plenary session, there was a series of smaller 1-hour workshops with facilitators from the department of psychiatry, who did not lead the discussions but rather guided or assisted as necessary.

Professor Strauss from New Haven, who attended as a guest of the authors, said of the conference:

The general atmosphere of the entire conference was of a meeting by a group of people with common interests and experiences. Although medical aspects of these experiences were discussed, there was no sense that this was a medical meeting or a meeting of medical patients. The participants freely shared their experiences, their many interpretations of these experiences, including religious views and a range of other human reactions, and their approaches to coping. Some people were obviously troubled by their voices and saw them as part of a mental illness, but many had very different ways of understanding these experiences and appeared to be competent, far from disabled, and - depending on one's view of the nature of voices - not in any way ill.

The considerable range of experiences described by the participants, and the many ways they dealt with these experiences - successfully or otherwise - can be viewed from many perspectives. It seems most useful to divide the common experience of their accounts into three possible phases with regard to coping with voices:

- **The startling phase:** the usually sudden onset, primarily a frightening experience;
- **The phase of organization:** the process of selection and communication with the voices;
- **The stabilization phase:** the period in which a more consistent, ongoing means of dealing with the voices is developed.

Many of the conference participants described phases which fell approximately into these types. For example, one of the speakers distinguished the following phases in the process of learning to cope with the voices:

1. Fear, anxiety and escape; 2. investigation of what the voices mean, and accepting them as independent entities; and 3. accepting myself, exploring what it is that I try to escape from, reversing the confrontation with the voices, and not trying to escape any more.

In the following pages, we will illustrate these three phases as found among people who had learnt to handle their voices.

The startling phase

Most voice-hearers described the onset of the experience as being quite sudden, startling and anxiety-provoking, and could vividly remember the precise moment:

On a Sunday morning at ten oclock, it was suddenly as if I received a totally unexpected and enormous blow on my head. I was alone, and was given a message - a message that would have shocked even a dog. I immediately panicked, and couldn't stop terrible things from happening. My first reaction was: What on earth is happening? The second was: I'm probably just imagining things. Then I thought: No, you're not imagining it, you have to take this seriously.

The age of onset for the initial experience of voices varied widely, as did the intensity of the startling phase, which appeared to be most severe when onset occurred during the vulnerable years of adolescence. The confusion seemed to be somewhat less total when voices had been heard from a very early age, or did not make their appearance until later in adulthood.

Many respondents stated that their voices had started in childhood. For 6% the age of onset was before the age of six; for 10% it was between ages ten and 20; and for 74% after the age of 20. One of the speakers recounted her first experience as a child:

For as long as I can remember I have had one, and later more, voices inside myself. My earliest memories of them go back to kindergarten. Perhaps it sounds funny, but I had two egos. A normal child-ego, in keeping with my age, and an adult-ego. The voice adapted itself to both of these. It spoke a child-language to the child-ego and an adult-language to the other. The adult-ego gradually disappeared in primary school. As a child, I didn't experience having these two egos as being strange. In fact, for a child, nothing is strange.

One of those who began hearing voices in adolescence - a period of developing personal independence - told us:

In 1977, after leaving secondary school, I decided to move into lodgings. I must say student life was fascinating, but I didn't sleep enough, and didn't eat regularly. After a few months, I fancied painting the large white wall in my room; this wall was a challenge to me. I began painting a dark forest on it, with a reptile in the foreground. Painting is something which is transmitted from your head to your hand, and I have always been able to hear colours; they are transmitted by vibrations. I hear black, red and dark brown. It was deathly quiet as I painted in the room, as I didn't have a radio on or anything. In the stillness, however, I felt something alarming beginning to grow - some threatening presence hovering, and I had the distinct impression that I was no longer alone in the room. Then I heard in my ears a monotonous noise which was not from myself and which I could not explain. It was a bit like the sound you hear when you put your fingers in your ears, only this sound was lower and more monotonous. It was an emotion, too, but even deeper than that, and I had the sensation that something was searching for me.

Circumstantial background

To the question whether the onset of the voices had been due to a certain event, 70% of the respondents answered that their voices had begun after a traumatic or emotional event, such as an accident (4%), divorce or bereavement (14%), a psychotherapy session (12%), or a spiritualist experience (4%). Others (36%) cited illness, love affairs, moving house, or pregnancy.

Impact of the voices

People who had first heard voices after a trauma described two main types of impact. For the more fortunate group, this was the perception of the voices as helpful, and representing the beginning of an integrative coping process. They evoked a feeling of recognition, or marked the start of a period of rest after an unhappy time. As time went on, these people felt the purpose of the voices was to strengthen them, for example, or to raise their self-esteem. The voices were experienced positively, and as understandable aspects of their internal selves.

For other, less fortunate people, the voices were experienced as aggressive and negative from the very beginning. One woman said:

The positive voices were suddenly accompanied by what I call real crooks, who could become very nasty. And, they came from everywhere: in my head, behind me, in front of me. It seemed as if telephone lines operated from inside my chest.

For these individuals, the voices were hostile, and were not generally accepted as parts of the self or as internally-generated phenomena.

People who suffered negative voices often felt them to be causing chaos in their minds, and demanding so much attention that they could hardly communicate with the outside world any more. One man reported:

In no time (through the voices), I made contact with family members, friends, neighbours, colleagues, my psychiatrist, the police, secret service, criminals, politicians, members of the royal family and other well-known people. I got in touch with plants, animals and objects. I even discovered robot people. Once, my brother came to visit me; his eyes were a bit glassy, and his skin seemed smooth, and I thought he had been replaced by a robot. I had to be careful, because robots are awfully strong. I chatted to him superficially and got rid of him as soon as possible.

The phase of organization: coping with the voices

Many respondents became confused by their voices and wanted to escape. For some, this urge lasted only weeks or months; for others, many years. It seems clear that, for the phase of organization to be at all successful, some form of acceptance must take place: denial does not work. During this phase, people reported varying degrees of success in the attempt to achieve a modus vivendi with their voices. Strategies included ignoring the voices (distraction), listening to them selectively, entering into willing dialogue with them, and making specific appointments with them. Attempts at distraction and ignoring were rarely effective.

From the interviews, it emerged that after the initial feelings of panic and powerlessness, there was often a period of great anger towards the voices. This anger, however, did not seem to be fruitful as part of any coping strategy. Mr R. told us:

Every time I thought I had telepathic contact with people, I would go to visit them. If these people denied having telepathic contact with me, then I argued with the voices. So we bickered with each other; there was a lot of negative communication, and this only made the voices stronger and more aggressive.

Ignoring the voices was another strategy employed by those with unfriendly voices. However, only 31% of our questionnaire respondents reported any success in this attempt: it seems that the effort involved often led to a severe restriction of lifestyle, as in the following account:

Finally, I decided to ignore the voices, and asked them to leave me alone. In my ignorance I handled this in completely the wrong way. You can't just brush aside something that is in yourself and manifesting so powerfully. In any case, the result - for the voices themselves - of any successful attempt to do this would be that they would lose their right to exist because of a lack of attention and energy, and of course this was not what they wanted. Until then, the voices had always been polite and friendly, but they now changed in the opposite direction: they said all kinds of strange things, and made the things that were important to me look ridiculous. It was a full-blown civil war, but I was determined to win and continued to ignore everything they said. I did this by keeping myself busy the entire day. In that period, I solved a lot of crossword puzzles, my house had never been cleaner, and my allotment was never better tended. The result was that life became more peaceful, but in a constrained way; I almost couldn't relax any more.

The most fruitful strategy described to us was to select the positive voices and listen and talk only to them, and try to understand them. The woman quoted above said:

In this period of ignoring the voices, to my surprise there were two voices that wanted to help me. My first reaction was to send them away, because the whole thing was getting on my nerves, but they insisted that I needed them, and to be honest, I realized this was true. The voices taught me how to watch, hear, and feel. For example, they asked me:
How do you hear us, and in what way do we talk to you?
I replied, rather cheekily:
Well, I just hear you with my ears, and you talk with your mouths.
Oh really?, was the answer, then where are our larynxes? And by the way, we would ask you to mind how you answer us.
I was very amused by this last remark. At first I took everything literally, which didn't improve my already strained relations with the voices. But then we agreed to say everything twice, at least the important things: once as we always did, and the second time in symbols, in an expressive way. The receiver would repeat briefly the essence of what had been said. At first this was rather stilted - I wasn't at all used to thinking in symbols. But I could immediately apply what they taught me, and as a result I began to feel better.

An important element in coping successfully proved to be acceptance of the voices; this appears to be related to a process of growth towards taking responsibility for one's own decisions. It is generally unproductive to try to blame others for one's problems, and this is also true with regard to a phenomenon such as hearing voices. As some people described it, you have to learn to think in a positive way about yourself, your voices, and your own problems. Another strategy that was frequently mentioned was setting limits or structuring the contact, occasionally accompanied by ritualized or repeated actions. An example was given by someone who heard negative voices and interpreted them as follows:

You must understand that I was attacked by a force of evil. With my ego-will, I choose not to be identified with the evil. The evil in myself, the evil in others, the evil in things surrounding me - I don't want it to be there. That's why I make gestures. You can also do that in your mind. I think you can only really turn your back on the voices by making a physical gesture:
This is not for me, I throw the message away. That gives me a feeling of relief, and then I think:
There, good riddance to bad rubbish. Next, I send the messenger away, and say aloud or in my mind:

You just go to your friends, don't bother me with this. That is the first step. The second step is choosing, with my own will, the things I want to be in contact with; to associate with the light in me, the most beautiful thing there is. I have a source of heat and a healthy core, consisting of pure healthy energy. I know that such a thing is present in every human being, and that we can choose whether to contact it or not.

The phase of stabilization

People who had learned to cope with their voices had found a kind of equilibrium. In this state of balance, people would consider the voices as a part of themselves and of their lives, and capable of a positive influence. During this phase, the individual is able to choose between following either the advice of the voices or his or her own ideas, and can say:

I hear voices, and I'm happy about it.

One woman told us:

They show me the things I do wrong, and teach me how to do them differently. But they leave it to me to decide whether I really want to change them or leave them as they are. For example, they think the way I listen to music isn't right. I lose myself in music, and they think I shouldn't. I tried listening the way they think I should, but found it too much effort. I didn't see the use of it. This kind of decision always involves consultation, but I have the final say and the voices always accept it.

Another speaker said:

Later on, it seemed as if life was slowing down a little. I was in calmer waters and I could concentrate on my own life again.

A third woman put it like this:

When you fall off your bicycle, you don't throw it away - you adjust your way of riding and carry on using it, with yourself and the bicycle in the proper relation to one another. You create a beautiful bicycle ride. It can be like this in your inner self, too. I have finally reached the point

where I feel myself to be neither winner nor loser, but rather as if a
dimension has been added to my life - a dimension that, with courage,
can be handled, and that can be useful in the end.

Personal approaches to understanding

In the introduction we noted that one of our patients who heard voices
had been somewhat reassured by adopting a specific frame of reference to
account for her experiences. We wondered whether others would share
her theory. This proved to be naive of us, because it soon became clear
that there were a great many disparate perspectives used by voice-
hearers. These included psychodynamic, mystical, parapsychological,
and medical models, often based to some extent on the published writings
of authors such as Jung, Ehrenwald, Roberts, Pierrakos, and Atkinson.
In an attempt to classify this enormous variety of explanatory
frameworks, we divided them into two main categories: those treating
the voices as a (broadly) psychological phenomenon arising from within
the individual; and those treating the voices as a phenomenon of non-
psychological origin.

Psychological

These perspectives have their origins in many scholarly sources. Carl
Jung, for example, offered a psychodynamic model suggesting that
impulses from the unconscious mind might speak to us through visions or
voices. We found that Jung's work in this field appealed to a great many
voice-hearers, who often reported having gained a deeper understanding
of their voices and what those voices were trying to tell them.

An associated theory (Putnam, 1987) focuses more specifically on
psychodynamic mechanisms for the processing of profound emotional or
physical suffering. It is assumed that a person may react to an extremely
traumatic experience - such as incest, parental abuse, accidental injury,
kidnapping, or acts of war - by isolating these memories from the
consciousness. The trauma then returns in the form of flashbacks,
feelings of persecution, aggressive voices, or terrifying images. This, too,
was found by many of our participants to be a fruitful interpretation of
their experiences.

Mysticism offers another possible explanation which assumes a
positive, developmental function for the voices - a model which
encourages the fearless embracing of the experience as a natural and
creative element in spiritual growth (Roberts, 1979). This view is notable
for its implication that hearing voices, far from being an affliction, is

indeed a privilege which may provide the means towards a kind of divine enlightenment beyond the confines of the ego.

Some parapsychological interpretations also treat hearing voices as a special gift or sensitivity deriving from a more subtle level of consciousness. Within this interpretation, the gift has a particular value in that it is also capable of being exercised for the benefit of others through the practices of clairvoyance or mediumship. In accepting this model, one would be anxious not to lose such a sensitivity, but rather to manage and direct it.

Non-psychological

Within this group, many participants sought to describe their experiences in terms closely allied to what has become known as biological psychiatry. This approach, as in classical psychiatry, treats hearing voices as the symptom of an illness, but in this case with the emphasis firmly on organic dysfunction - in other words, on a physical or chemical breakdown within the brain. The implication of this model is that proper biological treatment will put things back to normal. One speaker said:

I have never experienced the voices as something from outside myself; I know they are inside me and that I can do something about them. I take medication on a daily basis, and I know I will have to do so for the rest of my life. However, this doesn't bother me. I have been working for ten years as a secretary, and I feel good.

Another, very different, variety of non-psychological explanation was presented by the Dutch Society for Natural Medicine, a group which interprets voices as coming from the wandering spirits of the dead. Some religious groups, such as Jehovah's Witnesses, go further and consider hearing voices to be evidence of possession by demons. For example, one person said:

I heard three to five different voices. They were sexless and always threatening. I had to do exactly what they said. One day they even ordered me to kill my stepfather, but at the last moment I snapped out of it. Shortly afterwards I admitted myself to a psychiatric hospital. I got medication, but the voices remained. Then, as a result of my hobby, which is medieval art and history, I started reading the Bible. I now believe that Jesus healed people like myself, as in the story of the possessed man. (Matthew VIII, verses 1-5 and Mark V, verses 2-20)

All the frames of reference outlined above lead to certain therapeutic strategies associated with their theoretical assumptions. Some implied progressions are as follows:

Psychological:
- Psychodynamics: psychotherapy focusing on archetypes and blocked emotions.
- Mysticism: mystical training, eg meditation and transcendent practices.
- Parapsychology: learning to deal with different levels of consciousness and control one's sensitivity.

Non-psychological:
- Biological psychiatry: medication.
- Natural Medicine (as interpreted by the Dutch Society for Natural Medicine): creative interaction with the spirits of the dead.
- Religion: faith healing.

Whatever the perspective adopted, some kind of explanatory theory does appear to be essential to the development of a coping strategy. Unless some meaning is attributed to the voices, it is very difficult to begin the phase of organizing one's relationship with them in order to reduce anxiety. Generally speaking, however, those perspectives which encourage the individual from seeking mastery over the voices tend to yield the least positive results. Interpreting one's voices as the manifestations of electronic influences might be one such example. The explanation offered by biological psychiatry may also be unhelpful in terms of coping strategies, given that it, too, places the phenomenon beyond one's personal grasp.

Implications for the psychiatric profession

Much of what we heard at the Congress confirmed that the reduction of hearing voices to the status of mere pathology is not very fruitful in helping patients to deal with these experiences. It may also be an inaccurate analysis. Outside the world of psychiatry, there are many people who hear voices and manage to live with the experience; some, indeed, find it an enrichment to their lives. It could therefore be extremely worthwhile for those working in the mental health professions to examine in greater detail which frames of reference and coping strategies seem to be most helpful to such patients; we might, by doing so, be able to support and assist them much more effectively in their attempts to deal with their extraordinary experiences.

The main steps in this process are the following:

- – to accept the patient's experience of the voices. These voices are often felt as more intense and real than sensory perceptions.
- – to try to understand the different languages used by patients to describe and account for their experiences, as well as the languages spoken by the voices themselves. There is often a world of symbols and feelings involved; for example, a voice might speak of light and dark when expressing love and aggression.
- – to consider helping the individual to communicate with the voices. This may involve issues of differentiating between good and bad voices and of accepting the patient's own negative emotions. This kind of acceptance may make a crucial contribution to the promotion of self-esteem.
- – to encourage the patient to meet other people with similar experiences and to read about hearing voices, in order to help overcome isolation and taboo.

For most psychiatrists, these steps will demand a considerable enlargement of clinical perspective, and should broaden the generally accepted theories within the profession. We are very interested in hearing from fellow practitioners in the field about their experiences or views in relation to any of the issues and suggestions aired by the conference participants.

References

Atkinson, J.M. (1985) Schizophrenia: A Guide for Sufferers and Their Families; Turnstone Press, Wellingborough

Ehrenwald, J. (1978) The ESP Experience; Basic Books, New York

Jaynes, J. (1976) The Origin of Consciousness in the Breakdown of the Bicameral Mind; Houghton Mifflin, Boston

Jung, C. (1961) Memories, Dreams, Reflections; Pantheon Books, Random House, New York

Pierrakos, E. (1979) The Path; Phoenicia, New York

Putnam, F. (1987) Dissociation as a Response to Extreme Trauma; presented at a diagnostic workshop, Free University, Amsterdam

Roberts, J. (1979) Seth Speaks: The Eternal Validity of the Soul; Prentice Hall, Englewood Cliffs, New Jersey

Romme, M; Escher, A. (1989) Hearing Voices; Schizophrenia Bulletin, vol. 15, no. 2, pp.209-216

Romme, M; Honig, A; Noorthoorn, E.; Escher, A. (1992) Coping with Hearing Voices: An Emancipatory Approach; British Journal of Psychiatry, no. 161, pp.99-103

Acknowledgement

We would particularly like to thank Prof. Dr John Strauss from New Haven, who attended the first conference for people hearing voices in Utrecht in 1987, and who rewrote our article for the Schizophrenia Bulletin in which our experiment was first published. This chapter comprises elements from that article and from another in the British Journal of Psychiatry referring to the same experiment.

3. THE BRITISH EXPERIENCE
Paul Baker

The search for new explanations

In 1988 I met Marius Romme and Sandra Escher in Trieste at a conference sponsored by the World Health Organization entitled 'The Question of Psychiatry'. I was there to speak about Manchester MIND's campaigning and development work in the search for non-medical solutions to mental health problems; Marius and Sandra were presenting information about their work on hearing voices. During the conference, we discussed one another's work, and I was particularly enthusiastic about the approach they were taking with this issue. This was partly because I had a relative who experienced a form of voice-hearing, and partly because as a community development worker I was concerned to promote and support initiatives that helped people to maintain their own autonomy in the face of very distressing and little-understood symptoms. Perhaps because I was not part of the medical world of mental health, I was quite open to the proposition put forward by Marius and Sandra that voices were actually perceived by hearers, and that they had meaning beyond the accepted wisdom that they were merely hallucinations. We promised to keep in touch, and I went away from Trieste invigorated by the creative thinking behind this approach.

A short while later, in November 1988, I was invited by Marius Romme to attend a conference in Maastricht entitled 'People Who Hear Voices'. The conference was held in a prestigious national conference centre in Maastricht (Netherlands), and was organized jointly by a group called Resonance Foundation (a self-help organization of voice-hearers) and the Department of Social Psychiatry at Limburg University. This was an opportunity for professionals to listen to the direct experiences of voice-hearers alongside current theoretical frameworks. It also presented radical interpretations of the phenomenon, and proposed ways to help people to cope with the experience. At the heart of this pioneering approach was the drive to rescue the hearing of voices from the impersonality of the illness model. Such was the credibility of this campaign in Holland that the meeting was opened by the Chief Inspector for Mental Health from the Ministry of Health & Welfare for the Netherlands.

The conference followed three years of work which had presented many challenges to existing interpretations of hearing voices. When I interviewed Marius Romme just after the conference, he recalled:

The decision to hold a conference was not mine, but that of the Resonance Foundation. The patients felt that professionals were not accepting the reality of their voices. On this occasion, rather greater numbers of professionals than voice-hearers were invited. The voice-hearers hoped, by talking about their experiences, to explain what was actually happening, as opposed to the professionals' theory of what was happening. They were trying to bridge a very real gap by enabling the professionals to meet normal, healthy people who heard voices without being psychotic. These people had learnt to cope with the voices by forming their own theories to provide an anchor for them. (Baker, 1988)

The conference was fascinating and extremely useful. Fundamental to the approach adopted by Marius, Sandra and Resonance has been its emphasis on partnership between the voice-hearers themselves and the allied professionals, who followed their lead; this was indeed a refreshing change from most of the approaches I had come across before, which rarely - if ever - gave such importance to the views of those who actually experienced the mental health difficulties under consideration (Baker, 1989). The Dutch story is told in full elsewhere in this book, but I wanted to emphasize this starting point, as it had a powerful effect on me.

A brief history of the development of the British Network

I ask you to try to do the same in England. Groups need to be established in each country, where people can talk together about hearing voices... it takes groups of people with the same experiences to change attitudes... in America and England at the moment, psychiatrists are conducting themselves as parents. My goal is not to change psychiatry, not to change the parents, but to offer the hearers of voices an organization through which they can emancipate themselves. (Baker, 1988)

Following the conference, and with these words from Marius fresh in my mind, I wrote an article for the National MIND magazine OPENMIND, which was published in August 1989 (Baker, 1989), and this attracted some interest from voice-hearers and concerned professionals. Shortly before publication, Nigel Rose and Mark Greenwood (founder members of the National Hearing Voices Network) went over to Maastricht, and during that year other contacts were made with interested individuals across the UK.

This interest led to a visit to the UK, in the summer of 1989, by Marius Romme, Sandra Escher and a representative of Resonance, Ans Streefland. They spoke at a series of well-attended public meetings in the north-west of England (Greater Manchester, Liverpool and Sheffield) to discuss the results of their work. These meetings were attended by survivors and their families, mental health workers and members of the public. Individual responses varied, with a certain amount of professional resistance evident, but on the whole the reaction was positive. Certainly there was an enthusiastic response from voice-hearers themselves. One meeting, attended by over 100 people, proved an almost cathartic arena for many voice-hearers, most of whom were speaking publicly for the first time about their own experiences and own interpretations of their meaning.

As a consequence of this visit, other initiatives began to be developed in this country to raise the issue amongst voice-hearers, professionals and the public at large. A national group met in London to promote the various alternative perspectives offered by this new approach. Groups were set up in Manchester and London, and a meeting was held in Nottingham in March 1990. The London and Manchester groups planned further conferences similar to the first one held in Holland in 1987. To prepare the ground in Manchester, Alan Leader from Lambeth Link came in October 1990 to talk to a crowded meeting at the Town Hall about his own experiences of hearing voices. Alan had spent 20 years in various mental institutions as a diagnosed schizophrenic, and spoke of how he had learnt to live with his voices and even to use them to help him in everyday life. There were many voice-hearers at the meeting, and it was generally agreed that it was important for people to get together and talk about their experiences. Alan himself set an encouraging example by talking so freely in public about his own experience.

The first British conference

The first British conference organized by members of the Manchester Hearing Voices Group was held in Manchester in November 1990. The aims of the conference were:

1. To establish a network of people who have had this experience and are interested in self-help, and so bring people together to share their experiences and to discuss strategies for coping with them.
2. To try to broaden professionals' approach to the phenomenon.

Fourteen voice-hearers participated in the conference, which was organized specifically for them to share their voice experiences. It was also attended by Myrtle Heery (see chapter 7), a researcher from California who came to observe the day's proceedings. Myrtle's research interests paralleled Marius Romme's in many ways: her study was concerned to

dispel the common stereotype of the inner voice as the prerogative of saints and psychotics, and thereby encourage research into its liberating effect on our human capacities. (Heery, 1989)

The conference was audio-taped so that the rich diversity of perspectives for understanding could be reproduced in a report. (Grierson, 1991)

Many participants denounced the common view that hearing voices is somehow an unreal event. The classical psychiatric interpretation tends to mask the wealth of individual experiences and the many different ways of understanding and relating to them. Several speakers echoed the assertion that voice experiences are real experiences, parts of their lives that have to be taken seriously. One of the opening speakers put it succinctly:

It's an experience that I have, and its real.

The conference heard of the great variety of such experiences: for some, a number of voices engaged themselves in conversation in the hearers' heads; for others, the affair consisted largely of voices continually repeating nonsense, the tireless repetitions driving them to their wits end. Some experienced wonderful, even addictive voices that brought comfort. A number of people reported voices telling them incredible, fantastic things, making exaggerated promises. There were voices persecuting people, telling them they were wicked and evil. One man spoke of his voices playing a part in his sexual fantasies, and this led to a discussion in which other participants grudgingly revealed a similar role for their voices! Some people spoke about their voices as the manifestations of telepathic communication.

Many made the distinction between the voices they heard inside their heads and others that were clearly outside of themselves. For some, the voices were a mundane experience, and something that they didn't spend a great deal of time thinking about - the voices were just there. The voices were familiar and recognizable to some, while for others they were the voices of strangers. Many of the participants said that they would be terribly lonely without their voices, or that their voices were a good influence upon them.

There are many distressing problems that can arise from the experience of hearing voices, not least those caused by the present stigma attached to the issue. These can, however, be overcome if people succeed in developing the confidence and skill to affirm and describe their voice experiences. Those taking part in the conference were pleased to share with others the events and ideas that had, until then, remained all too private. The clear hope emerged that this meeting could be the beginning of a wider movement that might help to change our society's perception of the phenomenon.

Publicity and taboo

One of the most difficult obstacles to the acceptance of hearing voices is the social taboo that surrounds the subject. Consequently, good publicity is of the greatest importance in the struggle to remove this handicap, and we were glad that press and radio were willing to help this young plant to grow. Following the first conference, The Independent on Sunday (C. Azis, January 6 1991) published a sympathetic article on the topic. This generated a great deal of public interest, and further enquiries from the media led to members of the Network appearing on the Radio 4 programme 'Medicine Now' and the Capital Radio programme 'Philip Hodson Confidential'. Interviews were also broadcast by BBC Radio Wales, Radio Leeds and Greater Manchester Radio.

The London conference 1991

In March 1991, over 200 people attended a conference on hearing voices in London. This was the biggest UK event to date, and had been organized by the Network and Lambeth Link. Many of the participants were hearers of voices, and the remainder primarily professional mental health workers, with a scattering of relatives and people from voluntary groups.

The morning's proceedings included speeches from: Alan Leader and Anne Walton about their experiences of hearing voices; Marius Romme and Sandra Escher on the research they are doing in Holland; Mike Grierson, a sociologist from Manchester, talking about science and the way it can abuse people who hear voices unless research is carried out compassionately and sensitively; a psychiatrist who described her research on the use of earplugs, personal stereos and singing to oneself as methods of coping with hearing voices; and myself from Manchester on the politics of hearing voices. The afternoon consisted of workshops in which people could discuss their experiences and how they had learnt to live with their voices. Professionals and relatives had the chance to ask questions and join in the discussions. Following this, everybody got together in the main hall and was given the opportunity to say what they had thought of the conference and what they thought should happen next. Most people were very enthusiastic about the conference, and were pleased to have had the opportunity to listen to the experiences of voice-hearers. It was clear that these new explanations for the phenomenon had given many people new hope and determination to find their own ways of coming to terms with their voices.

The conference ended with a very positive message: that the work would continue, and that a network for voice-hearers had been launched. It was also decided that a further meeting needed to be organized during the year because of the overwhelming numbers of people who had wanted to attend this meeting but had to be turned away.

The third national conference

This was held in September 1991 in the Department of Sociology at Manchester University, and was attended by 30 people from all over Britain. It demonstrated once again the vital need for more understanding and acceptance of the experience of hearing voices. All those attending and speaking were themselves voice-hearers, with their own personal approaches and explanations, some people taking medication and others not.

Anne Walton (a member of the Manchester Self-Help Group since November 1990) spoke of how she had become involved with the Hearing Voices movement, and reported on the progress of the Network. Mickey De Valda (another member of the same Manchester group) spoke about the effects of medication abuse and the denial of basic rights in hospitals and other institutions. Sandra Charnock, a student psychiatric nurse, came from Doncaster to say that hearing voices was not an unusual experience in her family, and described how she had learned successfully to live with them. Afterwards, small workshops were held for people to discuss their voices and their theories about them. In the plenary session, many of the participants said how much they had enjoyed the conference, and it was agreed that Mike Grierson would produce a report on what had taken place.

The Manchester hearing voices conference 1992

This conference was held at a newly opened psychiatric hospital in North Manchester and was the first attempt to develop a dialogue between voice hearers and mental health professionals including psychiatrists. Professor Marius Romme, the psychologist Richard Bentall from Liverpool University, and Professor Alec Jenner from Sheffield, spoke to an audience of over 100 people. The key note speech was delivered by Sandra Escher who said the following about what really helps voice hearers:

Persons who hear voices and who have learnt to cope with them, all stipulate how important it was for them to have a friend, partner or relative who listened to them, accepted them and with whom they felt secure. A relationship such as this can offer security during those periods in which the voices are dominant. It is crucial to seek the proper support during these episodes... Giving support means that a person does not become dependent. The reason for this is to provide growth potential for self-confidence and self-management. Voices are a big challenge that can be seen as a threat or an inspiration. Either the voices can make a person helpless or they can act as teachers who can help one to live a more prepared life. Personal growth can only be realized in a stimulating environment with social possibilities. The final objective is to develop an identity as a person who hears voices.

The importance of a diversity of explanations - hearing voices conference, Manchester 1993

This was the most ambitious conference held so far. Over 150 people attended from all over the country to participate in a day that explored a range of different approaches that help explain voices and assist people to come to terms with them. Speakers included experts on the medical approaches and the use of medication, but there were also presentations on spiritualism, parapsychology, psychology and self-help. Participants explored practical applications of the above approaches in workshops, particularly the use of meditation, distraction and focusing techniques, managing medication, establishing self-help networks and the use of astrological charts.

The basis of this conference was to challenge the way psychiatry has narrowed the understanding of voices as being a problem, and to consider other perspectives. As Marius Romme said at the conference,

It is quite ridiculous to reduce our perceptional possibilities to our five senses and to reduce our communication to our motor speech activities. Everyone who ever loved somebody knows better. But the importance of the spiritual perception is that of inspiration, that of learning to grow; the possibility to open up beyond our daily hassles. The importance of parapsychology is that it has taught us that intuition and psychic perceptions need to be checked; that you have to learn to control the impressions, and that training is needed. We also need to realize that we are not able to control all the influences on us because we live in a grim society, with discrimination, aggression, injustice in so many different areas. I think it is of great importance to listen in a systematic way and to inform ourselves through dialogue with the person who hears voices about all aspects of those voices.

Establishing the British Hearing Voices Network

We had to establish a network of voice-hearers and interested individuals in Britain and by September 1993 the membership list had grown to over 350 people. All those on the list receive the quarterly National Hearing Voices Network Newsletter. First produced in the autumn of 1990, it is distributed free and provides information on Network activities, useful publications, and accounts from voice-hearers in the UK. We also produce an information pack, and have published four pamphlets: including the report of the first Manchester conference, an overview of the Dutch research on the subject and the development of their network. In addition to the Network contact list, there are now also several self-help groups in existence; the first of these was formed in Manchester, while others have been set up in London, Doncaster, Oxford, Liverpool, Huddersfield, Wakefield, Fife, Edinburgh, Oldham and Gwynedd.

The Network was set up to assist voice-hearers to find their own ways of coming to terms with their voices by showing that:

- there are various explanations for the experience of hearing voices which empower voice-hearers and enable them to live with the experience in a positive way;
- there are people who have found alternative explanations for their voices outside of the psychiatric model and ways of coping without the use of drugs;
- people who hear voices can be assisted in developing ways of coping better with their voices by participating in self-help groups

in which they can share experiences, explanations and methods of coping and benefit from mutual support.

People who hear voices, their families and friends can gain a lot from destigmatizing the experience as it will lead to greater tolerance and understanding. This can be achieved through promoting more positive explanations which give people a framework for developing their own ways of coping and by raising awareness about the experience in society as a whole.

Our aims are:

- to establish a large national network of people who hear voices and allies to gain a better understanding of the experience;
- to set up self-help groups of voice-hearers to share experiences and discuss strategies for coping with voices;
- to educate society about the meaning of voices to reduce ignorance and anxiety;
- to develop a range of non-medical ways of assisting people to cope with their voices;
- to bring together voice-hearers who have not been in contact with psychiatric services with those people experiencing distress.

The Manchester self-help group

The first meeting of the self-help group was held in February 1991. The group meets monthly and is run on a very informal basis, with its format based on that of similar groups in Holland. Up to 30 people attend. The group discusses people's individual experiences and theories, and provides the means for them to support each other in developing methods of coping. A researcher also attends the meetings and, with the full consent of the group, is drawing on some of the members' experiences for his work. A community psychiatric nurse is present to provide support and to act as a link between the self-help group and the planning group. Members have contributed to the newsletter and participated in a video project intended to promote the issues involved in hearing voices, and have gone to the Netherlands to meet representatives of Resonance Foundation.

Developing the Network

We are still at an early stage of development as a group, but the response so far has been very encouraging. Working entirely voluntarily, we have set ourselves the following objectives:

1. to hold a further national conference in 1992, with invited experts who will talk about their particular perspective on the phenomenon of hearing voices, eg religious, extra-terrestrial, spiritual, mystical, psychiatric, etc.

2. to produce a video about hearing voices for use by new groups, and to collaborate with the Mental Health Media Council in its production and distribution.

3. to seek funding for the employment of a worker, based in Manchester, to help the Network to cope with the increasing numbers of enquiries and requests for information. This is particularly important, as we expect the publication of this book to generate a great deal of further interest.

4. to send more members of the Network to the Netherlands to meet members of Resonance Foundation, particularly to learn more about the techniques employed by Dutch self-help groups, and to spread these practices in the UK where appropriate.

Ultimately, we hope to establish the Network as a comprehensive advice and information service for voice-hearers and self-help groups. We are excited by the prospects offered by this way of working, and intend to promote and develop it to the best of our abilities. If you think you might be able to help us in this ambition, please contact us: Hearing Voices Network, Swan Buildings, 20 Swan Street, Ancoats, Manchester M4 6JW, Great Britain.

References

Azis, C. Heard But Not Seen; Independent on Sunday, 6 Jan. 1991

Baker, P. (1988) Interviews with Prof. Marius Romme; notes from the conference of 11 Nov. 1989 (unpublished)

Baker, P. (1989) Hearing Voices; OPENMIND, no. 40, pp.16-17

Baker, P. (1992) Hearing Voices: A Different Perspective; National Hearing Voices Network

Grierson, M. (1991) A Report on the Manchester Hearing Voices Conference; published by the National Hearing Voices Network

Heery, M. W. (1989) Inner Voice Experiences: an exploratory study of thirty cases; Journal of Transpersonal Psychology, vol. 21, no.1

Romme M., Escher, S. (1992) Hearing and Accepting Voices - and Life is not a Problem that has to be Solved but a Mystery that has to be Lived; National Hearing Voices Network

Rose, N. (1991) The Dutch Experience; published by the National Hearing Voices Network

4. PSI[1], PSYCHOLOGY AND PSYCHIATRY

Gerda de Bruijn

There are vibrations or forces within the universe that touch us and offer us a knowledge of reality which our senses cannot give. The acknowledgement of this fact would start a revolution within psychology. (Charles Richet, 1923)

Walter's voices

During my training as a child psychologist, I worked for two years with a young man described in his file as schizoid and suffering from auditory hallucinations. The therapy was designed mainly to improve the social skills of this intelligent and retiring adolescent, and in the first 18 months I never saw any indication that he might be hearing things that I did not. Then one day, during the last few months of our relationship, an extraordinary episode took place.

My conversation with Walter was not going smoothly that day, mainly because I was giving him only half of my attention; the other half was still preoccupied with a recent, unrelated incident and a person with whom I had been very angry. In the course of our conversation, Walter became more and more withdrawn, until eventually it was almost as if he were listening to his own inside. Suddenly he said with great feeling that, behind the real, ordinary world of our conversation there was another, a frightening world, and that he heard voices coming from this other world. I did not hear these voices, but it was clear from Walter's trembling that he was genuinely scared by what he heard. After a while, he agreed to tell me what the voices were communicating: violent curses.

On the face of it, there may appear to be nothing remarkable about this story. But the words Walter heard spoken from the frightening world coincided exactly with the curses that I, during our conversation, had been phrasing in my mind with the other half of my attention. It was as if Walter's voices were literally saying what I had been thinking in silence. I was speechless.

I did not tell the child psychologist who supervised my training that Walter had hallucinated that day. Nor did I attempt to explain what had actually happened: I had no words to describe the experience - indeed, my profession had no words for it - and I was afraid to speak about it.

This took place 20 years ago. I now know - though none of this was ever mentioned during my training - that these incidents reminiscent of psi[1] have been recorded by other psychotherapists. Similar reports reveal several things: that the authors often find the incidents concern information which is being suppressed from the therapist's consciousness, or which is so personally relevant that he or she feels touched to the core; that such episodes happen more often when there is a strong positive transference and the therapist is not fully available to the patient, or the therapeutic contact is coming to an end; and that they are particularly prevalent amongst patients whose diagnoses suggest that they may be on the brink of a psychotic episode (Ehrenwald, 1977; Ullman, 1977; Wolman, 1986; Silverman, 1988).

I now believe - though I cannot be sure - that it might have been of help to Walter if I had told him matter-of-factly that the words he had heard corresponded with my own thoughts. My profession is still very lacking in language with which to describe these incidents, and there has been no systematic research in this area. Psychology and psychiatry on the one hand, and parapsychology on the other, have always shown little enthusiasm for examining one another's findings.

It seems likely that a change in this situation could be of benefit to those with mental health difficulties. It has been suggested that there is a correlation between voice-hearers with active, satisfying lifestyles, and parapsychological and/or spiritual frames of reference for the interpretation of their experiences (Heery, 1989). In the hope of widening the discussion of these perspectives, then, this chapter seeks to provide a historical summary of the relationship between psi, psychology and psychiatry.

Ancient beliefs

Before the birth of psychology and psychiatry, psychic and mystical experiences were a common element in many societies' understanding of humanity and of mental health. In pre-Christian polytheistic and pantheistic societies, it was commonly accepted that a person's inner life might give access to what was considered divine, and to miracles such as the inexplicable transference of knowledge or healing energy. Traces of such beliefs have been found in ancient Greek and Egyptian cultures, as well as in those of early Christian gnosticism. Socrates allowed his life to be directed by his demon, a voice of wisdom which he did not experience as an aspect of his own thoughts. He also knew that clairvoyant (or clairaudient, clairsentient, etc.) perception could coincide with madness:

in other words, that a person in the midst of such perception is understandably ill-adjusted to the routine demands of everyday space and time - as illustrated by the priestesses of Delphi and Dodoni. Socrates described this kind of madness as being of divine origin.

Rituals used in Greek and Egyptian dream-temples suggest that peoples in those times assumed the presence of a certain power and knowledge of healing within what is now called the human subconscious, but was then interpreted within a more spiritual/religious perspective. After preparation with ritual cleansing, a sick person would be visited in his or her dreams by the spirit of a divine healer (usually Asclepius for the Greeks and Imhotep for the Egyptians); this healer would either cure the patient by touch in the dream or explain what course of action was needed for healing to take place. According to some sources, Egyptian papyrus texts also reveal knowledge of the use of certain transcendental techniques of mental concentration: an image of light was used to contact the gods and, through them, acquire knowledge.

Similarly, the religions of the Far East had accumulated knowledge of human suffering and how it might be healed within the individual. The yoga sutras of Patanjali, which were probably formulated in the 2nd century, are a rich source of information on the psychic and spiritual dimensions of human existence. Patanjali defines yoga as the control of thought-waves in the mind or, in another translation, the restriction of the fluctuations of mindstuff - a kind of science of mental health. The aim of the control of thought-waves is the awareness of, and communion with, the divinity present in human beings and in all aspects of creation: achievement of this awareness brings the end of suffering (samadhi). One of the eight branches of yoga, concentration, may give rise to siddhis, or what we might call psychic powers. Patanjali gives a description of the siddhis, but adds that they are powers in the worldly state, but obstacles to samadhi.

The originators of the Western monotheistic religions (Moses, Jesus and Mohammed) all heard voices not apparent to others. Whether these inner revelations are testimony to their sanity or madness, I leave to the reader's judgement (we certainly know that Jesus's contemporaries occasionally considered him to be possessed). However, in those parts of the world where these monotheistic religions became predominant, and in spite of persecutions, the idea survived that the divine may be discovered within human consciousness, and may present opportunities for evolution. This notion was propagated both by individuals and by groups such as the Sufis in the Islamic countries, the Kabbalists among the Jews, and - long after the early Gnostics - by the Rosicrucians, Freemasons and Quakers in Christian countries.

Persecutions were especially vigorous against those who were believed to practise sorcery, soothsaying and necromancy[2]. Up until the birth of psychology and psychiatry, the Church claimed the right to classify and judge these individuals according to four main diagnostic categories: canonization, possession, heresy and witchcraft[3]. Joan of Arc, who heard voices, died at the stake in 1431; until the very last moment, the authorities tried to make her confess that the Saints' voices she claimed to hear were not real, but they were indeed real to her. In about 1600, Bruno was also burnt at the stake for proclaiming that humans have divine and therefore magical abilities which may be discovered through training of the memory. Around 1700, Gichtel voiced similar views in Germany, but his punishment was limited to being pilloried, exiled and barred from his profession as a lawyer. Fifty years later, Swedenborg was able to articulate the same ideas in Sweden and continue to be a statesman, despite a good deal of public suspicion about the voices he heard. By this time, Western society was beginning to move towards the birth of psychology and psychiatry.

The cradle of the humanities: magnetism

Around the beginning of the 19th century, a Viennese/Parisian physician, Mesmer, tried to help his nervously afflicted patients with the use of magnetism. He approached this therapy with an attitude which was probably unusual at that time: he took seriously his patients descriptions of what they felt within their bodies[4]. This resulted in a series of propositions in which he described his belief in the existence of a subtle and weightless fluid which pervaded the whole universe, and thus interconnected everything which existed (such as the planets, plants and human beings). In humans, this connection with the universal fluid was supposed to take place mainly within the nervous system; obstructions in the flux and reflux of this fluid through the body could result in illness. Magnetizing exerted influence on the circulation of fluid within the body and could, according to Mesmer, cure nervous diseases directly, and other complaints indirectly.

One of Mesmers pupils, de Puysgur, stressed the importance of human will and belief in the process of magnetization, and of the trance-like state shown by some magnetized subjects. Sometimes, psi-like incidents would be experienced by a patient in such a trance: for example, he or she might describe the nature of his or her own illness, and prescribe medicines or behaviour which could provide the cure - exactly as in records of the rituals in Mediterranean dream-temples.

It was this trance-magnetism in particular which then spread into the Netherlands and Germany. In these countries, the magnetic trance was described as something which reveals itself by degrees: initially, the attention focused on ordinary sensory perception becomes more limited; the person may become insensitive to physical pain, and may become very suggestible - more sensitive, for example, to suggested hallucinations. There may be an increase of inner clarity, in which the patient may look around inside his or her body and know what would provide a cure; there may also be telepathic incidents, limited at first to involving people in the patient's immediate vicinity. Ultimately, there may be a depth of trance giving access to universal clarity, a state of perception unbounded by time and space, which the individual may experience as ecstasy. These final degrees of trance did not occur very often: an 1815 text estimates that universal clarity and ecstasy occurred in only one out of a hundred people. The trance states described by these authors show a striking similarity to Patanjalis yoga sutras (which had not yet been translated) - a similarity which may well be no coincidence.

Even as Mesmer and de Puysgur were beginning their practices, the Inquisition in France had barely died out, and the Netherlands had just seen its last witchcraft trial. Part of the reason for the excitement generated by these two influential figures was undoubtedly that they openly promoted - and claimed to practise - heretical techniques tantamount to witchcraft. Cartoons depicting magnetizers on broomsticks were widely circulated in Paris. The (Roman) Inquisition, however, did not pass its first, damning judgement on magnetism until 1840.

This exciting period is now seen by many as the cradle of the humanities and psychotherapy. Something very important had happened: Mesmer had claimed the authority to define mental health, seizing the clergy's traditional prerogative on behalf of the developing medical professions. Ellenberger (1970) has written a beautiful historical novel tracing the development of the concept of the unconscious from events of this period; he shows the growth of insight into suggestive influence and the importance of the quality of contact between healer and patient, and how by the turn of the following century all this had developed into the concept of psychotherapy. But somewhere along this road, from about 1830 onwards, some important elements were lost from the mainstream progression: the art of magnetizing, and the so-called miracles of deep trance-states. By 1900, these subjects had been exiled to the domain of parapsychology.

The parting of the ways (1830-1900)

The 19th century saw a strong revival of interest in folk-healing, and some direct historical descendants of the early magnetism movement enjoyed enormous popularity: spiritualism, the newly-founded Christian Science movement, and the German chemist Reichenbach's investigations into auras of the nerve-spirit, to name but three.

One of Reichenbach's friends, the physicist and philosopher Fechner, sometimes perceived auras which he characterized as ethereal bodies. Fechner is now considered by many to be the originator of psychology itself. After a personal crisis, he developed a pantheistic view of reality which encompassed paranormal phenomena and spiritual experiences. He believed that each individual consciousness is connected with a universal soul which extends not only through space, but also time. This is a view similar to Patanjalis, and one that came to be shared by some 19th-century philosophers and a least two other early psychologists: the Dutch Heymans and the famous William James, for whom:

...one fixed conclusion dogmatically emerges: there is a continuum of cosmic consciousness into which our collective minds plunge as into a mother-sea or reservoir. Our normal consciousness is circumscribed for adaptation to our external earthly environment, but the fence is weak in spots, and fitful influences from beyond leak in, showing the otherwise unverifiable common connection. (James, 1909)

A French pioneer of psychodynamic psychiatry, Pierre Janet, developed a related idea: he believed that anything which ever existed continues to exist, but on such a plane and in such a manner that it remains beyond human understanding; he believed that it might one day become possible for humans to study history by means of this continuum. However, little of his impressive body of work suggests that he believed human consciousness - or the unconcious - to be an open system connected with a larger whole. For a brief period, while still a philosopher, he did experiment with suggestion-at-a-distance (interpreted by others as telepathic suggestion) with a healthy woman[5], but generally speaking he was more interested in working with people perceived as mentally ill. For this reason, he started to study medicine, and became a gifted therapist to whom we owe much of our modern understanding of how the individual may suffer a split within the personality, and how suggestive influences may help to re-establish contact between the parts. By this time, he was no longer posing the question of whether the extreme sensitivity he found in some individuals (such as the sensitivity to suggestion-at-a-distance) might increase their vulnerability to mental illness, nor did he wonder how such people could protect themselves against unwelcome impressions. He did, however, believe that massage could be a useful complementary therapy when psychological difficulties were reflected in muscle spasms, which he attributed to congealed emotion. He saw religion as something which was capable of strengthening a person's morale, and indeed morals, but which must also be irreconcilable with a more scientific approach to reality.

In the same year as Janet's reports on suggestion-at-a-distance, a group of Oxford scholars published a much more wide-ranging investigation of psi-like incidents (Gurney, Myers et al., 1886). They described about 700 cases of both experimental and spontaneous telepathy, with some of their information supplied by major figures in the history of hypnosis, such as Libault, Elliotson, Esdaile and Richet. The results of this investigation suggest that spontaneous telepathy occurs more often between individuals sharing an emotional bond, and when the receiver of the information is relaxed and the sender agitated or in danger. I personally believe this to be a significant finding for all those who are professionally involved with people in difficulties.

Separate realms (1900-1950)

In the first half of the 20th century, psychology's main preoccupations were with issues of sensory perception and learning theory. The latter in particular was later to prove useful in the understanding of caring or therapeutic relationships, although consciousness (let alone cosmic consciousness) appeared for the moment to have been expelled from psychology altogether. For a while, parapsychology continued to provide a link with the caring professions through the efforts by Myers, Hyslop and Prince to understand the possible connections between psi-like incidents and mental illness - in particular, the disintegration of the personality. By 1925, however, this link was lost, and parapsychology was reduced to laboratory research with cards and dice.

Perhaps the most promising avenue of exploration with regard to the integration of the two realms has been offered by psychodynamic psychiatry. For Freud, it is true, the phenomenon of religion could be satisfactorily explained in terms of wishful thinking: he believed that human helplessness gave rise to the longing for a strong father. Issues relating to parapsychology were, however, central to the relationship between Freud and Jung, as well as to its breakdown - Freud's plea to Jung not to lose himself in the mudstream of the occult is well-known.

Less well-known is that Freud, shortly after making this last remark, became a member of the Society for Psychical Research, and remained so until his death. During his last two decades, Freud became much more sympathetic to the hypothesis of telepathy as a possible phenomenon in the course of psychoanalysis, although he allowed his later biographer, Jones (1957), to dampen such speculation in his published work.

Throughout this period, however divergent their interests, psychology and psychiatry had one thing in common - an analytical and somewhat deterministic, mechanistic view of human development: problems in the present were usually seen as the result of earlier learning processes and/or unconscious psychological traumas. As a consequence of this bias, another important truth was almost lost: the fact that integrating and self-healing forces may be found in the present, and even in the patient's unconscious. Jung (1963), Maeder (1949) and Assagioli (1965) have all, in their own ways, stressed the presence of these creative forces in people experiencing mental suffering; each of them has also presumed a more or less open unconscious, in keeping with the earlier views of Fechner, Heymans and James. It may be no coincidence that all three of these psychiatrists received part of their training from Bleuler in the hospital at Burghlzli: Bleuler was generally known to be one of only a few in the field who could form therapeutically beneficial relationships with patients in psychosis.

Jung believed that archetypes (which may appear in psi-like incidents) emerged from the collective unconscious with greater frequency during psychotic episodes. Maeder made an effort to find each patient's wise and healing archaic image, which he likened to Socrates's demon; he believed that the proper use of this guiding image in psychotherapy could greatly reduce the time needed to effect a cure. Jung and Maeder were both of the opinion that patients' dreams may offer revelations of a healing wisdom and, at times, telepathic perceptions and precognitions - notions strongly reminiscent of the ancient dream-temples and 19th-century descriptions of deep trance. Assagioli showed a great sensitivity in his therapeutic work with healing symbols and with patients' projections of their higher self on to their psychotherapists, gods and lovers. As early as the 1930s, he wrote about spiritual development and its associated (mental) diseases. He stressed that it was essential to be extremely careful and delicate in any effort to open up the unconscious of patients who had shown any telepathic sensitivity; he warned that the unconscious of such a subject might contain information which has not been a part of his or her individual history, and which may be disruptive to the personal sense of identity.

Integration: the modern challenge

Since the end of World War II, there has been a refreshing cross-fertilization amongst the various theories and therapies of both psychology and psychiatry. A third, humanistic force has introduced the concept of organic self-regulation, and so helped reinstate a more creative view of consciousness and the unconscious. This has been a period during which we in the West have had to abandon our colonial arrogance and learn to revalue the spiritual traditions of the East, with its deep psychological wisdom, and acknowledge the common factors shared by the Third World's healing rituals, psychic healing and psychotherapy.

This has given rise to a contemporary revival of practices associated with folk-healing, with at least two particularly outstanding characteristics: the use of body-oriented techniques for mental health problems, and the conscious training of various possible perceptions of reality - the very features which 19th-century psychology and psychiatry had tried to abandon in the age of magnetism. There is now a great body of knowledge about meditation, and research is being carried out (by both patients and therapists) into its possible healing powers (Shapiro and Walsh, 1984; Kwee, 1990). Parapsychologists won scientific acknowledgement from the American Association for the Advancement of Science in 1969.

There is, however, still a need for research into questions which touch on both mental health and parapsychology: these are questions which, because of the old split between the two separate disciplines, have been largely neglected by researchers, but which may be of great relevance to the understanding and treatment of mental health problems. We need to explore, for example: whether and how a psychic sensitivity (conscious or otherwise) and a spiritual or transcendent dimension may contribute to psychological confusion or psychopathology; whether a psychological trauma may give rise to a psychic sensitivity[6]; whether those claiming to possess this sensitivity, and/or those trained in a spiritual discipline, can be of help to people who experience mental health problems; whether the practice of a spiritual discipline, and/or the more subtle body-energetic approaches (including self-help techniques) can be of use in re-establishing mental equilibrium.

The personal knowledge and understanding of those who hear voices is indispensable to this process, and this book contains a wide spectrum of their experiences. Clearly, there is an enormous difference between hearing an oppressive voice which delivers frightening or harmful messages, and hearing a voice which gives useful information and may be a creative influence upon one's life. Within the Resonance Foundation, those who are confused by the voices they hear are offered at least one important opportunity: the means to share these voices openly. My message, as I close this chapter, is that there may yet be further opportunities in the near future for those who are troubled by their voices: we in the Foundation are fully open to the widest discussion of experiences touching upon the transcendent, the so-called psychic, and the spiritual. In the process of sharing information about our experiences, the atmosphere of openness may produce surprising discoveries. Psychologists and psychiatrists may stand to learn a great deal from the personal knowledge of their patients - it has, after all, happened before.

Notes

1. In parapsychological research, psi is the collective noun used to indicate psychic phenomena such as telepathy, extrasensory perception, precognition and psychokinesis.

2. Sorcery entailed a mixture of what we would call today folk-healing, suggestion and possibly psychokinesis. The modern equivalents of soothsaying would be clairvoyance and precognition. Necromancy was similar to what we now know as spiritualism.

3. The honour of canonization was conferred upon pious individuals who represented no threat to the authority of the Church, and who might even serve to increase its prestige; consequently, saints were free to perform the very miracles for which others were persecuted.

The state of possession, according to the Rituale Exorcistarum, might be characterized by: speaking or understanding words in a foreign language that had never been learnt; by access to information about distant or hidden objects (this would also include precognition); and by an unnatural degree of strength. All these miracles were supposed to be the result of a forced and unwanted bond with the devil; for this reason, possession was considered an illness which could be healed by exorcism and prayer.

The categories of heresy and witchcraft were not mutually exclusive, and both heretics and witches could be sentenced to death. Heresy involved proclaiming a belief not in accordance with the doctrine of the Church; such a belief might be based on miracles, but it could also be inspired by sensory and intellectual perception. Witchcraft might be characterized by soothsaying and sorcery; in this case, however, these miracles were supposed to be the result of a voluntary bond with the devil.

4. Mesmer reports that one of his first patients perceived an almost painful subtle flow, initially in all directions within her belly, then suddenly moving towards both feet. Those trained in modern body-oriented psychotherapies may recognize what is now referred to as grounding. In Mesmer's day, however, the scientific and social climate was very unfavourable for any acknowledgement of these experiences. Historians are generally agreed that the period between 1500 and 1800 was characterized by increasing alienation from physical and tactile experience, including sexuality, and that the voices of women (who tend to be more sensitive to their internal bodily experiences than men) were increasingly silenced as their educational opportunities became fewer and fewer during this period.

5. These experiments have also been summarized by Richet (1923), who participated in some of them.

6. A hypothesis earlier formulated in the 1930s by Ferenczi. See Masson (1984), pp.184, 283-295.

References

Achterberg, J. (1985) Imagery in Healing: Shamanism and Modern Medicine; New Science Library, Boston

Assagioli, R. (1938) Spiritual Development and its Attendant Maladies; Hibbert Journal, vol. 36; reprinted as chapter 2 in Assagioli's Psychosynthesis (1965); Penguin

Colquhoun, J. C. (1833) Report of the Experiments on Animal Magnetism; reprinted 1975 by Perspectives in Psychical Research, New York

Edge, H. L.; Morris, R. L.; Palmer, J.; Rush, J. H. (1986) Foundations of Parapsychology; Routledge, London and New York

Ehrenwald, J. (1977) Psi, Psychotherapy and Analysis; in Wolman, B. (Ed.) Handbook of Parapsychology; McFarland, London

Ellenberger, H. F. (1970) The Discovery of the Unconscious; Basic Books, New York

Gurney, E.; Myers, F.; Podmore, F. (1918) Phantasms of the Living; Kegan Paul, London

Heery, M. W. (1989) Inner Voice Experiences: an exploratory study of thirty cases; Journal of Transpersonal Psychology, vol. 21, no. 11, pp.73 - 82

James, W. (1909) The Final Impressions of a Psychical Researcher; originally published in the American Magazine, October 1909; reprinted in Mishlove (1975)

Janet, P.; see Pierre Janet and Psychological Analysis; in Ellenberger (1970)

Jones, E. (1957) Sigmund Freud, Life and Works, vol. 3, pp.402-436; Basic Books, New York

Kwee, M. G. T. (1990) Psychotherapy, Meditation and Health. A cognitive-behavioural perspective; East-West Publications, London & The Hague

Maeder, A. (1949) Selbsterhaltung und Selbstheilung; Waldstadt, Einsiedeln

Masson, J. M. (1984) The Assault on Truth; Farrar, Straus and Giroux, New York

Mishlove, J. (1975) The Roots of Consciousness: psychic liberation through history, science and experience; Random House, New York

Patanjali (1969) The Yoga Aphorisms of Patanjali, with a commentary by Swami Prabhavanda; Vedanta Soc., New American Library, New York

Reichenbach, K. von: Letters on OD and Magnetism; in Regush, N. M. (Ed.), New York

Richet, C. (1923) Trait de Metapsychique; Librairie Flix Alcan, Paris

Shapiro, D. H., Walsh R. N. (1984) Meditation: classic and contemporary perspectives; Aldine, New York

Silverman, S. (1988) Correspondences and Thought-Transference during Psychoanlysis; Journal of the American Academy of Psychoanalysis, vol. 16, no. 3, pp.269 - 294

Ullman, M. (1977) Psychopathology and Psi Phenomena; in Wolman, B. (Ed.) Handbook of Parapsychology; McFarland, London

Wolman, B. (1986) Protoconsciousness and Psychopathology; in Wolman, B., Ullman, M. (Eds.) Handbook of States of Consciousness; Van Nostrand Reinhold Company, New York

5. TALKING ABOUT VOICES
Sandra Escher

The need for discussion

People who hear voices find themselves having to deal with another world which may overwhelm them and claim their attention to the exclusion of all else, in much the same way that all of us, from time to time, become engulfed by violent emotion. As a result, the power of reason may be virtually extinguished, at least initially, making it impossible for those concerned to go about their daily lives without being affected by such a penetrating and confusing experience.

Throughout our many interviews and discussions with the hearers of voices over the last few years, we have been struck by the clear evidence that open discussion with others offers one of the most important means of creating some kind of order in the attempt to come to grips with these experiences. In particular, we have seen that communication has greatly helped many people to accept their voices; as a result, their self-confidence has been much improved, freeing them from their isolation and reaffirming their sense of involvement with those around them.

Unfortunately, voice-hearers all too often find their family and friends too embarrassed or afraid to listen to their experiences, and it can prove impossible to find anyone genuinely interested in what the voices have to say. Even when someone is prepared to listen, the phenomenon is so extraordinary that it can be very difficult indeed to convey to anyone entirely unfamiliar with such experiences. Mutual communication amongst voice-hearers themselves is a practical solution to these problems. The sharing of similar experiences, using a common language, provides real opportunities for all concerned to share and learn.

This is an extremely important area, and we have devoted this entire chapter to the positive outcomes of such communication, as reported to us by people who hear voices. Potential benefits of discussion can be summarized as follows:

1.   clearer recognition of patterns;
2.   easing of anxiety;
3.   discovery of alternative theoretical perspectives;
4.   improved acceptance of voices;
5.   clearer recognition of the meaning of the voices;

6. appreciation of potentially positive aspects;
7. better structuring of the contact with the voices
8. more effective use of medicines;
9. improved tolerance and understanding within th
10. personal growth.

1. Recognizing patterns

People who hear voices say it is very important to them to be able to discuss the voices in much the same way one might talk, for example, about disagreeable relatives. In the process, it is possible to learn to recognize their games and tricks, as well as their more pleasant aspects, and to identify patterns which are specific to given situations. Such knowledge can help the hearer to be better prepared for any subsequent onset of the voices. A 35-year old woman, regularly admitted to psychiatric hospital, commented:

The questions people put to me made me reflect on the voices I heard, which I had never really thought about. I was surprised to discover a pattern - whenever I think negatively, I find myself hearing a negative voice.

2. Easing anxiety

Most people who hear voices initially imagine that they are alone in doing so. This in itself can make the experience an anxious or unpleasant one, and also often produces feelings of shame, or the fear of going mad. A good example of reduced anxiety was given to us by 36-year old man who spoke at the first conference. He had first heard voices at the age of about 20, when they had frightened him terribly. Six months after the conference, he lost his job, and was amazed to find himself beginning to hear voices again. This time however, he did not find the experience nearly so disturbing or shocking: the conference had given him the comforting realization that he was not alone in hearing voices, and this helped him greatly.

Anxiety often leads to the avoidance of situations which might trigger the hearing of voices, and this avoidance seriously blocks the development of self. Thus, some voice-hearers no longer dare to go to parties, drive a car or go into a department store. Such a degree of anxiety severely restricts freedom of movement, and strategies of oidance often seem only to exacerbate the problem. One woman told us:

The moment the voices disappear, I start worrying that they will return.

This woman now has regular telephone contact with another voice-hearer, who encourages her to overcome her fears. This encouragement from someone familiar with her experiences enables her to break the vicious circle of anxiety and fear.

3. Finding a theoretical perspective

Like professionals in the field, voice-hearers themselves look for a theoretical explanation to account for the existence of their voices. A 50-year old woman who began to hear voices five years ago told us:

After my son died, I began to hear his voice. But what does one do with these messages? I thought others with similar experences could help me, and began to seek them out, but at first my search was fruitless. At the conference, I met people involved with The Path (see chapter 7), a spiritual movement based on lectures by the medium Eva Pierrakos. These people advised me to read her books, which I did. I recognize a good deal of myself in them, which helps me to carry on.

Personal experience can be of the greatest help in offering advice to others. For example, in a conversation with another hearer of voices, Mr X said:

I have been diagnosed as schizophrenic, and hear voices - why do they cause such pain?

The woman responded by asking:

When do you feel the pain?

He told her that this mainly happened when he found himself surrounded by great numbers of solitary people in large spaces, for instance in a department store. The woman helped him to realize that he tended to absorb the pain of other people. Although she could not teach him immunity to this pain, she was able to advise him on exercises to help him to acquire the means to close himself off, and so ward off the pain. Learning to close oneself off - and subsequently reopen oneself - is a technique associated with parapsychology: sealing the boundaries of one's ego. Mr X reported that the woman's explanation made good sense of his situation.

We should mention in passing that it must not be assumed that all the advice offered by fellow voice-hearers will be automatically sound. We have been told by some people that advice they were given led them into even greater difficulties. Our investigations and interviews have suggested, for example, that visits to spiritualist meetings or psychics can sometimes confuse the novice voice-hearer even further. Some, too, have described how well-meaning help in the form of confinement in the isolation ward of a psychiatric hospital was the precursor to hearing voices, or else caused the voices to become more aggressive, rather than affording the intended protection. Generally speaking, one must always be wary of advice or explanations which are purely personal convictions and make no allowance for any other interpretation. It is most important to be fully aware of the wide variety of individual situations and circumstances. The least hazardous advice tends to be that which may serve to increase the individual's own influence over his or her voices, rather than intensify powerlessness. Self-knowledge and self-determination are the keywords.

4. Acceptance

A 38-year old woman told us:

When I talked with others about their experiences with voices, I realized I could cope better with mine by acknowledging them rather than denying them. I have stopped fighting the voices. I still couldn't say I'm happy about them, but life has become easier as a result.

In the process of developing one's own point of view and taking responsibility for oneself, the essential first stage is acceptance of the voices as belonging to me. This is of the utmost importance - and also one of the most difficult steps to take.

5. Recognizing meaning

A young woman told us of several instances in which she had spoken out loud what her husband had been thinking. This was not always particularly remarkable, given their intimate knowledge of each other's circumstances and moods, but sometimes this would happen even in the absence of any overt indication of what he might be thinking. This irritated the husband, but he did not allow his annoyance to show. His wife then found herself picking up his anger; the voice she heard intensified it, and told her that her husband would murder her. Consequently, she became afraid of him, much to his confusion. In this woman's case, the voices expressed what she herself was feeling: aggression was a particular problem in her relationship, and something of which she was afraid.

Whenever voices volunteer information in this way, the challenge posed by their presence is often less significant than the problems in the relationship concerned which are being reflected or echoed. In cases like this where the voice imparts information about the hearer's sensitivity, it should be particularly fruitful to discuss the nature of the messages. This approach is described more fully in the section on Functional Analysis in chapter 9.

6. Positive aspects

When people hear voices that are truly malicious - ridiculing or belittling others, or even abusing the hearers until they are driven to injure themselves - it may understandably be difficult to persuade them to accept the existence of a positive, helpful dimension to the experience. Contact with others can lead to the surprising discovery that positive voices do exist, and to the realization that these may arise, or be detected, as a result of a proper acceptance of the hearer's own negative side. An example was given by a 40-year old woman:

Through communication with others, I had to learn to accept there are both positive and negative sides to me. It is very difficult to explain, but by accepting my negative side, I can devote more attention to my positive side. I can learn to care for myself.

7. Structuring contact

A 28-year old woman, who had originally heard voices all day long, commented:

I have made an agreement with the voices that I will keep my evenings

*free for them. I am not available to anyone else after 8 pm, and have
asked my friends not to call me after that time. My husband, fortunately,
accepts this arrangement. The advantage of this system is that the voices
seldom become difficult during the day, and I can function much better.*

The imposition of this kind of structure on the relationship with the
voices can help minimize the common feelings of powerlessness. It can be
extremely valuable in helping people to see that they can set their own
limits and restrain the voices from excessive intrusion.

8. More effective use of medicines

Sharing experiences also enables people to get to know what medicines
others are using, how useful these are, and what their side-effects may be.
It is important, for example, to know whether a particular medicine has
been found helpful in reducing the hearing of voices or in easing the
associated anxiety and confusion. Questions can be aired and reactions
assessed in a way that may not be possible in discussion with doctors,
where opinions tend to become unduly polarized, with both sides
painting the situation in black-and-white terms. Both sides must always
understand that the effectiveness and acceptability of any prescribed
medicine are matters of individual experience. A young woman who still
receives out-patient treatment said:

*I took neuroleptics for some time, but then chose to stop taking them
because I felt like a zombie. I could no longer even read a book. I do still
use medicine, but these days its more of a maintenance dose with fewer
side-effects. When voices threaten to overpower me, I increase the dosage
temporarily.*

9. Family understanding

A 30-year old woman told us:

*As a result of the conference, both my parents and my husband came to
accept my voices, and this made my life much easier. Also, my social life
has improved, because people around me now realize that sometimes -
because of voices - I am not open to communication with them. My
family are more supportive towards me, and accept me more readily
when I behave differently.*

10. Personal growth

Almost all voice-hearers who have learned to adjust to their experiences report that, with hindsight, the process has contributed to their personal growth. Personal growth can be defined as recognizing what one needs in order to lead a fulfilled life, and knowing how to achieve these ends; it could, perhaps, be described as a process of emancipation.

Mrs X provides a good illustration. She began to hear voices in 1980, at the age of 26. She lived with her parents, rarely went out and was extremely dependent. After one of many suicide attempts, she was admitted to a psychiatric hospital; within 24 hours she began to hear voices, which quickly came to dominate her, forbidding her, for example, to eat, drink and sleep. However, six months later the situation changed completely; she had made a resolution to become independent. Now the voices became a helpful influence, supporting her in something of an identity crisis. They gave her greater insight and awareness, and enabled her to experience life in greater depth. Four months later she left hospital and began to live independently, studying and working.

We met this woman in 1987, when we interviewed her as a possible speaker for our first conference. At this stage she was still receiving out-patient treatment, and could not as yet work. She told us that she had had three episodes of hearing voices, but thought that she dealt best with them by ignoring them. In the course of our interviews and conversations with other voice-hearers, she began to reconsider this approach, and to ask herself new questions about the voices. After the conference, she became an active member of the Resonance Foundation, and worked on its telephone helpline service for people in difficulties due to hearing voices. When we spoke to her again later that year, her attitude to the voices had changed significantly:

I have learned to regard them as a warning sign; whenever they materialize, I know things are going badly for me and that I must take notice.

The previous year, she had fallen passionately in love with a man who fully returned her affection. Mrs X had then begun hearing her friend's voice addressing her in abusive, insulting terms. This time she was not swamped by panic, but was clear-headed enough to avoid the mistake of confusing the voice with that of the actual person; she confronted her friend and asked him whether he had ever entertained such thoughts towards her, and he was able to reassure her that he had not. By checking with him, she succeeded in gaining more insight into her problems:

There is a part of me that cannot accept people being nice to me, and wants to destroy me.

She came to realize that her voices, when they appeared, were part of a paranoia in which she imagined that everyone was talking about her - even to the extent that if she saw someone laughing on television, she felt herself to be the object of ridicule. When this happens nowadays, she simply turns off the television. With the help of her many activities, Mrs X has managed to leave her voices behind. She can now cope much better with her own emotions, which used to be extremely volatile and make contact with her difficult. She remains extremely sensitive - for example, tuning in immediately to the moods of others - but no longer bursts into tears at the first sign of anything alarming.

Mrs X noticed that her abilities as a telephone adviser improved consistently, and she is now considering setting up a study group. She has also succeeded in finding a training course for leaders of self-help groups. She is amazed by the discovery of her own potential, and has gradually learned to trust her own judgement. She is now working again, as well as being busy acquiring further qualifications, and says that she feels better than ever before. She has begun to talk about voice-hearing with those around her: she distributed copies of the conference report containing her own story amongst her friends, and presented a copy to her mother for her birthday. She also tries to talk about it with her father, and commented:

Conversation doesn't have to be limited to his passion for football.

Disadvantages

Communicating about hearing voices does, of course, have its disadvantages.

Exposing oneself in this way can make one feel very vulnerable. It feels like hanging out one's dirty laundry.

Some voice-hearers find great difficulty in opening up about their experiences, though many find it somewhat easier amongst themselves. In particular, those who have never been psychiatric patients need real courage to face a world that will all too often call them mad when they talk about their lives. For those in this situation, it can be hard to see what may be gained by doing so, and often their only motive is to help others who are unable to cope with their own voices. Another possible drawback to disclosures about hearing voices is that the voices may occasionally become temporarily more acute. One 30-year old woman told us:

Whenever I talk about hearing voices, that night they are more active. But even so, the advantages are much greater.

Conclusion

We have seen many examples to confirm that the sharing of voice experiences is extremely helpful to the necessary process of acceptance and reconciliation. Those who have learned to deal with their voices testify that, whatever the drawbacks, the positive effects outweigh the disadvantages.

Of course, for some whose lives are being made intolerable by voices, it will clearly be very difficult to say, philosophically, It is only temporary, or to begin to shape a manageable relationship with their voices, or to see a clear way forward. When anxiety is especially severe, none of this may be possible. Anxiety management techniques (see chapter 10) may be a solution in these cases.

Successful copers report that it is imperative to treat the voices as a third party, and to learn to say 'No', as one would to any outlandish suggestion.

Learning to cope is a complex internal process that cannot be accomplished unaided. Those who hear voices must find the opportunity to talk about it, exchange experiences, and even complain about it, in order to become stronger in themselves.

References

Chamberlin, J. (1988) On our Own: patient-controlled alternatives to the Mental Health System; MIND, London

Strauss, J. S.; Estroff, S. E. (1989) Foreword in Schizophrenia Bulletin, vol. 15, no. 2, pp.17-18

Romme, M.; Escher, A. (1989) Hearing Voices; Schizophrenia Bulletin, vol. 15, no. 2, pp.209-216

6. HEARING VOICES: EXPERIENCES OF NON-PATIENTS

Introduction
Marius Romme

In the course of our experiment (chapter 2), we met a considerable number of men and women who heard voices but had never been psychiatric patients nor considered themselves to be mentally ill. Nor, for that matter, were they seen as mentally ill by their family or friends.

When we first met these people in the wake of the TV programme, we were quite astounded because, like most psychiatrists and indeed most lay people, we were used to regarding anyone who hears voices as mentally distressed. We were forced to change our ideas when we were confronted with well-balanced, healthy people who simply happened to hear voices: voices which were not heard by those around them, and which they experienced as coming from outside.

The voices heard by such people meet the criteria applied by psychiatry in defining auditory hallucinations; put simply, these are that the voices heard by the individual are experienced as not me. The designation auditory hallucinations is unfortunate in that it presumes the existence of pathology, of illness; it would therefore perhaps be less prejudiced to call voices extrasensory perceptions. This is, in fact, one of the reasons for publishing in this book the experiences of those who hear voices but have never felt like or been labelled a psychiatric patient.

A second reason for publishing these experiences is in order to learn from them: to learn, for example, how it may be possible to manage the hearing of voices without becoming a psychiatric patient, and how some people - after a period of difficulty - can discover in these voices a source of inspiration (what Jung called vocation) or simply of good advice. These experiences have much to teach us about how people may cope, both with voices and with their lives, during the process of integrating the voices. People appeared to apply five main principles to integrate their voices:

- keep strictly to your daily routine;
- concentrate on your positive attributes;

- get to know yourself and thus accept the negative in yourself;
- accept the presence of an influence lying outside yourself, but grasp fully that it is not more powerful than yourself;
- do your utmost to find support and acceptance from those around you, and talk with others about your experiences.

A further reason for publishing these accounts is to suggest that the real problem is not so much hearing voices as the inability to cope with them (see the section on Parapsychology in chapter 7). These stories reveal a wide variety of degrees of success in terms of coping, and an equal variety of individual frames of reference.

All seven of these contributors have managed to accept their voices. It is notable that they also accept the existence of another, non-material realm: all share a parapsychological or spiritual perspective for the interpretation of their voices (see the section on Inner Voice Experiences in chapter 7).

First Contributor

Before discussing how hearing voices has affected my life, let me first introduce myself. I am a woman of 61, married, with a son and daughter-in-law and two grandchildren. For many years, I successfully combined a career as a social worker with running a home and raising a family until I was physically incapacitated. I now receive state sickness benefit.

I have heard voices since childhood. They foretell the future, as well as advising and directing me. Sometimes they talk about other people - for example, the outcome of someone's illness. Although it can be difficult, I have learned to take notice of these voices, because they have invariably been proved right. I have adopted them as travelling companions. I do confide in others around me about my experiences, although this can cause problems.

I received my first definite message at the age of nine. We were living in a harbour town at the time, and one day a Greek tanker moored in the harbour began to explode. The noise of the first explosion was so loud that it carried to my school. My father was a member of the fire brigade, and rushed to the scene. News of the disaster quickly spread through the town, and my mother feared greatly for my father's life. We were brought up as Christians at home, so my mother and I began to pray for his safety. Several hours later, I heard an inner voice say: 'Your father will return', and told my mother about this. Just then, our neighbours came in and said that the tanker was expected to blow up completely. I was terribly afraid, but again I clearly heard a voice repeat: 'Your father will return'. This turned out to be the truth: a complete stranger grabbed hold of my father and pulled him clear, while a colleague standing next to him was killed by flying iron bars.

I kept quiet about this incident, though I heard voices more and more frequently. I was puzzled as to their significance - I did not believe in spirits - and didn't know whether to resist them. In any case, ignoring the voices proved fruitless. They were there all the time, which I found tiring. Finally, my only hope of relief was to confide in my parents. They did not understand, but did not make fun of me; they listened attentively, although they were unable to advise me what to do. I found it impossible to resign myself to my predicament, and continued to hear voices constantly both before and during the second world war.

When I was a child, people were amazed at my confidence, especially when I answered their questions with great conviction. This marked me out from other children, and my mother just assumed that I was precocious; luckily, my parents paid little attention to the comments of others. I myself was accustomed to this phenomenon - I heard voices which opened my eyes and helped me to form my opinions.

One example of this concerned an uncle of mine who was obsessed with politics and how the war would be fought. I heard a voice contradict him, and surprised everyone by announcing that the war would end with the fall of Berlin. My mother declared 'Now I've heard everything!', and my uncle dismissed my pronouncement as childish fantasy. I was 14 at the time. This incident was never again referred to in the family, perhaps rightly so. For my part, I learned to trust my voices.

Another wartime example happened following the move of a friend and her parents to Ede after heavy bombing. In August of that year, I and another friend visited her. On an outing near Castle Doorwerth, near Arnhem, we were walking along the old Roman road when I heard aeroplanes approaching. This was nothing unusual in those days, except for the absence of gunfire or air-raid sirens. I checked with my friends, but they had heard nothing. Suddenly I heard a voice tell me, as we walked home over the Rhine bridge: 'The Allied invasion will take place on this very spot'. In spite of misgivings, I told my friends what I had heard, but their response was that this was just typical of me. My girlfriend repeated my remark to her father, who laughed dismissively, and said: 'What childish foolishness. Get this straight: we here in the east are in no danger. It's you people living near the coast who should worry.' He expounded on how he saw the war progressing. I kept silent, but knew better. When the invasion came, the information from my voices was proved correct; the invasion started out on that same bridge.

Hearing voices did also cause problems. For instance, we found ourselves working under a new supervisor at work - someone already familiar to some of my colleagues, including my husband-to-be, who admired him for various achievements. Judging by what they had told me, I was looking forward to meeting him. However, when we were introduced - although he greeted me warmly and charmingly - a voice declared: 'He is a devil.' Then something incredible happened: the director's face contorted into that of a devil. This was a very difficult moment for me, though I kept my composure and responded cordially. I was reluctant to mention this incident, out of loyalty to my colleagues, but in the end I did tell my husband. He fully accepted my explanation, even though it was completely alien to him. Because my voices were not a problem for me, but something in which I had faith, he accepted them as a part of me. This has not always been easy for him. Later my voices proved to have been right again; the man was indeed a devil.

On another occasion, one of my husband's colleagues fell ill. My husband told me he had just over-exerted himself and would recover in time, but I was immediately prompted to comment: 'He is going to die.' We discussed this no further. We visited this man, a close friend, regularly; after six weeks he had to be admitted to hospital, where he died. How do you cope with such information? We have chosen not to talk about it, but just to accept it.

I continued to hear voices after the birth of my son. I told him about this when he was old enough for secondary school, and he saw a connection between my hearing voices and the fact that I have many acquaintances. He told his friends: 'People seem to sense that my mother has a special gift. Wherever we are, even on holiday, complete strangers approach her and confide in her or ask her advice.' I myself had not made this connection.

After getting married, I returned to temporary work, still hearing voices. My colleagues did not know what to make of my experiences when I spoke of them. On one occasion, a computer was installed - something I welcomed, except that my voices were warning me repeatedly that using the computer would endanger the confidentiality of my clients. I was worried, even though the system seemed secure. Finally, I insisted on using a code to protect my clients; this was confusing and tiresome to administer, and got me branded as stubborn and opinionated, which made life difficult for me. Recently, though, a colleague commented: 'We were jeopardizing the confidentiality of our clients. You foresaw that.'

I was also helped through a critical period - both in terms of my own life and because my husband was ill - by hearing voices. Having worked for twelve-and-a-half years (an important anniversary in Holland), I was given a party by the management and all 123 fellow-workers. Two of my dearest wishes were fulfilled: I was presented with a gold watch and a silver toiletry set. As I accepted the latter, the glass in the hand-mirror broke of its own accord. Everyone was shocked, and immediately offered to exchange it, but a voice impressed on me that I should leave it as it was. I was reluctant to do so, but insisted on keeping the mirror. Within a year, I found myself forced to accept that I was physically no longer capable of working. Had the cracked mirror been a portent? This was a dreadful time during which I heard many voices, and also saw a ghostly form as I lay in bed. I tried to dispel it, but without success. 'Come', the figure said. Eventually I realized this meant I should forge a new life for myself, and relaxed. I blossomed again, and in spite of my ailments I am now even happier and more fulfilled than I had been in my career. Could this be seen as a process of growth and a form of self-realization?

Another difficult period for me was when I became aware of my husband's growing ill-health. I was first alerted to this on holiday in Greece. After a midday nap, we were on our way to visit an old church when a voice said: 'Isn't your husband looking awful?' I looked at him but could see nothing wrong. I started fretting about this as I drove mindlessly along a four-lane highway. I was unable to confide in my husband, and had to cope with my anxiety alone. After several anxious weeks, we returned home, and my worry continued to grow. I knew my husband was eager to visit the ruins of Minoan civilization, so on impulse I booked a trip to Crete as a surprise. He was thrilled by this, but my mind was still uneasy, because the voices warned me incessantly about his health. Shortly after our return from Crete, he had to be rushed to hospital, where a suspected tumour was diagnosed. He took this news in his stride, and somehow I, too, managed to find the strength to stay calm. Autosuggestion, you might say. After my husband was discharged, we began to rebuild our lives, and followed the doctors advice to relax and take another holiday. We went to Vienna. There, I was woken one night, not only by a voice but by a hazy figure saying emphatically: 'They will destroy the health of your husband. You must fight for him.' I was in turmoil, but there was my husband beside me, sleeping peacefully. The next day, as we wandered pleasantly through a wood, a voice repeated: 'Fight. They will destroy his health.' You can imagine how I felt!

I was reluctant to leave Vienna, and managed to arrange with the specialist for radiotherapy treatment to be given locally. My husband himself sensed that he was getting worse, and suffered great pain at night. Again and again I heard a voice repeat: 'Fight. They will destroy his health.' You can imagine how painful this was for me: must I cause my husband further anxiety? Finally, I found the courage to confide in him. He did not argue, so I grabbed the phone and made an appointment with the doctor who was treating him. Radiotherapy and chemotherapy were both stopped, and together we successfully overcame this difficult time.

I have never ceased to hear voices. They are intrusive, but friendly; they heighten my awareness, and are part and parcel of me. I shall say no more, but hope you have grasped what I am trying to convey. I have never dismissed the voices as supernatural forces, magic, witchcraft or anything of that sort. The voices have transformed my life, and I ask you to respect that fact.

Second Contributor

For the past 14 years, I have been aware of telepathic contact with the voice of my guiding spirit.

When this dialogue first began, there was a period lasting several months during which I had many and various paranormal experiences, such as automatic drawing and painting, clairvoyance, premonitions, and healing by means of what I call magnetism. Although parapsychology had already been an abiding passion of mine for ten years, I had always viewed it purely as a field of study, and had never envisaged becoming personally involved. Now I found myself transported, without warning, from studying paranormal phenomena to the experiences themselves. It was initially very difficult to learn to recognize that I was hearing a voice, as I did not literally hear it with my ears, but more as an imprint on my consciousness; this was telepathic communication. Sometimes - for example in the process of doing automatic writing - I have had difficulty in distinguishing whether this was genuine or a projection of my own imagination. On the whole, though, this voice - my guiding spirit - has felt like an integral part of me, and has been there since birth.

Once I became aware of its constant presence, my life took on an extra dimension, at times enriching, at other times troubling. In retrospect, I can see that both peak experiences and painful ordeals have all been part of the phenomenon, and equally to be endured. The first year of this period was particularly harrowing, because I alternated between the heights and depths almost daily. Naturally, this had an effect on family life, but I found it essential to try just to carry on as usual, for no one could be expected to put up with the disruption I was experiencing and causing.

I often had the sense of being engaged in a mission impossible! But time and time again, when I most needed relief I found deliverance, however defeated I had come to feel. The explanation given by the voice for my having to suffer so much hardship was that it was essential to my training, and that once I understood what work the voice had in store for me, any suffering would pass away. It explained: 'The work must proceed, you must be steadfast - what I have to teach you is difficult.' Despite such encouragement, I found it difficult to accept my trials without occasionally becoming infuriated. Life seemed to me to be exceedingly hard; but courage and patience were the watchwords by which I lived. Timing was of the essence.

After two years like this, I came across the collected works of Teresa of Avila. I wished I had found it sooner. This book corroborated and confirmed for me what I had been going through, as Teresa had undergone a similar process. She had intended this book for those searching for God, as a guide for their use on the journey. She wrote of the problems she encountered as a result of hearing a voice: she was warned by those around her that this was the work of the devil himself, and these aspersions made her doubt the existence of God, as happened with me. In her books, Teresa depicts a journey penetrating the seven dwelling places within one's interior castle. On reaching the seventh, one comes into contact - through the voice one experiences - with God, and is filled with life. She summarizes the seventh dwelling place neatly:

To be God's violin is something other than to play the violin for God. At present He is preoccupied with refining the final composition. He can bring this to completion when he has the violin in His hand, when I have surrendered myself to Him, not partially but wholly.

With the help of my reading, I can now offer some hints from my own experience for others to follow:
- Choose goodness, light, God. Having made your choice, allow nothing and no one to deflect you. Above all, trust that whatever suffering you encounter will further the growth of your soul.
- Think positively. This escaped me for a long time, especially as the times of difficulty can sometimes be overwhelming.
- Engage in creativity. To escape from depression, first voice your complaints firmly (through your guide, for example), and ask for help from above, in order to emerge from the Slough of Despond. Harness whatever energy you have released by crying out, and start using your hands creatively.
- Commune with nature frequently. Nature is the tangible presence of the Godhead. When your soul is in torment, nature has its own healing powers.

- Be discerning and alert. A discerning disposition, especially at first, is important in distinguishing the voice. It keeps your spirit awake! You are not meant to be a passive tool.
- Be discreet. Avoid chattering to your family, friends or acquaintances about your experience of hearing a voice. Attempt to lead as normal a life as possible, however difficult this may be. Cultivate the company of similar souls in whom you can confide; they alone can comprehend your experiences.
- The full flowering of the soul: everything revolves around this. The soul must be fully perfected before union with God can take place. Its sanctification seems to be both the goal and the means: as my voice put it: A striving towards union with God involves suffering as its prerequisite and eternal love as its outcome.

Supplement: written three years after the above.

In these last few years I have found immeasurable support from the mystical works of John of the Cross, a contemporary and close friend of Teresa of Avila. He too was a Carmelite. His writings are now available in his collected works, including 'Ascent of Mount Carmel', 'Dark Night of the Soul', and 'Living Flames of Love'. These three works demonstrate how to approach union with God. Teresa's writings depict how to enter the seven dwelling places of the interior castle, and John amplifies and clarifies this process. His works sustained me through critical times. It is paradoxical but true that one must suffer to arrive at this point: suffering fosters spiritual growth, and leads to the experience of ever-increasing godly love, which is limitless; suffering forges the soul, spirit, mind and body.

The voice, which even now I still do not perceive aurally, helps me in this process in various ways; I even feel at times that it carries me along. Sometimes I find that things work out without help on a human plane; at other times it seems impossible to persevere, and indeed I could not do so without encouragment.

Nowadays the notion of suffering is generally rejected and regarded as senseless, something to be avoided at all cost. Yet suffering has a function which is beyond the imagination of most people. John of the Cross sums this up in his writing: suffering leads to purification, and a new spiritual man emerges who can rejoice in God's presence throughout eternity.

References

Collected Works of Teresa of Avila (1976);ICS Publications, Institute of Carmelite Studies, Washington

Complete Works of St. Teresa of Jesus (1975);Sheed and Mard, London
John of the Cross: Ascent of Mount Carmel (1983) Burns & Oates,
   Tunbridge Wells
John of the Cross: Living Flames of Love (1987) Burns & Oates, London
John of the Cross: Dark Night of the Soul (1976) Burns & Oates, London

Third Contributor (Anna Hofkamp)

I am paranormally gifted in the realms of clairaudience, clairsentience,
intuition, and to a lesser extent clairvoyance. For as long as I can
remember I have had at least one, and later several, inner voices. My
earliest memory of this goes back to nursery school. At that time I had
two selves: an ordinary child-self growing up in the usual ways, and a
fully-developed self. The voice I heard matched whichever self was
predominant, speaking in childlike terms to the child and in adult terms
to the mature self.

As a child, I accepted this unquestioningly, as children will. My two
selves would alternate abruptly, without any transition. The inner voice
was not, I think, unaffected by the changeover; the character of the voice
definitely altered. Generally, it would warn my child-self against certain
actions, such as the danger of playing near a ditch. It was more explicit to
my adult-self, for example warning me not to mention that I heard a
voice, as this would be misunderstood, or explaining why a teacher
behaved in a certain way. The difference in its tones was so distinct that it
remains vivid to this day. As I grew up, the adult-self waned, until it
receded altogether by the time I was about ten. The voice remained, like a
guardian angel and best friend combined. It was always recognizable,
sometimes warning, sometimes comforting, and always loving.

During secondary school, I once benefited greatly from my voice: it
supplied all the answers to a Dutch test. What an ideal way to crib - no
teacher could detect that! Unfortunately, when I looked forward to
similar assistance in a German test, nothing happened, and I still recall
only getting grade 3. From this experience, I realized that I was not to rely
on voices to help me in matters that I was quite capable of sorting out for
myself. One must never become dependent on voices, and certainly not
out of laziness.

I had, in fact, already vowed not to exploit the voices in this kind of
way, but one quickly forgets this sort of resolution when it is convenient
to do so. The lines I was given as punishment for doing badly in German
were a stern reminder of this vow. The experience was a formative one
for my inner self. Years later, I had a similar experience: when I played

cards, I would hear exactly which card to retain and which to discard. Consequently, I always won. Then I realized this was not honest, and promptly stopped following the voices' advice. As a result, I lost completely. Even now, I receive no intimation of what to do if money is involved.

The exchanges between the voice and myself went on in this way for years. As a child, I would sometimes find it warning me, for example, that it was time to go home or I would be late; as an adult, against staying in a particular hotel. I was always left the choice of whether or not to heed its advice, but with hindsight the voice aways proved correct. Sometimes it took a teaching role, explaining things that happened to me, especially up until I was six or seven, and again after the age of 26. Sometimes its advice was intensely practical, such as whether I would be able to find a parking space somewhere or should take a train.

Having grown up with a voice, I experience it not as an external phenomenon but as part of myself. In this respect it is like a conscience, although when it proves problematic one cannot simply ignore it. I myself had no real difficulty with the experience. However, I fully realize this is the exception rather than the rule.

In 1976, I took a course in spiritual psychotherapy given by an Englishman named Beesley. I learned a great deal from him about the human being as a spiritual being, and about reincarnation. Such matters could be considered paranormal. Incidentally, so many people today are confronted with the paranormal that it has become quite commonplace. Amongst other things, I learned about the significance of hearing one or more voices. Such voices can be inner guides, but are not always so - there are negative voices, too. (These voices can originate from the dead, but could also be a projection from one's own unconscious.) Negative voices usually play upon fears or other negative emotions. The unconscious is very complex, and - as with the normal world - can be a source of both ugliness and love.

After I took this course, I noticed that the character of the voice began to alter. For example, on one occasion it insisted that I should no longer smoke or eat meat. I was outraged, and protested that it was my life and I would smoke if I wanted to. A loving, gentle voice then answered, I am your inner counsellor. I was stunned and drained by this, and found myself sitting open-mouthed and staring into space. Since then, the earlier voices have disappeared, but this one has remained.

Since 1976 this voice, my spiritual guide, has taught me many philosophical lessons, lessons in living. Amongst other things, I have learned how to work with the positive and the negative and the golden mean between these two poles.

It is, of course, wonderful to have such a voice and companion, but not always easy. Being so preoccupied, it is all too easy to lose contact with reality. At one point I found myself torn between two worlds: I was involved with the social sciences academy, whose atmosphere and demands were on a completely different wavelength from my inner world, and this conflict became so difficult that I finally lost interest in both realms. I became physically ill and was totally sapped of energy, although my symptoms were rather vague and the doctor could not account for them.

Through an acquaintance, I came into contact with Zohra (Mrs Bertrand-Noach), who gives lectures and writes books derived from her spiritual awareness. When I studied with Zohra (1982-1988) and contemplated her teachings, I was amazed at the way she was able to shed light on my inner guide; she is the only person who has been able to explore and illuminate my experience. Her approach could be called psychosophy: *psycho* meaning soul, and *sophy* meaning wisdom. It is a means of contacting one's own inner wisdom and strength.

This woman has helped me, then and since, to integrate the spiritual with daily life, and to know when to leave well alone. When I was caught between two worlds, I was alienated and drained of energy by the dilemma. I could not cope with this until finally I recognized my weakness: my relations with other people. The unseen world, its voices and images, were all familiar to me and gave no cause for anxiety. I have learned to adjust to this, incorporating elements that I agree with and rejecting - respectfully but firmly - those I disagree with. This can often be hard, especially when fear has the upper hand and rules everything with its constriction. It is not in itself a voice, but a pervasive and terrifying threat when negative circumstances arise. Hence it is important to foster positivity and thus gain strength; this gives confidence, and helps those of us who are receptive to be less easily swayed by negative forces.

In seeking to understand the phenomenon of hearing voices, it can be difficult to find logical explanations for their content. It is, perhaps, easier to make some sense of the phenomenon by considering the circumstances in which the voices appear to arise. Mr Bosga, in his section on parapsychology (see chapter 7), refers to the British developmental psychologist Spinelli, who has formed the hypothesis that until one has a stable identity one will be more susceptible to distorted perceptions. His observations are drawn chiefly from work with children. Personally, I have particularly noticed that people with these identity problems also find difficulty in handling paranormal phenomena. I believe it to be of paramount importance, when dealing with the paranormal, to emphasize the formation of one's own identity, the development of love and appreciation for oneself, and the full acceptance of oneself with all one's faults. This is true for everyone. Where self-esteem is lacking, a person is easily suggestible, and can readily be swayed by the influence of others. This is especially so in the hearing of voices, which can issue absurd orders or threats, or conjure up confusing images, thus arousing feelings of guilt and unaccountable fear. The only value I can see in negative voices and images is that they reveal weak spots in one's unconscious, and give clear evidence that there is far more to our lives than the five senses suggest; this is an important truth which may lead us to greater insight and knowledge.

The following is a simple exercise which, in my experience, can be helpful in increasing strength and positivity:

Try to relax, and imagine that there is a light burning in your heart, radiating both light and heat. This light need not be large, just whatever size feels comfortable for you. Know that the light and warmth are a source of strength, infusing you with life. They radiate from your heart, filling your bloodstream and spreading throughout your entire body. You feel very secure in your own warmth. This light cannot be affected by anything outside of yourself, and is under your complete control; it cannot be extinguished, but will always exist. This is the source of your strength, the power that enables you to be what you want to be. Let the light and the warmth flow through your body for a while, and feel it strengthening you, like a battery being recharged.

You can repeat this exercise as often as necessary. Don't worry if it seems not to work the first time. With practice, it becomes easier and easier to concentrate, and the feelings of light and warmth will increase.

There seems to be a wave of particular interest at the moment in various forms of contact with unseen worlds, both positive and negative. As a result of this, the positive forces influencing our lives are increasing in strength: I myself have seen negativity successfully confronted and overcome by positivity. This is the way forward. A clairvoyant often perceives fear in the form of a great barbed hook: after each victory over fear, the hook straightens out, becomes clearer in colour, smaller and less substantial, and less can cling to it. You actually feel lighter.

I do not believe that problems with hearing voices can be resolved by denial or suppression - these can cause even worse problems. Hearing voices has its positive side, so long as you hang on to your own judgement. Make a pact with yourself: if the voices want you to do something, try suggesting that they ask you three times. If their demands or advice are important enough, they will be repeated, even though several weeks may pass. Meanwhile, just remember: when all is said and done, it is your life and you are answerable for it. You need not let the voices rule you, but can enter into a dialogue with them - there is nothing to stop you doing this. If you treat the voices with respect, they will respect you all the more.

A final word: the better we all learn to handle our emotions, the lighter and more positive the atmosphere surrounding us will become. This will, indirectly, nourish the souls of the dead and other forces, enabling them to come closer to their own light. So long as disturbed emotions are not involved, the hearing of voices is quite remarkable. To everyone who experiences voices, I wish much love and wisdom in their work with them.

Fourth Contributor

It all began with the ghostly messenger who appeared to us in the garden, and who came, I knew, to announce that Marc's time with us was almost up. Marc, my son, was then 28 years old, and suffered from Hodgkin's disease - cancer of the lymph glands. This messenger was very nice and courteous; he was huge, with a dark complexion and a presence that commanded respect. He communicated messages telepathically, which I understood without his uttering a word.

During Marc's death struggle, I saw his spiritual being separate from his actual body: a vapour issued from his mouth in a spiral form. When he partially recovered, this vapour sank down around his head. There were other periods when I did not see anything, and then Marc had briefly regained consciousness. This spiritual body later appeared in several different guises, and all of this was beautiful.

After Marc was taken from us, I found myself surrounded by noises - creakings and suchlike. When I talked about this, people told me that all houses creak and make various noises, but I knew this was something quite different. Subsequently there was one occasion when friends were forced to agree with my interpretation, and this confirmation delighted me. I now had proof that I was not alone. I received many signs and warnings that I knew could only come from Marc, they were so clear and miraculous.

However, the noises continued to disturb me. It reached such a pitch that I didn't dare to go to sleep: just as I was beginning to drift off, the noises would start up at their loudest and worst. This went on for some time. Then one night, thoroughly exhausted, I cursed them violently and turned my back on them. From that moment on, I was always able to slip easily into a long, deep sleep. I refused to give in to fear, and whenever I heard a creaking or grating noise I faced up to it directly and demanded my right not to be disturbed. As a result, both the fear and the noises have faded.

I wanted to know the significance of all this, and after searching for a long time I found a woman - Simone van Vel - who was a spirit medium. She told me immediately that my son and I were in telepathic communication. Through her, Marc told me that in the course of a few months I would go through a period of learning, and would then understand better. It all seemed so amazing and incredible, and I wanted so much to believe that Marc still existed, well and happy. Nevertheless, I did not want to cling to a hope based on pure illusion. Having exhausted the immediate possibilities, I was determined to know more, and this spurred me on to proceed with my quest.

I took a course in self-development given by the same medium, who repeatedly instructed me to sit at a table with a candle and photo of my son, and to note down what came to mind. I tried this, but couldn't make any sense of it. Was I just hearing my own words and thoughts? It all seemed too simple. Later on, however, I realized that messages were, in fact, being transmitted and received. To my own great amazement, I found myself in the situation of receiving messages from another world, where my son now resides, and where everyone continues to exist after discarding their earthly bodies.

During the course, we learned to develop the use of our senses, and in the process I realized that I had always seen into the future. I now knew that I was more sensitive than most, and that I had possessed these abilities even as a child - indeed, they had been the cause of some difficulty between myself and my parents, though I think they eventually understood what was going on. I was always rebelling against situations which were self-evident to me, but unseen and unknown to others. At the time I interpreted their inability to share my understanding as pure spite.

I had always viewed my parents and those around me as being much nicer, gentler, kinder, but above all more sensible and wiser than myself. This made it hard for me to understand why they sometimes acted as they did, making what seemed to me to be gross errors. It was almost as though they acted out of sheer perversity and ill-will, with harmful effects for myself and the other children. I have always wondered how, at the age of six, I could have understood so well how an adult should behave, given my limited life experience. I now know it was because I perceived everything from a different dimension.

I realize now that what I used to call my conscience - the voice that has been with me for my whole life - has been a Higher Helper (as I now refer to it). It has seen me through circumstances which others have told me they could never have endured. This power (for that is what it is) has governed my whole life without my knowing it. Deep within each of us lies that part of ourselves that is the true source of wisdom and knowledge, waiting to be tapped. The terms we choose to describe this power depend on our individual outlook on life.

Thus I began a slow and laborious process of growth, a study of all aspects of the supernatural - above all, its wonder and beauty - punctuated by breaks, yet progressing increasingly further. Meanwhile, I learned to contact Higher Beings consciously to bring out the best in myself, culminating in joyful vibrations filling my entire body. I learned to close off my aura so that only Higher Entities could reach me; this meant I was not at the mercy of lower, earthbound influences which have their own spiritual needs and demands and so have no insight or guidance to offer.

Undergoing this process changed me radically. Over a number of years, my views on life and death, people and society, altered so completely that everything once familiar to me was open to question. Even before I knew it myself, I came into contact with a support network, with wondrous results. I was also showered with many penetrating insights which have, in a sense, guided me for my ultimate good even up to the present. This fresh vision of people and of the world contains a profound philosophy of life which enables everyone to function at their deepest, most insightful level. We can all draw on our own inner source of energy to realize ourselves to the full, and be delivered from the trials of illness and confusion. Each of us has the capacity to understand our own suggestibility, and to learn how to fulfil our destiny by nurturing our true selves.

I have learned from this process to help people, drawing routinely on the suggestions of the Helpers which we all have. I discovered that if I was run down, distressed or despondent, I could not work. I recognized that if I gave of myself to people who were filled with fear, anxiety or alarm, I was incapacitated by these emotions; I had to face the real difficulties of adverse conditions, and learn to be discriminating. Faced as I was with many communications, I had to learn to preserve my equilibrium and to detect whether I was on the right wavelength.

The experience of making conscious contact depends greatly on one's own inner strength. To begin with, I always used to emerge in a daze from an encounter with another person. Each of us is affected by the inner strength of others; this keeps us earthbound, and is the realm from which all the decisions determining our earthly lives flow. But once there is a sufficiently strong will present in the soul, we can learn to respond to the expectations and demands of the supernatural, and work with it. This must take place without one just being used like an automaton, or else it is impossible to build up a counter-force. This can also happen in the case of other random influences. It is essential to hold on to a full sense of one's own identity, without any clouding of the vision by one's inadequacies and imperfections, for this may lead to weakness.

When one begins to confide in people, one acquires quite a different circle of friends, and quickly discovers that not everyone is open to such matters. I must admit that if I had not been predisposed by the death of my son, I myself might not have been sympathetic to this line of enquiry, and might even have resisted it quite vehemently. Consequently, I am careful to respect the opinions of friends and others, and do not press my point of view. When they find themselves in difficulties, they realize for themselves soon enough.

I have made considerable progress, but also have to break off from this work from time to time due to terrific fatigue, and to distance myself - sometimes I have simply had enough. I am also very concerned that I might make mistakes, and cause even more problems for those people in need who come to me. I am extremely warmed by the great confidence people have in me, especially as I myself was very hesitant at the outset. Strangely enough, my predictions always come true - if not immediately, then in the long-term. I suggest to people that they jot down or tape-record what takes place between us, and then report what I hear, as literally and honestly as possible; I am concerned, as much for myself as for them, to be as accountable as possible. I am always moved when, perhaps years later, people tell me that the messages I had passed on turned out to be fulfilled, and were helpful to them.

Through the conference held in Maastricht, I became acquainted with Pathwork and various other organizations. Pathwork and the illustrations given by Eva Pierrakos's were particularly close to my own experiences. Pierrakos's entire perspective, and the terms she used, warmed my very soul; until then I had not come across anyone who had evolved their own approach to this matter. It goes without saying that I heartily recommend this remarkable medium's books and articles. With their help, I underwent a new surge of growth, and I can now work with people again, with renewed confidence.

Looking back over my experience, I can conclude that my most important gain, ultimately, has been the development of great inner strength; I realize that, although I have been helped and guided in the ways I have described, it has to be my own initiative that sparks new growth. The impetus for action must come from within myself; I must take the risk and the responsibility of launching myself forward. Those who have travelled this road will know what this entails: all the pitfalls, the anguish, the fresh starts. Through all of this, though, one can learn to acquire the courage to carry on.

Fifth Contributor

I will tell you right from the start that I am one of the lucky ones: I have never been confused by the voices I hear. This is not because I am any sort of heroine, but because I had read about hearing voices before it began; this, and various other occurrences, prepared me for the phenomenon.

I realize with hindsight that this new phase in my life had already begun in 1979. At that time I underwent a dreadful crisis, and experienced great despair about myself: everything I did seemed like an accusing placard telling me that I was useless. A conviction like this quickly reduces you to hopelessness, and so I approached a psychotherapist for help.

Looking back, I see that by giving me his time and attention, the psychotherapist helped me to build up a healthy sense of self. He would ask, 'What do you gain from that?' or 'Why do you assume that?' When I had to make decisions about anything that affected me personally, I could never make out how he felt about things. He put me back on my feet again. He also helped me to develop the ability to make conscious choices, weigh up the pros and cons of each decision, and assume responsibility for the consequences of my choices, including the less pleasant aspects; at the time, this was a completely new concept for me.

One day, after I had been talking about myself, the therapist asked if I would like something to read, and gave me nine typed A4 pages entitled Lecture 60, to take home. This was an account of an aspect of psychological development. I was impressed by its clear-sightedness, which illuminated my own negative attitude. All this was and is very clear to me, but it is still very difficult for me to describe here. I could understand this text both intellectually and on an emotional plane. The illustrations showed how to work for self-improvement. I was 43, and had never read anything on what seemed to me to be such a high plane, so naturally I asked my therapist who had written this. He told me that the contents were voiced by Eva Pierrakos, but were not her own words; that she was a medium who could enter into a trance and become the mouthpiece of another personality or spiritual consciousness. I did not believe in this sort of thing at all, and said so, and we talked about it no more. However, I continued to read up on all this. There were 260 lectures in all, examining every conceivable aspect of human psychology. Little by little, I found myself beginning to wonder whether there had indeed been a spirit at work.

A couple of years later, my attention was caught by a book written by Jane Roberts; she too could enter into a trance and speak on behalf of spiritual beings. Both women impressed me as being totally normal: for example, they liked disco-dancing, had a sweet tooth, and enjoyed lying in the sun and drinking wine. This showed me that they were ordinary people. But they were also capable of something extraordinary.

Jane Roberts was all of 32 when she heard a voice in her head for the first time. Her reaction was that this was all very well, but that she wanted to be satisfied that this was no illusion, or product of her sub-conscious or unconscious. She therefore spent a year testing out this voice, and wrote an account of this in her book 'Seth Speaks'. She and her husband, as well as others who were involved, became convinced that she can indeed speak on behalf of an entity named Seth. I next read, in quick succession, the other five books about her and Seth. There was a striking similarity between her accounts and those of Eva Pierrakos, who also had a Guide who spoke through her. During this time I abandoned my disbelief in spiritual entities.

I cannot remember in which book I found it, but Seth introduced a relaxation exercise to help one realize the possibility that there is more. I followed this exercise, and after a couple of times I saw or felt an image before my closed eyes; immediately, I understood that this was a warning about a thought that had just gone through my head. I was pleasantly surprised by this, for it represented help in a psychological realm that I had some practice in. After this, I spent a year and a half assuming that, with help and practice, other people were capable of similar experiences. In due course, more images - and later, words - followed. I kept all this to myself because it was so personal. I was also, of course, rather afraid that some people would find it strange. When, later on, I confided in others who were themselves spiritually developed, I had quite a job to convince them that these experiences were not available to everyone. One can call this phenomenon being a channel.

It is difficult for me to say whether I hear or feel words. Sometimes they seem to come from a long way away; often I understand immediately, while at other times I don't. I have always known for sure that some messages do not originate from the world of my own thoughts; thinking feels different. At worst, my experiences in this period were unexpected or surprising, but there was never anything frightening about them. The language used tended to be rather formal and unlike my own speech; the content would normally be something I myself could never have come up with: an idea, a tip, a suggestion, or the answer to something I had been wondering about. This source knew me better than I knew myself, and I suspected that I had no secrets. I found this strange, and it took me time to get used to it.

After about a year and a half of positive experiences, something quite different happened. One Sunday morning two years ago, I suddenly felt a roaring against my forehead, accompanied by a long stream of words predicting a terrible event. All this was completely out of the blue, and I felt panicky and didn't want to believe what had happened. At first I thought perhaps I had imagined it, but then decided I had better take it seriously and do something about it. I was at a complete loss, though, until I remembered Seth. I got out one of his books to see whether he had offered any advice on how to dispel such negative thoughts, either by using the imagination or by actual physical gestures. This was all new to me, but fortunately I was alone and in no danger of looking foolish in anyone's eyes. In his books, Seth does give instructions for rooting out and throwing away such negative thoughts, and I immediately acted on his advice. I will return to this later.

My reaction after that was rage - I would not be used for such purposes. Seething with indignation, I went through the action recommended by Seth. After this, the incident seemed to be over and done with, but it soon became clear that this was only the beginning of a whole series of similar episodes. I can't remember how often these happened, but I know I was preoccupied with them for some time. There were several voices: a harsh, man's voice in my head or right behind me; a shrill, shrieking, woman's voice, whispering loudly in my chest or lower down, or below me to my left, or above me to my right; and a nasal voice sniggering and ridiculing me. These would appear singly or together, and gave destructive commands or made inane comments. They also made some witty observations, some very astute, others more cruel, and these would hit home very painfully. I was stunned by the subtle, sharp intelligence shown by some of them. All had mannerisms which I recognized in myself. It was very confusing when good advice was given in an unpleasant whine, or a nasty comment was made in a friendly tone of voice. I was at a loss as to what to do, and what to believe.

I have always preferred certainty to uncertainty, and refused to do anything unless I myself was convinced that it was right; if I felt something to be wrong, I would politely but firmly (sometimes angrily) send the messenger back to his friends. If in doubt, I would say that I was not sure and would have to think it over, and that the messenger should leave me alone in the meantime. Then the voice would always leave. I knew that even if I was frightened, I must never ask for clarification or act intimidated. It became clear to me that it was ridiculous to believe that the voices could overrule my own will. I never asked them questions in case it encouraged them; I was convinced that I was dealing with potentially dangerous forces. Of that I am afraid.

A central issue for me is how to deal with uninvited and undesirable visitors, and the heavies are the worst of these. Let me give an example. With time, I came to see that there is a relationship between the nature of my thought patterns and the type of visit I can expect. Whenever I entertain negative thoughts, negative voices appear. I know this, but still sometimes forget it. Two weeks ago, I was extremely angry with someone, and spent much of the day grumbling to myself. That evening, I was alone at home when suddenly a shrill voice cried out, 'Hello darling.' At the same moment I saw two large, fiery, drooping eyes staring at me, and I felt as if all my energy was flying away in all directions, as if I was exploding with fright. I knew from experience that if I did nothing I would be restless and completely shattered for days, responding tensely to people and events, and unable to concentrate.

I therefore made a point of doing something about this, using Seth's advice. I trust him, and don't know of anyone more competent to tell me how to deal with the voices in my head; he himself always appears as a voice in one's head. Having emitted largely negative forces that day, I attracted evil. I knew that I had negativity, and thus evil, in me, but that I am not myself evil. So when I heard the voice that Sunday, I immediately resolved not to identify myself with evil - whether in myself, in others, or around me. I threw all evil away from me, as far as I could. Through Seth, I had learned to make an actual physical gesture which gives me strength and enables me to pronounce, 'There, that's gone.' Afterwards, I call out to the messenger: 'Go to your friends, you may not stay with me.'

I know now that other people carry, besides evil, good and light within themselves. There is a higher self, a source of heat, composed of pure positive energy, and it is from here that I make constructive decisions. I have always known that I am actually, for all my faults, a good person. A baby moves me because it radiates sweetness. My discovery of goodness has been beset with misconceptions, negative interpretations and suchlike, but I have decided that whatever happens I will cultivate the good in me. Personally, I do this by filling my thoughts with images of light. I breathe light in through the crown of my head until it fills my whole physical being. This relaxes me and gives me feelings of pleasure, and I continue until I feel as if I am smiling from the inside. At the same time, I think of the source within me, and say short phrases of affirmation such as, 'I live in a safe world', 'I am worthwhile', and 'I like people and they like me'. After a while, I feel my energy flowing again, and am filled with inner peace. Sometimes I sense a rumbling in the background, and restlessness threatening to return, but only when all around me is peaceful do I stop; this may take anything from two to 20 minutes, depending on how well I can concentrate. Afterwards, I can think clearly again without emotional disturbance.

At this point I feel complete, but my work is not finished yet. As I have said, there is a connection between my negative thought patterns and the unsavoury behaviour of the voices, and I am understandably terrified of facing this reality. We humans prefer not to believe that we ourselves may be partly responsible for our own unpleasant life experiences. We all like pleasure, but nastiness appeals to nobody. Nevertheless... This is quite well-known in Pathwork.

This is how I see this issue. Whenever I send evil away, I have peace for a while, but sooner or later it returns into my life in some form. After the second year of our lives, we construct inner convictions, a mixture of positive and negative, truth and misconception. The negatives are such things as resentment, fear, suspicion, disbelief, hatred, cruelty, and other destructive urges. Life experiences and other impressions are usually interpreted, correctly or incorrectly, at an unconscious level; misunderstandings that remain unconscious cause us our problems. For what is unconscious is inaccessible to us, and cannot be tested against reality. We are blind to the ways in which our misconceptions fail to correspond to reality - a reality that varies from individual to individual, to the extent that our lives vary. Thus one may be lucky in love but penniless, while for another, things may be the other way around. We react according to our conclusions, and simultaneously also create our own personal radiation, with which we attract similar people, events, and also voices. For these reasons, everyone at the Pathwork school works according to this vision of themselves, whether or not they now hear voices. Once we become conscious of our destructive urges and the ways we give them expression in our lives, we can, if we so choose, transform these into something constructive on behalf of ourselves and others. In company with people equipped for this task, we help ourselves and each other not to deny the faults within us, with varying degrees of success.

All this may sound threatening, but happily the effect is that people come to like themselves more - and, by extension, other people too. This is because relief floods every aspect of your personality that comes under scrutiny when you know that this is your prevailing reality. Denial only promotes a sense of guilt. As belief and the desire to change increase, it becomes easier and easier to express one's better self spontaneously. I myself have become gentler, and my experiences with unhelpful voices are separated from one another by months at a time.

You may conclude from all this that I am a medium, but this is not the case. I still have a great deal of purifying work to undergo, and do not know what may lie in store for me.

References

Pierrakos, E. Guide Lectures for Self-Transformation; Centre for the
    Living Force, Sevenoaks Pathwork Centre, Madison, US
Roberts, J. (1979) Seth Speaks: The Eternal Validity of the Soul; Prentice
    Hall, Eaglewood Cliffs, New Jersey

Sixth Contributor

To tell the story of how I became conscious of hearing voices both
positive and negative, and how I learned to deal with them, I must go
back to when I was 28 years old, when my husband, myself and our son
Lex lived with my parents.

My stepmother had been to the doctor complaining of stomach pains.
She had been referred for X-rays to investigate this, and came to tell me
about it before she went for her appointment. When she had left, I sat
quietly, wondering what might be wrong with her, and at that moment I
heard and saw that it was cancer. I also heard that it was her liver that
was affected, and that she would die. I saw the funeral, and heard that it
would be in the new year; the skies would be overcast and the ground
would be covered with leaves. This is exactly what happened.

It was not until later, in adulthood, that I first consciously heard
voices, and although the information they communicated was terrible,
they aroused my interest. I began consciously to talk with them. What I
had done unconsciously ever since I was a child now happened
consciously.

As a child, I was aware of something unseen being in contact with me,
though I didn't know how. I also knew that I played and chatted with
invisible children. Once my mother asked me who I was talking to, and I
answered, 'to myself', but knew that I was lying. I was said to have a
lively imagination.

After my mother died, when I was 13, my father made me go to the
graveyard every week. There I would pray (grown-ups seldom know
what their children are up to). On one such occasion I heard voices
talking to each other. I pretended it was only the wind rustling in the
trees, but secretly knew better: unconsciously, I knew there were actually
voices. I recited a Hail Mary to my mother in her grave, and added: 'I
will talk to you more at home.' Then I heard a voice say: 'That's good,
child, be off with you now.' It was most definitely my mother speaking.

When I chose to relate consciously to voices, I would sometimes
receive information which initially made sense; these were positive
voices. There were negative voices too, though, which stopped me from
doing things or did things to me. For example, they might make my arm

heavy and raise it up in the air; then I would go over to the wall and begin writing on it, without a pencil, describing what I heard from the voices. I wrote the most awful things, the most dreadful desires on the wall. The voices also sent me to the shops, where they said I would see or experience something, but of course this would not be the case. They would also make me tell lies to people. When my sisters asked whether my stepmother was really as ill as the doctors made out, I answered calmly, 'Of course not, she is just imagining things', when I knew this was not the case. I knew already from my positive voices that she had cancer, which the doctors confirmed from the X-rays.

The voices continued relentlessly for some time. I could no longer ignore them, and went along with them because I did not know how to put a stop to them. One day they announced that I was terribly ill. I certainly felt ill - by now, I could hardly walk for the pain I felt in my leg. When my husband asked me what was the matter, the voices informed me that it was polio, and that my husband should put me to bed. But far from feeling sympathy for me, my husband exploded with anger: he swore at me and shouted that this nonsense of hearing voices had to stop. So I had to try to stand up by myself and get myself to bed, and to my great surprise I found that I was able to stand unsupported, and could walk.

I learned from this incident that I could choose either to give the voices free rein or to set them aside, and in the years that followed, I exercised this choice according to the situation. When the voices were negative, I rejected them. When they were positive, I took notice of their messages - for example, a warning that I would lose my wallet or my keys - which were always accurate.

I still had a longing to do something with the positive voices, but was at a loss as to where to go to learn this. I found an avenue opening up for me when my son Lex became ill. Immediately after his wedding, he was stricken with severe back pain, and I wanted to do something to help him. I recalled another time when he had been extremely ill and had been cured with help from the spiritual world. Let me tell you how this came about. Lex was two-and-a-half at the time, and when he became ill, I took him to the family doctor. He was admitted to hospital, and after numerous investigations, it was confirmed that he had osteomyelitis of the hip. Injections had no effect on the illness, and the doctors told us that he would never recover. My sister-in-law went to visit him in hospital when he was looking his worst, and was shocked because she thought that Lex was dead. When she got back home, she called on a neighbour who she knew was involved with a group of people who had contact with the spiritual world.

The spiritual world is so-called by those who believe that there is life after this earthly life. In this other world there are, of course, the souls of doctors and medical specialists, and the group this man belonged to had contact with such people. My sister-in-law told him about Lex, and asked if he could help through his contacts. This he did, and he told my sister-in-law that she was in the nick of time to save Lex. To our utter amazement and joy, and for no visible medical reason, Lex brightened up. Everyone was at a loss to explain his improvement, including myself - I only learned the full story some years later. After two months, our son was able to return home. Once again I want to thank the specialist who said, very honestly: 'Don't thank me, it's not my doing. It's a miracle. Thank the Lord above.'

Naturally, I thought back to this incident when I became worried about Lex's back pain. Meanwhile, he had been told by the specialist that he must do no heavy work for two to five years, otherwise he could find himself confined to a wheelchair. I wondered at this point whether he was suffering from some kind of paralysis. I wanted to contact my sister-in-law's neighbour, but after making some inquiries, I heard that he had died. Someone gave me the address of the people he had worked with, and this is how I first came into contact with a spiritualist association. I attended an open evening where participants were invited to place an object or a photograph on the table, and a medium would comment on it. When the medium began, I was amazed, because what she saw and heard, I also saw and heard.

After this, I attended several similar open meetings, and eventually joined a group from this association in the hope of developing my awareness. In this group, I learned particularly to tune in to my feelings and recognize whether or not they were positive. I also learned that we all have a spiritual leader or guide, and became conscious of my own helper. This guide puts you in touch with things that you cannot otherwise know, bringing them into your awareness, and what he says makes complete sense. This fills you with an immediate and loving feeling; because what he says is so right, you come to trust him, and by building on this you learn to work with positivity. This is how I have learned to work with my guide.

I also learned during the association's meetings that there are voices belonging to those among the dead who remain attached to the earth. These earthbound spirits are unaware that they are dead, and that after their earthly life they must progress to another world. As a result, some of them identify with, and thereby take possession of, living people who resemble them in their appearance and thoughts. For example, the spirit of a dead wheelchair patient may inhabit the mind of a living person in a similar position, having concluded that they are one and the same person.

I had been with another association for about two years when someone recommended I go to the Association of Spiritual and Natural Healing (ASNH). There, they told me, I would be able to develop my skills as a magnetizer - a gift that was strongly present in me. I found myself attracted to the ASNH because its spiritual attunement was similar to my own. Besides magnetizing, I also learned how to make use of positive voices, and to avoid involvement with the negative ones which can make earthly human life truly unbearable. I later came to realize that dealing with negative voices is a field of work in itself. I learned that negative voices can arise out of good ones, a confirmation of something I already knew. I discovered the importance of remaining stable in order to keep the upper hand, and of avoiding physical exhaustion. I learned to hold fast to the positivity in myself and build upon it: in this way it is possible, amongst other things, to transmit energy to others.

At the meetings of the first association I had learned about earthbound souls of the dead; at those of the second, I learned how to direct the voices of such spirits to the hereafter or eternal life. One way of doing this is to explain to them that something has happened to kill them suddenly, and that their spirit has therefore departed from its earthly body. I tell them that although they cannot see their earthly body, they are still caught up in the moment of their dying. When they understand this, I am able to make them see that there is another, better life awaiting them.

Let me describe an example for you. I was sitting in a group where we were discussing some photos. Superimposed on the photograph of a child who had had some accident, I saw a dead child, a young boy. I began talking with him, and found that he had stepped out of the school bus and been run over by a car. He thought he had only fallen over, and so was still standing by the bus. He was crying and searching for something; when I asked him what he was looking for, he said, 'I've lost my cap.' I asked him, 'What do you want with your cap?', and he answered that he could not go home without it. I showed him (symbolically, of course) where his cap was, and his tears turned to laughter. I talked some more with him, and explained what had really happened. When he had grasped this, I was able to lead him towards the light.

I also learned that the souls of the dead communicate from the afterlife - paradise, heaven or whatever you choose to call it - and give guidance to those still on earth, and help them to do good; such a soul can be called your helper, leader or guide. This was familiar to me, as I was already working positively with the voice of my own leader.

I succeeded in getting my qualification as a magnetizer, and in my practice I found that I heard both where and what the subject's complaint was. Thanks to my leader, I heard and became acquainted with doctors from the spiritual world. They advised me about specific illnesses and ailments, and were always spot-on. This was a wonderful time for me, until one day I realized that negativity, envy and jealousy were rife in the group I was working with. I saw this showing itself in arguments in which comments were made that did not ring true. I could feel that all was not well, and that there was a negative undercurrent which was uncomfortable to my spiritual intelligence, especially as I had assumed that all the others had attuned themselves to this work in the same way as myself.

Meanwhile, I had got to know a woman who I discovered was paranormally gifted. We discussed things together a great deal; she had developed the faculties of clairaudience and clairvoyance, as well as being able to distinguish positive and negative voices. She came to the group with me a couple of times, and told me that some of the members were terribly negative. This was further confirmation of what my leader had told me - that I must leave the group to start one of my own.

At about this time, I found myself getting negative voices again. As yet, I had not learned to cope with them. I had learned to talk with them, and to point out the wonderful realm awaiting them in the afterlife, but these voices were not receptive. They were aggressive, and threatened both the existence of my spiritual helpers and my own belief in myself. I sensed that my magnetizing deteriorated, as well as my relationship with my spiritual leader; the questions I put would be answered wrongly because of the way I was feeling. Anyone who hears voices will recognize this.

I felt I was powerless, and became demoralized to the point where I felt I really could not go on. Luckily, the woman I mentioned - Ann - was still around. She too was burdened with negative voices, which told her that it was bad for her to be involved with me, and that I was vindictive and told lies. They also suggested that I was less spiritually attuned than Ann thought, and that she should have no more to do with me. Ann and I spoke with the voices together, and succeeded, in spite of their lies, in realizing that they were sent by the thought powers of others. It is possible to transmit harm or self-destruction to a person by means of negative powers, which can be sent through feelings of hate, jealousy or envy. This was what was happening to me; later on, well-disposed spirits told me by whom and why.

Together we persevered, trying to set aside negative thoughts and to discuss things in positive terms. We kept indicating to the negative voices what a wonderful world lay ahead after earthly death. We constantly reiterated that they must let go of the earth and earthly people in order to reach joy, love and light. Ann and I also learned a great deal during this period, particularly that the positive always triumphs over the negative. We learned that, however terrible the influence of voices may be in your life, there is always an end to it if you yourself are prepared to fight for it. Together we were able to engage in this struggle, and fortunately we have now learned to cope with negative voices.

As for myself, I went through hell for a couple of years, but have survived, thank God. I have learned so much from this period that, together with Ann, my greatest friend and colleague in this work, I can now offer more and more help to those still enduring such hell.

Seventh Contributor

In order to explain how I have learned to cope with voices, let me first tell you how I heard them for the first time, and how they influenced my life.

After finishing secondary school in 1977, I started training as an ergotherapist. In order to follow this course, I had to go and take lodgings in rooms in another city. A brief sketch of myself: I am male, an only child, and probably because of this, am excellent at keeping myself amused. You could say that I am a loner. I am extremely creative, and love painting, amongst other things; in my new rooms, I had plenty of space for this. My girlfriend stayed behind in the place where I was born, but although I had few new contacts, I must say that student life did not pass me by; indeed, I slept very little. For the first time in my life, I could decide for myself what I wanted to eat, and either cooked my own meals or ate in the hospital canteen. In short, I was free to come and go as I pleased, with no ties or constraints other than the question of what to do with my future.

After a few months, I fancied painting the large white wall in my room; this wall was a challenge to me. I began painting a dark forest on it, with a reptile in the foreground. Painting is something which is transmitted from your head to your hand, and I have always been able to hear colours; they are transmitted by vibrations. I hear black, red and dark brown. It was deathly quiet as I painted in the room, as I didn't have a radio on or anything. In the stillness, however, I felt something alarming beginning to grow - some threatening presence hovering, and I had the distinct impression that I was no longer alone in the room. Then I heard in my ears a monotonous noise which was not from myself and which I could not explain. It was a bit like the sound you hear when you put your fingers in your ears, only this sound was lower and more monotonous. It was an emotion, too, but even deeper than that, and I had the sensation that something was searching for me.

In fact, what I was hearing was a cry for help from a group of people. If I had to be more specific, I would describe it as the sound of aboriginals, of primitive voices: a very menacing, eerie sound. It would begin to whine, and then tail off, repeatedly badgering and goading me. Something wanted to take possession of me, and did so. I heard no Dutch (my own language) being spoken, nor any foreign languages; instead, everything was spoken in emotions. I couldn't utter an intelligent syllable in reply, only noises. For the sake of this account, I will call these sounds that I was hearing voices.

I had often had similar experiences in the past, but the sound had always been more distant and less threatening. After this episode, I felt threatened and hunted. It was as if there was something inside me that could suddenly appear at any moment: this feeling was consciously and unconsciously always present. In fact, I felt mad. I didn't dare to tell anyone about the voices, and was too afraid to be alone and express my emotions, for example on paper. I never knew when the voices would appear; often they did so at the most inappropriate moments.

I have always been religious - not only because of my upbringing, but also on my own account. Prayer is a part of contemplation; prayer is communication with a power, which I call 'God', though others may give it different names. I asked that power to help me. How long it took before I had the courage to say 'STOP' to the voices, I don't know exactly, but I do remember the emotional moment. I think it must have been about three years later. Not much had changed in my situation; the voices were not so active, but I continued to feel pursued - they could suddenly overwhelm me at any time.

The first time I dared to say 'STOP', I will never forget as long as I live. I was driving from Zwolle back to my work. I had just had a very emotional conversation in which I had opened myself up completely. I drove on to the motorway, and was suddenly totally aware that I was afraid: afraid of the power of the voices. There and then, in the car, I said out loud, I am scared, not just once but several times. Alone in a car, you can carry on without anyone hearing, and that is what I did: it was a kind of primal scream. It was as if I was casting something out from inside me, and this gave me a sense of liberation which made me happy; this was the moment when I felt I was becoming fully mature. I accepted myself as I was, and as I still am. I did not have to run away, but could accept the existence of the voices. I said 'STOP' to them, while accepting them as independent spirits, as something outside of myself. If I had to describe the process I went through, it would be in terms of the following phases:

- shock;
- fright and flight;
- research into the significance of the voices;
- acceptance of the voices as independent spirits;
- acceptance of myself;
- research into my reasons for flight;
- confrontation with the voices;
- compromise between acceptance and rejection of the voices messages.

After all this, it looked as though the turbulent rapids had disappeared from the river of my life. I was in calm waters, and could decide my own course. I still hear or feel that cry for help, but now I send it away, and that liberates me. I am myself, and can maintain my selfhood.

I hope that I can help to set other people on the road to this same feeling. You have to be able to say, 'I'm OK; you're OK.'

7. HEARING VOICES: NON-PSYCHIATRIC PERSPECTIVES

Introduction
Marius Romme

Psychiatric explanations for hearing voices represent only a small part of the substantial number of theories devised to account for the phenomenon. Given the broad base of this book's conception, we thought it appropriate to include a number of contributions which outline some of these other theories. In our choice of subject matter, we have been guided by the histories related in the previous chapter, and have included the conceptual frameworks used by these contributors. It should be pointed out that the explanations adopted by voice-hearers themselves seldom correspond completely with any single existing theory, but instead combine various elements from different models.

We have already seen, in chapter 6, a wide variety of personal perspectives. The first contributor ascribes the voice to a guiding mentor. A fair number of those who hear voices hold this view, and not only amongst those we met; several examples can be found in the literature of the field, for example in the research of the American psychologist Myrtle Heery. We have therefore included a brief description of her research with 30 voice-hearers.

The second contributor characterizes the phenomenon as mystical in nature, and identifies strongly with the mystical experiences of Teresa of Avila. This has prompted us to select a contribution on mysticism in religion.

The third contributor offers an interpretation of voice-hearing as both a paranormal gift and a means of achieving spiritual growth. Parapsychology has become an important contemporary movement appealing to many who hear voices, and we have included a section to reflect this.

The fourth contributor's account illustrates another way in which voices can represent a phase in the striving for spiritual advancement. The Path, as it is known, is a significant representative of those branches of spiritual thought in which a medium plays an active intermediary role.

The fifth contributor's central belief is that there is life after death, and that it is possible to communicate with the dead; this not only has an impact on the grieving process, but also shapes the life of the mourner. This type of approach called for a contribution about the metaphysical school of thought.

Voices are interpreted by the sixth contributor as deriving from the spirits of the dead which are not at peace, a view developed by psychics. In acknowledgement of this important approach to the phenomenon, we have included a section written by a psychic, outlining his personal rationale within this perspective. Theories of reincarnation are of particular significance here, with the assumption that the human soul is reborn several times, each time with a fresh task to accomplish (Karma).

There are various other issues and theories associated with the phenomenon of hearing voices which we have not been able to include here. In particular, we would refer any readers interested in voice-hearing in so-called primitive cultures to anthropological literature such as the writings of Professor Erika Bourgignon.

References

Bourgignon, E. (1970) Hallucinations and Trance: an anthropologist's perspective; in Kerp, W., Origins and Mechanism of Hallucinations; Plenum Press, New York

Inner Voice Experiences: A Study of 30 Cases
Myrtle Heery

Throughout human history, there have been descriptions of the voice within in religion, history, psychology, fiction, and myth. The psychological literature on these experiences has largely focused on individuals considered to be pathologically afflicted, while the religious literature concentrates on those thought to be divinely or demonically inspired or possessed. Surprisingly little attention has been given to the inner voice experiences of people who fall into neither of these groups. This study of selected reports of such experiences represents an exploratory investigation, and suggests a foundation for further research into the phenomenon.

The term inner voice describes a significant subjective experience: the actual perception of a voice speaking internally, and/or a vaguer felt sense of some inner communication. Just as the physical voice communicates between one human being and another, the inner voice may communicate intra-psychically - that is, between one level of the psyche and another (Van Dusen, 1981).

The history of the world's major religions makes it clear that saints, sages, prophets, and teachers (such as Moses, Muhammad, and Teresa of Avila) have relied heavily on inner voices for their inspiration, their guidance, and their authority. The experiences of these men and women have had tremendous impact on our world. But just as people diagnosed as psychotic and schizophrenic have no monopoly on the inner voice, neither do saints and sages. There are a great many ordinary men and women in that broad continuum between these two extremes who also report hearing inner voices. This study deals with the inner voice experiences of 30 adult men and women who are neither saints nor diagnosed as psychotic.

Method

30 subjects, all of whom had reported hearing inner voices, participated in this study. Fifteen were selected personally by the author, and 15 taken at random from amongst 50 respondents to a questionnaire on inner voice experiences, which had been mailed to 200 people on a psychological/educational mailing list in California. The subjects' experiences were explored in a deliberately naturalistic manner, allowing their various aspects to emerge with as little observer contamination as possible. My particular intention was to examine in depth the positive relationship between their voice experiences and their exterior lives.

Categorization

In order to define some categories, nine subjects were selected as a representative sample of the 30 to be interviewed, and each was interviewed twice. This selection covered a variety of inner voice experiences occurring under disparate circumstances, and a wide range of occupations, incomes, levels of education, and lifestyles. The resulting material was analyzed by the author and a colleague with extensive experience in the evaluation of subjective interview data. We independently read verbatim transcripts of the interviews, along with my notes on their intonation patterns and silences, and subsequently met to discuss our respective findings. There were some very obvious areas of agreement, and where there was doubt or uncertainty, we returned directly to the transcripts and tapes for clarification. Fairly clear groupings of types of inner voice experience soon began to emerge.

Three major categories arose out of the first nine interviews, and we then used these as guidelines to analyze the data from the remaining sessions, refining and redefining them as we went along. These three categories were as follows:

1. inner voice experiences revealing fragmented parts of the self;

2. inner voice experiences characterized by a dialogue providing guidance for the individual's personal growth;
3. inner voice experiences opening channels towards and beyond a higher self.

Three case studies

The following case studies include a representative from each of the above categories. The respondents' identities have been disguised to protect their anonymity.

1. Inner voice experiences revealing fragmented parts of the self

Eric is a 33-year old liberal arts graduate, married, with two children. He was previously employed in managerial work, but is now unemployed and living with his wife and children at his in-laws' home. He has started studying to be a teacher, and is also studying social work. His reluctance to commit himself firmly to a career and the support of his family suggests that he is still fragmented in major areas of his life.

Eric reported that his inner voice had control over some situations, including his leaving his last job, as though he had surrendered his free will to the voice.

I was absolutely a victim of the whole thing. I just sat back, and the thing (inner voice) did it to me and I didn't have a vote about it. I was another takeover.

Eric's experiences led him in a positive direction, but he denies that the inner voice is any part of himself. He sometimes questions its guidance, but feels strongly that it has the final say in any matter.

I had stopped some relationships that were getting real negative, and I didn't have the courage to do that, but I got myself into the situation and a voice-over just came out of my voice and I said things that destroyed the relationship. I mean it (inner voice) finished the relationship, which was the appropriate and healthy thing to do at the same time. I, in my individual personage, didn't know how to do that, so the voice took over.

This strongly suggests an expression of fragmented parts of Eric's personality, and this fragmentation seems to be leading him towards integration.

2. Dialogues providing guidance for personal growth

Ruby is 38 years old, married, and a former educational consultant.

Within the last year she has given up her consultation, and is devoting her life to painting.

My inner voice is what tells me when to paint, when it's the right time and when it's not time, and when it would be futile. And my inner voice gave me the direction about quitting my job and doing what I'm doing with painting.

Note that the emphasis here is on dialogue with the inner voice, rather than submission to its dictates, as in Eric's case.

I check that (what I'm doing with painting) out a lot. Last spring I was given an opportunity to apply for a state grant and become a consultant, and it seemed on the outside to me a real exciting possibility, but when I checked it out with my voice, my voice said absolutely not, that it would get in the way of my painting... it wouldn't have given me time for painting, so what I see it (inner voice) really doing a lot now is directing me more towards my original intent, which was to paint.

Ruby's change of profession is a direct result of her inner voice experiences. Note her phrase, 'I checked it out with my voice'. Ruby engaged in dialogues with the voice, actively using it for guidance in the liberation of creative energy; this is quite different from Eric's resignation to the commands of his inner voice.

3. Channels towards and beyond a higher self

Rob is a 63-year old writer and counsellor, with three grown-up children. He lost a fourth child 24 years ago after a sudden illness, and it took him a long time to get over this loss. He feels that parenting has been the most rewarding and humbling experience of his life, and that his 38 years of marriage have enriched him. Certainly these things seem to provide a firm foundation for Rob, and give him the sense of being deeply rooted in life.

Rob's beliefs have led him to perceive his inner voice as 'a deeper level of my own being'. Experiencing this was a significant part of his life at the time when he finished his divinity doctorate and became involved in work that was notable for its non-violent, selfless nature. He recounted an experience he had at the age of 33:

It operated once, that I can remember, in the civil rights movement, when I was in Mississippi in 1961, and I was part of a visitation to Jackson, where the Freedom Riders were. There were a group of 40 or 50 of us in

this room in a black college, and they were asking for people to volunteer to go with seven or eight into the airport restaurant, which meant we'd be arrested and go to jail. They needed a white Protestant minister, and they asked two or three times. They were about ready to leave, and the Rabbi who was heading up the delegation said,
'Well, we haven't got a white Protestant minister yet', and then I heard this voice say,
'Well, you've got one now', and that was me. I was so surprised that it was me, that I had said that. It came from some very deep place in me. I was hearing it and saying it at the same time... I wasn't uncomfortable about it. That's what I wanted to do, what I believed in, and that's what in my deepest self I wanted to do. I was never dissatisfied or upset or distressed by what I had said, but it surprised me.

Rob feels a spiritual dimension, which he defines as 'the I being part of a larger process', at work in his inner voice experiences. He sees the phenomenon as closely related to intuition, but makes the distinction that his voice experiences have consistently been a part of his spiritual life and being. For him, there is an element of volition and choice in these experiences. He finds prayer and meditation helpful in contacting the inner voice when he makes a conscious decision to do so. Rob does also have such contact when he has not deliberately sought it, but intention is nevertheless an important aspect of his relationship with the voice.

Summary
All of the individuals in the third category practise some form of meditation on a regular basis, and express a deep sense of spiritual connection through their inner voice experiences. The sense of certainty they enjoy is very similar to that reported by Arbman with regard to comparable experiences on the part of mystics. It is possible that the subjects in this category have attained a certain level of mystical experience which happens to embrace an auditory element, and which leads to positive selfless action, as described above in Rob's case.

Three reactions to spiritual awakening
Assagioli (1986) outlines three reactions to spiritual awakening which parallel the three categories of inner voice experiences emerging from this study. He describes these in terms of energies and levels of organization with regard to peak experiences. According to this framework, superconscious energies work with the individual according to the levels at which he or she is capable of receiving and integrating them. Assagioli observes that one possible outcome of a peak experience is that

it may fail to bring about a higher level of organization. In this case, the experience is often painful, and the individual may not recognize its transpersonal origin.

The positive outcome of this kind of experience is that the individual can be directed to the next steps that are necessary for fuller integration. This idea parallels our study's first category of inner voice experiences revealing fragmented parts of the self. For example, Eric has not yet recognized the transpersonal origin of his voice experiences, but they have continually led him to piece together various fragments of himself: he is searching for a career that will reflect his talents as well as help him support his family; he is no longer content just to do any job, but has developed a commitment, through his voice experiences, to find work that reflects his personality.

The second possible outcome of peak experiences, according to Assagioli, is less intense, and involves a temporary neutralization of personality patterns. What remains is very important: an ideal model, and a sense of direction which the individual can use to complete the transformation through his or her own purposeful methods. This sense of direction is precisely what we saw in subjects falling into our second category of inner voice experiences, where a dialogue was established and served to further the hearer's growth and development. Ruby's experiences, for example, guided her in the direction of changing her career to one of painting. This change, she reports, has been extremely fulfilling for her, and she continues to change and to grow in a positive direction.

The third outcome described by Assagioli is a higher integration of personality, in which the individual's life is permanently transformed as a result of the experience. This type of integration is rare, and may be compared to our third category of inner voice experiences. Those in this category find themselves integrated and opened to their higher selves by their experiences, and undergo a permanent shift in their lives. In our study, we found this enduring shift in personality to be also associated with selfless service - work without financial reward or apparent ego gratification.

An inner curriculum

These findings suggest an ongoing interior education, with the inner voice as the teacher. Alschuler (1987) has made a study of religious figures who had inner voice experiences, and postulates an inner curriculum. The experiences reported by subjects in our third category, where channels opened towards and beyond a higher self, showed some similarities with this inner curriculum.

Firstly, according to Alschuler, contact with the inner voice calls into question the individual's former beliefs about reality. Next, he or she goes through a process of intensive instruction, which may involve periods of isolation. The last stage of the curriculum is union, characterized by a fuller identification with the other world, a tour of heaven and hell, and a spiritual marriage with the inner teacher. Those who have experienced this level of inner education set out on missions of unification in the exterior world: their knowledge of the other side is so clear and powerful that they want to do what they can to make this side resemble it more closely. Although none of the subjects in this study reported this level of experience, those in our third, most integrated category were consistently involved in activities of selfless service. Sometimes this may have pre-existed the hearing of voices, but it was always intensified after the onset of these experiences. These subjects were in touch with something that transcended their individuality.

A foundation for further investigation

These findings suggest that psychotherapists might do well to consider quite a wide range of possibilities when a client reports hearing an inner voice. These possibilities might include such diverse processes as a fragmented voice, psychotic or integrated dissociation, extrasensory perception, intuition, vocation, or a spiritual awakening. The three categories emerging from this study may provide a starting point and a much-needed map of sorts for the exploration of the phenomenon of inner voices. They may also serve as a foundation for further investigation into a little-understood but widely-reported experience.

Finally, this study may help to dispel the common stereotype of the inner voice as the prerogative of saints and people diagnosed as psychotic, and thereby encourage research into its potentially liberating effect on our human capacities.

References

Alschuler, A. (1987) The World of The Inner Voice; unpublished data

Arbman, E. (1963-1970) Ecstasy or Religious Trance, vols. 1-3; Scandinavian University Books, Stockholm

Assagioli, R. (1986) Self-Realization and Psychological Disturbances; Revision Journal no. 8 (2nd edition), pp.21-31

Van Dusen, W. (1981) The Presence of Other Worlds; the Swedenborg Foundation, New York

Voices, Religion and Mysticism
Aad van Marrelo and Ton van der Stap

To apprehend the truth of one's life, external voices must be silenced. (E. Drewermann)

Mysticism is primarily an experience. Although descriptions of this experience - where available - are inevitably time- and culture-bound, they all share one central assertion: namely, that the object of the experience is not merely a part of reality, but reality in its entirety, as a unity. The subject of the mystical experience believes him or herself to be communing with a realm embracing everything that exists; a realm not separate from reality itself, but not wholly knowable in everyday perception. This realm seems to reveal to the subject a self-evident truth, beyond the reach of reason and the senses, representing the culmination of everything.

In all religions, from the very first, mysticism has preceded all else: it is impossible to conceive of any form of religion - whatever its culture of origin - coming into being without the foundation of a mystical experience. Ancient Japanese Shintoism was based on the experience of the godly in nature; Buddhism was born at the instant of Buddha's enlightenment; Christianity arose from people's individual encounters with God in the form of a human being, Jesus of Nazareth. In every case, the experience comes first: only later is it followed by doctrine, structural form within a given society, and coherent codes of morality.

Although the mystical experience itself, given the nature of its object, is not amenable to rational explanation, it is not in itself in contradiction with the powers of reason. However high our society's esteem for reason, it is not yet so exalted that experiences beyond its ken are automatically dismissed as unreal. Over the centuries, there have been attempts in both East and West alike to find a systematic philosophical basis for the mystical experience. Perhaps the best-known example is that of the Kyoto school of Buddhism in Japan, where the centuries-old tradition of Zen Buddhism is married to a Western philosophical inheritance. Within Christianity, the 13th-century Meister Eckhart is notable among those placing their personal mystical experience within a convincing theological and philosophical framework.

Whatever the culture, though, all mystics repeatedly emphasize that the experience itself remains inaccessible to reasoning, and that it is both inexplicable and incommunicable. This means that the content of such an experience is necessarily unverifiable, and can only be known by those with similar perceptions and by those who are open and receptive to mystical experience. This characteristic of unverifiability by reason is shared by various other fundamental human perceptions, which tend to be best recognized when expressed in the language of the body or in poetic terms.

The object of the mystical experience - the apprehension of reality as a living, significant oneness - is called God in Western religious traditions, and has always had a personal character. This personification of the ultimate reality is not, of course, exclusive to Western culture, but the version of it found in Christianity can be traced back to the monotheism of Judaism. According to this model, the assumption of the existence of a God leads to the belief that He will make himself known to people, and will be sought out by people; thus it follows that this God is manifested through speaking. Throughout the entire Jewish Bible, God is found addressing humans in speech: He calls them to account, enters into dialogue with them, and listens to their questions. Despite cross-fertilization with religious traditions from other sources (for example, Neoplatonism), Christianity has always retained its concept of the personal God. Consequently the mystical experience has, without exception, always been expressed in terms of a personal encounter. In the popular Christian consciousness, God is an external reality while the perceptible world, creation, is, so to speak, not-God. This dichotomy, peculiar to Western monotheism, sets the terms for the formulation of the mystical experience - even though the experience itself gives the lie to the dichotomy. This creates an odd dilemma for Western mystics, and one which is alien, for example, to Buddhism.

Since the ultimate reality in Buddhism is not characterized as a personal God, it is clearly inconceivable for this reality to speak. We confine ourselves here to the most highly-developed form of Buddhist mysticism, namely Zen, which does not allow for any kind of voice-hearing. Certainly, the experienced Zen master is aware that his disciples may occasionally have the impression that they are hearing voices, and understands that these voices may seem so convincing that the hearer can identify the very spot from which the sounds originate. But the master knows that this, like the perception of unusual images or other paranormal experiences, is simply a part of a particular phase that must be undergone by a pupil in the course of his or her training in meditation. The master will invariably advise anyone encountering such experiences to remain calm and centred, and above all to attach no significance to the phenomenon. Contemporary Zen masters explain that these perceptions are sensory in origin, and released by the unconscious. The calm certainty with which these masters advise their disciples probably stems from this school's centuries-old familiarity with mysticism. They know from long historical experience what may be helpful to their disciples on the road to enlightenment, because they are familiar with the goal and the means for its attainment.

This is quite different from the Christian tradition, where the mystical experience so often takes the form of a dialogue with a speaking God. Generally, Christianity has been notable for its suspicion of all the varieties of unusual experience which appear to affect the mystic, such as ecstasy, speaking in tongues, levitation, and so on; but it has been far less resistant to the seeing of visions and the hearing of voices, provided that these clearly originate from God, Jesus or another revered, holy figure such as the Virgin Mary. In order to determine whether any such voices do indeed originate from an authentic godly source, the Christian Church has evolved a special tradition known as Discernment of Spirits, which is essentially a kind of psychological health test conducted by the Church authorities. Mystics have often contributed to this assessment process by drawing upon their own experiences. Thus the English mystic Julian of Norwich declared that a sense of inner certainty about mystical insights was itself a guarantee of their authenticity. Similarly, Ignatius of Loyola advised his clients to decide for themselves whether or not a particular inspiration, which might in itself seem very wise or exalted, actually bestows inner peace. Generally speaking, the Church's own basic criterion for judging the validity of mystical experiences is whether those experiences are shared by others.

With few exceptions, mystics claim to see visions along with the voices they hear, and this is often cited as proof of their conviction that these voices are received internally. On the whole, the voice offers an explanation of the vision, which is seen with the inner eye. Sometimes the voice will make mysterious, obscure pronouncements which prompt meaningful reflection. Sometimes the voice may supply the answer to a deep, long-standing question about life, or satisfy more or less unconscious spiritual longings. Invariably, the common elements concern what may be termed the hidden meaning of reality (for example, the oneness of creation in God, the nature of evil, or the certainty that the individual, even in his or her loneliness, is shaped and nurtured by God). Sometimes the voices may inspire feelings of deep sorrow over such things as sin and suffering, but when this does happen, the experience always culminates in an overwhelming feeling of blessedness stemming from the realization of the goodness of reality in God. The course of this process depends on the disposition of the individual concerned: the intensity of the insights is largely a function of the degree of personal commitment to this area of experience. But peace, once attained, never deserts the mystic, who is notable for his or her lucid moral perspective and the protection of the same optimistic vision of life. In short, the hearing of voices imparts a remarkable self-confidence to such individuals, a peaceful certainty that is truly felt rather than merely believed in accordance with Church teachings.

The voices heard by mystics tend to speak in the idiom of the day. Those reported by mystics in the Middle Ages, for example, are strongly coloured by the contemporary forms and manners of worship. There also appears to be a close connection between prevailing social structures and the culturally related utterances found in any given period. To Hildegard van Bingen, in the 12th century, God appears as an organizing principle throughout the entire cosmos; in retrospect, we can see in this the image of the well-organized society of the Hohenstaufers (12th and 13th centuries). In the mid-13th century, at the height of the troubadour era, Hadewijch sees mysticism in terms of a noble adventure, with particular emphasis on the experience of unconditional love and absolute fidelity. Catherine of Siena, in the 14th century, is preoccupied with the suffering of Jesus, and her association with God is accordingly experienced as baptism in the blood of Jesus.

Around the 16th century, mystical phenomena seem to become more marginal, with only occasional reports of divine visitation by voices and visions, although those that are recorded continue to reveal the same imprint of cultural and social factors. By the 19th century, there is evidence to indicate that the messages imparted in visions of the Virgin Mary no longer deal with the immense, existential questions common to all mystics everywhere, but tend to be restricted to the issuing of moral imperatives - commands and warnings reflecting the status quo, and issued through a conservative clergy working within small, simple, and closed environments. Under these circumstances, the hearing of voices is kept confined within the framework of religious visions, unaffected by the profound mystical foundation which might otherwise underlie it. This attitude, it could be argued, has persisted into modern times: voices and visions have long been regarded as limited religious experiences. Although to some extent accepted within this framework, they are viewed as having only individual significance, and - contrary to the experience of the great mystics of history - having no function within society.

A Metaphysical Perspective
Ingrid Elfferich

I am a gerontologist by profession. You might wonder, then, why on earth I should be writing about metaphysics in a book about the phenomenon of hearing voices. It all began when I was at college, conducting research into the ways in which people who had suffered a great personal loss managed to find a new meaning to their lives. Those who had most success in this all appeared to be people who - as they put it - had found contact with something higher. It was amazing to see how much more easily these people managed to deal with their problems once they had had what might be termed a transcendental experience.

I have also had the privilege, in my work, of counselling those approaching death. In the course of this, I discovered that the dying often find the process eased and calmed by what has come to be known as a near-death experience. Some of these people managed to let me know that they were hearing voices. Usually, they would recognize the voice as that of someone who had died before them, someone they had known and loved, although I am well aware that many other voice-hearers do not always have such a definite idea about the origin of their voices.

These experiences prompted me to search for a frame of reference that would do more justice to those who hear voices but are mentally perfectly healthy - more justice, that is, than is done by the orthodox psychological framework.

This search has been inspired by at least three considerations. The first is that, in at least some cases, voices give a concrete, sane message which is in accord with the facts of our visible world, and indeed adds new information to that world. These messages contain material which, as far as can be traced, cannot possibly have resided in the consciousness of the person hearing the voice. The second is that these people are fully aware of the fact that they hear messages which cannot be heard by anyone else: there can be no fault found with their so-called reality-testing, which is more than adequate. The third fact is that some of these people clearly acknowledge the difference between their own thoughts and the voices: even while they are actively engaged in talking or thinking for themselves, completely occupied with concrete matters, the voices may announce themselves.

These three facts do not fit into the usual model for understanding hearing voices, which declares that it is an intra-psychological phenomenon. We are in need of a new hypothesis, and we must acknowledge this need.

Those who hear voices find themselves in difficulties when either they or the people close to them do not have an adequate frame of reference. Matters may become worse still if they adopt a theory which serves to render them powerless. Clearly, an alternative perspective might help them to come to terms with their experiences. Even the simple knowledge that hearing voices may be the result of a form of perception not understood by orthodox psychology and psychiatry might provide considerable relief.

In the course of meeting these people and studying these issues, I became increasingly aware that our conventional view of the world and of people is simply too limited. Many other scientists have come to a similar conclusion, and begun to venture into areas normally considered to be outside their profession, in their search for a new understanding.

A wider view

I would like to propose a metaphysical perspective which encompasses the phenomenon of hearing voices within a broader vision of human existence in the world.

To begin, I would like to quote two Dutch philosophers. The first, Berger, wrote an introduction to metaphysics in which he stated that the literal meaning of metaphysical is aiming beyond or carrying beyond. The metaphysical hypothesis implies a layered reality: a reality composed of various interconnected time-and-space dimensions that cannot be apprehended with our normal, everyday senses. The second philosopher, Poortman, suggests that our mind or spirit may have its own energy that is, in some sense, physical. If this were so, it would be plausible to assume that this spiritual energy completely pervades the physical level of our existence.

According to this philosophy, there may be planes and dimensions surrounding and interpenetrating our physical lives, influencing us in ways which are not yet fully understood. This metaphysical view suggests that, on some level of our consciousness, we are interconnected not only with the living but also with the dead, who may still exist in another dimension of reality and in a more subtle body. Within such a perspective, hearing voices may be understood as an act of communion with fellow human beings on a different plane of reality such as some clairvoyants claim to be able to perceive. It is possible that emotional trauma may rupture the familiar boundaries of our field of existence, creating a hole through which voices from another dimension may take hold of the person concerned. Clairvoyants and clairaudients sometimes claim to be able actually to see these holes, but given that these are not ordinary, physical, sensory experiences, it may be more correct to speak of extrasensory perception. Nevertheless, within a broader perspective, these extra senses may very well be the ordinary senses of a meta-organism - an organism composed of a different kind of matter.

Our search is not, however, limited to these parapsychological domains; it may also be fruitful to venture into the realms of physics and of new research into the nature of consciousness.

Physics

Contemporary physicists are at pains to point out that our inherited, accepted view of reality is quite inadequate: the underlying structures of our universe are proving to be far more complex than we have tended to assume. As one physicist puts it:

Quantum theory has shown that the sub-atomic particles are not isolated grains of matter but are probability patterns, interconnections in an inseparable cosmic web that includes the human observer and her consciousness. Relativity theory has made the cosmic web come alive by revealing its intrinsically dynamic character. The image of the universe as a machine has been transcended by a view of it as one indivisible, dynamic whole, whose parts are essentially interrelated and can be understood only as patterns of a cosmic process. (Capra, 1982)

Several other contemporary physicists have tried, like Capra, to apply this view of modern physics to the fields of physical, mental and spiritual health (Bohm, 1985; Wolf, 1986; Hayward, 1987; Zohar, 1990). According to some of these, mysticism - particularly eastern mysticism - expresses the nature of reality more adequately than the explanations we were all given at school, which persuade us that the world is made up of entirely self-contained entities, and that our mind is somehow separate from the universe. It seems that on the contrary, the structures we perceive in three-dimensional space are woven into the totality of the universe. The holographic model, for example, is a pioneering theory which uses mathematics and logic to show that the so-called supernatural is probably a part of ordinary nature after all.

We cannot escape the conclusion that there must be a transcendental order, a spiritual principle that has a formative influence on matter. It is significant that physics is being forced to resort to metaphysics - an outlook which presupposes an entirely different order to the universe than that offered by traditional science. Perhaps the time is ripe for us to become aware of the metaphysical questions hidden behind the apparent laws of nature, to consider a version of reality that embraces quite different principles of time and space. Certainly, many physicists now seem to agree that modern physics has important implications for some of the fundamental concepts of psychology and psychiatry: it calls into question accepted notions of the self, feelings, mind, and - last but by no means least - reality.

Research into consciousness

Until recently, Western science was convinced that all aspects of human consciousness could be explained in terms of the physiological interaction of cellular brain-processes. There is now, however, a growing belief that these electrochemical activities must themselves be explained by reference to an autonomous spiritual principle. The brain-researcher G. R. Taylor gives numerous examples of perceptions arising without any perceptible prior sensory stimulation. He concludes that cerebral activity alone is insufficient to account for the dynamics of consciousness: sometimes our mind seems to have an energy at its disposal which is entirely its own, and quite different from that characterizing normal observable brain activity (Taylor, 1979).

Some scientists engaged in research into the human mind have found strong indications that we might do well to regard the human mind as a spiritual principle connected with other dimensions of reality, an energy which, during our physical life, is at least partially independent of brain activity. Stanislav Grof, the American psychiatrist, conducted 30 years of research into altered states of consciousness, and contributed a great deal to the study of so-called transpersonal experiences. He developed a method of penetrating into the deeper layers of consciousness, and discovered that in these layers our psyche may touch upon a concrete reality which is inaccessible to our normal, waking mind. Grof echoes many of the ideas of modern physics, and regards altered states of consciousness as sources of information on the nature of the universe and the human mind. His observations on psychosis are particularly relevant to the subject of hearing voices:

All Western definitions of psychosis emphasize the individual's inability to discriminate between subjective experience and an objective perception of the world. The key phrase in the definition of psychosis is accurate reality-testing.

It is therefore obvious that the concept of psychosis is critically dependent on the current scientific images of reality. Traditionally, psychiatry has defined sanity as perceptual and cognitive congruence with the mechanistic world-view. If an individual's experience of the universe seriously deviates from this model, this will be seen as an indication of a pathological process involving the brain, or a disease. Since the diagnosis of psychosis cannot be separated from the definition of reality, it will have to be drastically influenced when a major shift in scientific paradigms changes the image of the nature of reality. Grof concludes:

According to the new model presented here, functional matrices that are instrumental in psychotic episodes are intrinsic and integral parts of

human personality. The critical problem in understanding psychosis is,
then, to identify the factors that distinguish the psychotic process from
the mystical one. (Grof, 1985)

Mystical experience

Mystical means in direct communion with absolute reality, or experiencing the oneness of the universe. A mystical experience is the perception, beyond communication, of a higher reality, and the most powerful way in which human beings may receive strength from a source beyond themselves. Through this experience, we may discover that our ordinary view of reality is only one of many modes of perception. We may be lifted on to a higher plane by forces from another dimension, and be led to the conviction that our consciousness is indestructible. We may touch a reality which transcends that which we have always accepted. Those who have undergone such experiences tend to describe them as states of knowledge, but this knowledge is seemingly difficult to reconstruct within the limitations of our ordinary state of consciousness; the consequence of this is that the new knowledge cannot be passed on to others. But the psychological impact of the experience is clear: direct contact with universal oneness leads to the immediate conviction that there are more things in heaven and earth... than are dreamt of in our philosophy.

The mystics' version of reality is very much in agreement with that advanced by modern physicists. In 1966 the psychologist LeShan conducted a revealing experiment. He selected 62 different statements about how the world works: half of these were by physicists (Einstein, Oppenheimer, Bohr, Heisenberg, Planck), and the other half by mystics (Eckhart, Aurobindo, Vivekanada). He shuffled these together and gave them, with no indication of authorship, to a group of people, all of whom were trained in either physics or a mystical discipline. When asked to identify the author of each statement as physicist or mystic, their guesses were no better than 60% accurate: the similarities of viewpoint were too great, the conclusions about the nature of reality too close to one another.

A striking example of the awareness of an existence beyond the individual psyche is the near-death experience. Research into the perceptions of the dying has shown that people may have experiences similar to those of the mystic. Perhaps the most striking revelation, however, of the autonomous, dynamic nature of our mind, and the existence of other dimensions within our universe, is offered by the experiences of those who have been clinically dead. There is no scientific explanation to account for the fact that such people, after resuscitation, may give a precise description of events which occurred around their dead body at a time when no brain activity was registered. In almost all cases where the facts could be verified independently, the perceptions of the dead have matched the details of the actual events. There is no sensory explanation for this accuracy. Moreover, the contents of such experiences are quite consistent with one other - far more so than one would expect if they were simply the products of individual, isolated brains. Many of those who have had such an experience are convinced that they have been granted a glimpse of another form of existence.

The many scientists who have studied this subject in depth tend to view the near-death experience as a strong indication that the human mind may be active and aware within another dimension of reality, independently of any brain activity. Science as a whole must not neglect the facts that face us.

Conclusion

Contemporary research into both physics and human consciousness appears to offer confirmation of the metaphysical view of the world: namely, that a human being may transcend his or her physical existence and find access to other dimensions which are as much a part of the reality of creation as is the visible world.

What use, though, is this metaphysical perspective to the person who hears voices? Its potential benefit lies in the fact that it opens up the possibility of the voices representing a phenomenon which transcends the individuality of the hearer. This model places our perceptions in a broader framework of understanding, one which implies a capacity to make and maintain contact with other planes of being. In the case of negative voices, this would suggest that one may be fighting something which actually exists, even though its reality is not perceived by others. This being the case, it is clearly necessary for hearers of voices to develop the mental power and capacity to shut themselves off from these perceptions.

The main psychological implication of this perspective is the necessity - especially in the case of negative voices - of working through emotions or events which were not properly dealt with in the past. The harmony resulting from self-acceptance may be the best protective shield one can have when confronted with these negative energies.

Those who are afraid of being regarded as crazy because they hear voices may find great relief in the simple assurance that their experiences are nothing abnormal, but are shared by many mentally healthy people. The worst thing that can happen to a voice-hearer is to be put in the hands of someone who does not know this, and who regards any case of hearing voices as pathological. On the other hand, a psychologist or psychiatrist who is aware of the possible impact of transcendental experiences may be able to help others towards healthy integration of these experiences, a process which will enrich the meaning of their lives.

We need to bring about a shift of viewpoint which would help us to clarify the fact that we live within a universe composed of interpenetrating levels of reality. Hearing voices - because of the richness of information carried by some of these voices - may even help us to bring this shift about. With the help of the hearers themselves, we may discover the laws governing our capacity to attune ourselves to other dimensions of this space-time reality.

References

Bohm, D. (1987) The Enfolding-Unfolding Universe; Revision Journal; reprinted in Wilber (1982)

Bohm, D. (1985) Unfolding Meaning; Routledge & Kegan Paul, London

Capra, F. (1982) The Turning Point: science, society and the rising culture; Simon & Schuster, New York

Grof, S. (1970) Beyond Psychoanalysis: implications of LSD research for understanding dimensions of human personality; Darshana International, New York

Grof, S. (1985) Beyond the Brain: birth, death and transcendence in psychotherapy; State University of New York, Albany, NY

Hayward, J. (1987) Shifting Worlds, Changing Minds: where the sciences and Buddhism meet; Shambala, Boston

LeShan, L. (1966) The Medium, the Mystic and the Physicist: towards a general theory of the paranormal; Thurstone Books

Pribram, K. H. (1982) What the Fuss is All About; in Wilber (1982)

Taylor, G. R. (1979) The Natural History of the Mind; Martin Secker, Warburg

Wilber K. (1982) The Holographic Paradigm; Shambala, London

Wolf, F. A. (1986) The Body Quantum: the new physics of body, mind and health; MacMillan, New York

Zohar, D. (1990) The Quantum Self; Morrow, New York

Parapsychology and Hearing Voices
Douwe Bosga

It is misleading to generalize about experiences of voice-hearing as though all were equal. Closer analysis shows that the umbrella term 'hearing voices' covers a wide range of highly divergent experiences. An individual who cannot cope with these voices usually ends up needing psychiatric help, and such help has long been based on the view that the client would benefit most by the total disappearance of the voices. This view has gradually begun to change: people are starting to realize that the real problem is not so much the hearing of the voices, but rather the inability to cope with them.

This is certainly true of the form of voice-hearing associated with parapsychology, which is known as clairaudience. As the term suggests, this is closely related to the much more widely-known phenomenon of clairvoyance. To illustrate what kind of light parapsychology might throw on hearing voices, we shall first deal briefly with the phenomenon of paranormal perception in general.

Extrasensory perception

Parapsychology is concerned with the study of extrasensory or paranormal perception. In this context, para- means beyond; paranormal perception, then, refers to a perception that is additional to normal perception, ie that occurring via the five physical senses. The implication is that individuals so gifted are capable of obtaining knowledge, by extrasensory means, about events in the world around them and about other people's experiences: they see, hear, or know something that could not have been perceived solely by means of their own eyes, ears, or any other known organ. Extrasensory perception is usually divided into two groups: telepathy and clairvoyance.

Telepathy and clairvoyance

Telepathy is defined as the ability to acquire information about the contents of another being's consciousness - human or animal - without the use of the five senses. Contents of consciousness consists not only of thoughts, but also of feelings and emotions; in short, all those factors constituting human consciousness. Since this knowledge is obtained without recourse to the ordinary senses, it follows that the perception is not restricted by space: telepathic messages can cover large distances.

Clairvoyance is the ability to acquire information about people, things or events without the use of the five senses. The difference between this and telepathy lies primarily in the object of the knowledge gained: where this knowledge is concerned not with the contents of another's consciousness, but instead with events either involving or not involving people (or animals), we speak of clairvoyance. These perceptions may relate to events in the present or the past, and sometimes in the future.

By definition, telepathy and clairvoyance are closely related - so closely, indeed, that it is often impossible to distinguish between them.

This explains why, in practice, people tend to refer to any of these phenomena as ESP (extrasensory perception). Clairvoyance is, in any case, a somewhat unsatisfactory term, because it suggests that a psychic sees clearly; as will be shown, many cases of extrasensory perception do not involve seeing, and even where they do, the image is seldom very clear. A paranormal impression may be quite vague, or correspond only partially to reality. The well-known psychic Warner Tholen once put it like this:

Let me give you an example of how clairvoyance works. Imagine that you have just walked through Piccadilly Circus in London, and then you try to visualize the scene immediately afterwards. In all probability, what you summon up will only be a vague impression, or you will see one part of the area very distinctly and other parts not at all. One person will see the monument clearly, another the steps and the pigeons, another the entire place crowded with people, and so on. This is very similar to the experience of clairvoyance. On one occasion you may see only a small part, another time you'll see something vaguely and get a certain feeling, another time you may see several fragments without knowing how they interrelate.

Classification of extrasensory perception

Various attempts have been made to classify the phenomena of extrasensory perception. One such system was introduced by the parapsychologist Frederic Meyers in 1904, and is still widely used today. Meyers divided the modes of ESP into two basic categories: sensory automatisms and motor automatisms. Within these categories, he distinguished several types, each representing a more precise definition of the mode of expression of the extrasensory perception. Since the motor automatisms are of no interest to us in the present context, we shall not discuss them here.

Sensory automatisms

In sensory automatisms, paranormally-obtained information is unwittingly transformed into a sensory perception. Six types of sensory automatism can be distinguished, five of which correspond to the five senses, while the sixth relates to paranormal knowing or what we might call clair-knowledge.

1. **Clairvoyance**. One of the most frequent modes of expression of ESP is visual perception. Here, the extrasensory information is transformed into a visual image.

2. **Paranormal feeling**. While clairvoyance is undoubtedly the best-known manifestation of ESP, paranormal feeling probably occurs the most often. By this we mean that an individual takes on the physical pains and feelings of others, and the extrasensory information is transformed into a bodily sensation.

3. **Clairaudience**. This entails the hearing of an inner voice communicating a message relating to reality.

4. **Paranormal smelling**. When smell plays an important role in some matter, this can appear in paranormal perception. Thus, a psychic might suddenly smell (for example) cow dung during a consultation, indicating that the person for whom he or she has a message has some connection with cows.

5. **Paranormal tasting**. Given that the incidence of ESP is fairly widespread with regard to the four senses so far considered, we must suppose that there are also more instances involving taste than have been documented. One such example concerns a mother trying to decide what to feed her family the next day; her son already knew what she did not yet know herself, because he experienced the taste of spaghetti in his mouth. Such cases, however, make scant appearances in the literature, and it may be that parapsychologists have not given this area sufficient attention.

6. **Paranormal knowing**. There are cases reported in which extra-sensory information is not transformed into an image, a sound, or any other sensory impression, but in which the perception nevertheless somehow penetrates the consciousness. In these cases, we speak of paranormal knowing. The individual may have a certain feeling without knowing its significance, or become suddenly aware that something is happening. Here, we are on a borderline shared by such phenomena as intuition and inspiration, which science is similarly ill-equipped to explain.

Clairaudience

In parapsychology, the hearing of voices without any sensory basis is routinely linked to the seeing of images, the smelling of odours, etc. Under what circumstances, one might wonder, should we consider the phenomenon to be the proper subject of parapsychological study? Clearly, only when the messages heard can be demonstrated to correspond to actual events in the material world. A rather dramatic example may serve to illustrate this.

A clergyman was urgently warned by an inner voice not to go to the theatre that evening. He obeyed the voice, and did not go. However, as he had already bought the tickets and it seemed a shame to waste them, he offered them to a friend. His friend was very pleased by this generous offer, accepted the tickets and went to the theatre in his place. During the performance, the theatre caught fire and burned down; the clergyman's friend died in the blaze.

The Dutch parapsychologist W. H. C. Tenhaeff (1976) considers clairaudience to be a phenomenon of veridical pseudo-hallucination. In our example, the clergyman could be said to be hallucinating inasmuch as he hears something lacking a sensory basis. In fact, though, we are dealing here with a pseudo-hallucination, because he is aware of the fact that he hears something which is not actually present. Finally, it is a veridical experience because the contents of what was heard corresponded with later events.

Favourable conditions

There are certain conditions that appear to be particularly conducive to the experience of extrasensory perceptions. Studies have shown (Schmeidler, 1988) that when people are in an altered state of consciousness (such as hypnosis, dreaming, deep relaxation, or extreme stress), there is an increased occurrence of spontaneous experiences of clairvoyance or clairaudience. It has also been demonstrated that instances of ESP are especially common between individuals sharing an emotional bond, such as partners, relatives, and therapists and their patients (Schwartz, 1980; de Bruijn, 1992).

In 1987, the British developmental psychologist Spinelli formulated an interesting hypothesis. He suggested that we are in a position to speak of registering the thoughts of others only if we are conscious of our own, and can thus distinguish between the two: in other words, only when the individual has his or her own identity can he or she appreciate that the thoughts or experiences of another are involved. This foundation led Spinelli to the hypothesis that, for a given individual, extrasensory perception is likely to be especially frequent until a stable identity has been established. Until such time, the boundaries between self and other have not yet been defined. Indeed, anyone in this position is, as it were, wide open to others: the impressions belonging to the other person are experienced as being one's own. This is unlikely, under these circumstances, to be experienced as threatening, because the need to protect one's own identity has not yet developed. Clearly, according to this model, we would expect to find many instances of extrasensory perception amongst young children in particular. This was indeed confirmed by Spinelli's study, which also showed that the number of such experiences decreases in proportion to advancing age.

There are, of course, many adult experiences of clairvoyance or clairaudience, but these seem to occur primarily in altered states of consciousness and within emotional relationships. In both these circumstances, the individual is less inclined to seek to protect his or her own identity, and will therefore be more receptive to the other party. Within the context of any such relationship, strange thoughts will obviously not be experienced as being quite so threatening as might otherwise be the case. It would, of course, be an oversimplification to claim that any ESP experience taking place outside either of these special circumstances is evidence of weak identity; however, Spinelli's approach provides an interesting perspective for further investigation.

There remains the question of whether a person is likely to gain any benefit from the knowledge that his or her voices are producing information derived from paranormal perception. In our experience, this is only partially the case. In practice, such experiences often appear to be felt as a great burden, and this can give rise to severe problems. At the Counselling Department of the Parapsychology Institute in Utrecht, we try to help those who believe themselves - rightly or wrongly - to be experiencing psychic or paranormal phenomena, and who do not know how to cope with them. Many kinds of problem may arise; one of our staff, Martine Busch, has grouped these into five main categories:

1. **Problems arising from the experience itself.** The contents of the experience itself are unpleasant. Information is received about unpleasant matters such as illness, death, etc. This may give rise to feelings of guilt, but also to confusion, because it is so difficult for people to understand the nature of such experiences. Many feel as though they are actually living in two separate worlds.

2. **Problems arising from the reactions of family and acquaintances.** People are made to feel peculiar or misunderstood, and the reactions of their peers make them feel alone in having such experiences. Already aware of being different, they may suffer great insecurity, confusion and loneliness.

3. **Problems arising from playing paranormal games.** The attempt to contact the spirits of the dead has always been a popular pastime. Leaving aside the question of whether this is really possible, it is clear that, for some people, such games can lead to quite extreme fears, obsessions, and states of alienation.

4. **Problems mistakenly presumed to be paranormal in origin.** When, in the midst of genuine mental distress, a single paranormal experience occurs, the individual may seek to use this as a general explanation for all else. Similarly, psychosomatic ailments may be ascribed to a presumed paranormal sensitivity.

5. **Problems of assimilation.** The subject does not know what to do, or what can be done, about the paranormal experiences, is looking for spiritual growth, wants to develop his or her paranormal abilities, or wants to find a way to incorporate the paranormal into the totality of his or her personal development.

If we accept that there may be voice-hearing phenomena reflecting an active capacity for paranormal perception, it is still necessary to control the influence of the voices. Such mastery is of the essence, for all those who are truly paranormally gifted are confronted by unwanted impressions. It seems to be impossible to prevent this from happening; it is, however, possible to learn how to cope with it. This leads into territory beyond our present scope, so let one brief remark suffice here. Those who are, or believe themselves to be, consistently oppressed by extrasensory impressions can benefit greatly by sitting down quietly for about ten minutes once or twice a day; this will allow the space to acknowledge and accept all the current impressions. Together with positive instruction on how to tackle these perceptions effectively, this type of exercise will relieve a great deal of pressure.

References

Meyers, F. W. H. (1904) Human Personality and its Survival of Bodily Death; Longmans, Green and Company, New York

Schmeidler, G. R. (1988) Parapsychology and Psychology; McFarland, Jefferson, NC

Schwartz, B. E. (1980) Psychic Nexus; Van Nostrand Reinhold, New York

Spinelli, E. (1987) Child Development and GESP: a summary; Parapsychology Review, vol. 18, no. 5

Tenhaeff, W. H. C. (1972) Telepathy and Clairvoyance; Charles C. Thoman, Springfield, Ill.

Pathwork and Hearing Voices
Marga Croon

Pathwork was founded in 1952, although this name was not used then. Eva Pierrakos (then known as Eva Broch), had found herself, at the age of 37, literally taken by the arm and launched into automatic writing. She was not at all distressed by this, but was sensible enough to contact a friend who was more familiar with such matters. Eva initially felt it unwise to undergo such experiences alone, and took daily guidance from her friend.

The individual who is sensitive to phenomena such as these has, so to speak, an opening in his or her energy field through which entities can enter. Eva learned that these beings exhibit various characteristics: good and evil, pleasantness and deceit, gentleness and cruelty. When one is receptive, all of these characteristics are capable of being manifested: one can be influenced for good, or become thoroughly entranced and lose oneself in the process. Evidently there is a world of beings beyond our customary, everyday perceptions, one which is just as multi-faceted as our own, human world. Eva was first exposed to this other world through automatic writing - this was its means of entry into her. She learned from her friend that, whatever the temptation, one must never surrender control to these entities: such an exotic, magical world can be extremely alluring, a realm of wonder to which it is all too easy to yield. None are happier about this than lower beings, who are delighted by the chance to enter and occupy a human being. Over a period of many years, Eva learned to be receptive only to one high, noble entity which offered her peaceful, loving companionship. With this being's help, she underwent a process of extremely deep and penetrating analysis, which lasted for five years until publicity forced her to give it up for the sake of guiding others. Eva wrote about this in an article describing her transformation into a medium (Broch, 1965).

As a result of the process she underwent at the hands of her Guide - as she later named her companion - and through her own role as guide for many others, Eva learned that one's progress depends on the type of entity that comes in search of a dwelling-place. Each of us is a field of energy which attracts other energy. The negative characteristics we all carry in our energy fields enable other undesirable energies - which may be even more extreme - to enter. In order to be the best possible medium, it is important to be as purified as possible; the process of purification lasts years, even a lifetime. Unlike orthodox analysis, which may be relatively short-term, it is a continuous growth process (Pierrakos, 1978).

In this situation, there are important choices to be made from amongst the various possibilities: if the entities are to be used for higher purposes alone - that is, in the service of one's own process of growth and that of others - one must choose to remain attuned exclusively to benign beings. Those entities which are full of deceit, rule one's actions, and have no respect for free will, should not be entertained. Beings that flatter and fawn excessively are also unworthy of attention, though this is not to say that a good spirit will not provide affirmation of self and help one to see one's better qualities. One should also be on guard against prophesying spirits: these can be very draining of energy, and should be expelled.

It is essential, when learning to work with voices or other paranormal phenomena, to seek the help of a capable therapist in the field. Attempting to brush entities aside is no solution; once one has attained such sensitivity, it cannot simply be disregarded. Above all, this sensitivity is a gift, and it is vital to recognize one's negative traits, conquer them as far as possible, and learn to work with the good without falling victim to the pitfalls involved. However difficult it may be to accept, each of us is responsible to him or herself. In learning to handle voices, therefore, a primary requirement is to become a free and responsible agent with complete choice between affirmation and dissent.

I would now like to consider the matter of hearing voices within this framework. There are plenty of people who will suggest that voices represent fragmented parts of the personality, and that the entities I refer to do not actually exist. Eva Pierrakos herself admits that she cannot be absolutely certain of her own interpretation. Is the Guide with which Eva was so familiar for 23 years a separate entity, or part of her own higher being? There is, I believe, an element of truth in both viewpoints. Other mediums of my acquaintance admit, in their best moments, that they sometimes blend with their Guides, and at other times experience a kind of distancing. Eva describes this as positive schizophrenia, a phenomenon that is part of the growth towards integration. I certainly believe that, for many of those with tendencies towards mediumship who experience this somewhat split character structure, the proper task is the pursuit of unity.

In my own experience, I am inclined to think that I myself am on a higher plane when I hear voices. To put it more accurately, the event takes place on a plane where no actual myself exists: in a dimension of existence where my form is of a higher energy and there is no distinction between the I and the other. For a long time I have used a pendulum as a means of making contact with this plane. When doing so, I get the clear feeling that the energy is lower when I am giving guidance than when I ask for direction for myself or another, and this higher plane is far more difficult to work with. The inner hearing that fills my daily life lies between the higher and lower planes, and is frequently very concrete; perhaps surprisingly, it is usually concerned with everyday matters such as which route to take somewhere, when the time is ripe to do something in particular, or when to snap up a bargain in a department store. I often struggle against this. For instance, I may hear that I should buy something that I have no use for - a bottle of milk, say, which is something I don't normally drink. A few days later, someone will turn up and ask for a glass of milk, and then I am either glad I took notice of the inner voice, or regret that I ignored it. I may react either way to the voice's suggestions, for although it is very dear to me, I am convinced that I must be responsible for my own actions.

Some of the things I hear are very striking, especially when they refer to things I could not possibly know in advance. I have several friends who experience exactly the same thing; it is not so unusual a phenomenon as some might think. It is also true that the more one is preoccupied with the process of purification, the more one form or another of extrasensory perception develops. I have the feeling of living within a much broader perspective, much to my delight, and know that there are other, innumerable realms surrounding my own. Although I know that this is felt as a great burden by some, its enormous potential should not be forgotten; I hope we can succeed in creating a climate in which people can learn to work with it. I sometimes hear of instances like this, but have never heard of lessons being learned from them.

A number of therapists, burdened to a greater or lesser degree by their voices, are aware that they have a hole in their energy field, through which entities can freely enter. Sealing such a hole is a considerable challenge. This can sometimes happen as a result of an experience of healing, when the aura may be made whole again. During therapy, too, it may become clear after a while which traumatic experience is responsible for the hole; closure is often achieved when the trauma is identified and properly processed. I have read about a South American hospital which has a team of paranormally-gifted therapists; where necessary, these specialists will converse with a troublesome entity and ask it to leave the sufferer for ever, and this is exactly what happens. There are a few such therapy groups in Holland and England. For an excellent account of the human energy field and its corresponding psychological structures, I would refer readers to 'Hands of Light' by Barbara Ann Brennan, who was my own teacher for some time.

Another important point is that it is essential to pay great attention to the physical body. In order to create a sound, solid basis for working with these energies, it is crucial to be properly earthed, and to remove all blockages. For this reason, Pathwork emphasizes the need to teach people to work well with their bodies, and the method favoured is known as core-energy work. The central principle of this approach is that the physical body, the emotions, the intellect and the spirit are all integral parts of a whole: everything is interrelated and interactive, and therefore one must work appropriately with all aspects. See Ad Reks Padwerk en Core-Energetica (1989) for a fuller description of these techniques.

What does the Pathwork or the Path have to offer the hearer of voices, whether the experience is enjoyed or endured? Firstly, with the help of a compilation of lectures by Eva Pierrakos, Pathwork provides a broader perspective on life's possibilities; this in itself can be very effective in reducing feelings of uncertainty, and can be the springboard for a process of positive forward movement. There is also the option of getting involved with Pathwork group seminars, and Pathwork days are held twice a year in Holland. Guidance is always available from expert helpers, a number of whom have personal experience of voices or other forms of extrasensory perception (although few regard such experience as being the most important element in their guidance). Pathwork helpers will receive training, and of course, for therapists, there is always the possibility of holding consultations. Fuller information on all of the above, including the annual syllabus and a full book-list, can be obtained by writing to the secretary's office: Postbus 7839, 1008 AA, Amsterdam, Netherlands.

I hope this brief outline of Pathwork's approach will be of use to any hearers of voices who are themselves seeking ways of learning to work with them, or to anyone who would like to help others to do so.

References
Pierrakos, E. Guide Lectures for Self-Transformation; Centre for the Living Force, Sevenoaks Pathwork Centre, Madison
Brennan, B. A. (1988) Hands of Light; Bantam Books, NY
Roberts, J. (1979) Seth Speaks; Bantam Books, NY

A Karmic Perspective
Han van Binsbergen

I will assume in this discussion that all human life is animated by a spirit which takes up residence in a body and inhabits it until death. In the course of its occupation, the spirit must complete a number of assignments in order to fulfil the destiny allotted to it by the laws of Karma. When the body dies, the spirit returns to its own realm in readiness for subsequent reincarnation in another bodily form.

Psychics, especially those who are sensitive to voices, are in the habit of communing either with the spirits of the living or with those that have already returned to the spiritual realm. The hearing of voices, in this context, is not the unwelcome intimacy it may often be for those in different circumstances. For a psychic, the ability to converse with spirits is of the greatest importance, in order to receive messages that may be passed on and to gain insight into problems arising from any imbalance between spirit and body. Should this balance be disturbed, the spirit signals the fact to its body by means of an otherwise inexplicable pain or illness. A voice-sensitive psychic like myself can assist in the understanding of such signals by helping to translate them into human speech, so that the trouble can be resolved in the shortest possible time.

With the severely ill, tormented by pain and approaching death, a sensitive can contact the sufferer's living spirit. This, of course, can take place only with the express consent of the individual or the person responsible for his or her care. The sensitive can ascertain how close the spirit is to the completion of its Karmic duties: the spirit reveals the precise state of affairs, and by co-operating closely with it the psychic can ensure that the body is freed of pain. An agreement is then made with the spirit that it will be given an escort for its return to the spirit realm. This spiritual support, in all its aspects, is one of the most wonderful and miraculous experiences granted to the paranormal healer.

I am anxious to stress, through all of this, that there are a great many voices which are neither malicious nor painful but can provide great satisfaction.

Voices associated with uncompleted Karmic duties

Any of us can lose our lives at any moment in any one of a number of ways: accident, suicide, war, murder, and so on. In all these situations, the spirit is presented with a fait accompli: except in those few cases where Karma has already been fully satisfied, the spirit's mission in that particular incarnation will not have been fulfilled. Nevertheless, it is obliged to return to the spirit realm, for it has, after all, no body in which to live. As in all cases, though, the spirit cannot return until preparations for its reception have been made in that realm, and until then it can only roam restlessly. It is quite conceivable, under these circumstances, that such a spirit might communicate to another still resident in a body, imparting messages through the unconscious - messages which may then be brought into consciousness by their transformation into human language. Initially, the person concerned may be terrified, being unfamiliar with such spirit contact and only used to talking with people. The phenomenon is often assumed to be entirely imaginary, and other explanations are sought for what is heard. Only when the experience recurs repeatedly is it understood that the imagination cannot be responsible, and that this really is an audible voice; the difficulty, of course, is that the voice is completely inaudible to anyone else. In due course, such voices generally disappear once they have communicated their important message, and find their way back to the spirit realm.

Voices of Karmic completion

When a spirit has fulfilled the assignments of its incarnation and thus satisfied Karma, it receives permission to vacate the body. This is the precise moment at which death occurs, whether the process of dying has been gradual or sudden. In the approach to death, when the time is near for parting from loved ones, the spirit is busy performing the duties necessary for the satisfaction of Karma, and death by natural causes takes place only when the spirit has completed these tasks and abandoned the body. It is hardly surprising that, in most such cases, the spirit does not continue to manifest itself, although there are exceptions, as we shall see. When the spirit's departure is sudden, this can often be extremely distressing for relatives: nothing is arranged, no goodbyes have been said, and they are left confused and uncomprehending. Occasionally a relative will, without warning, hear the unmistakable voice of the deceased giving instructions, for example about important documents; it may also reassure them by telling them how happy it is to be in the spirit realm.

Voices in response to grief

A person's death naturally causes great sorrow to relatives. Intense feelings of pain, emptiness and loss are common elements in the difficult early phases of the grieving process.

From the spirit's point of view, matters are quite different. After vacating the body, the spirit approaches the spirit realm (assuming that Karma has been satisfied). Its entry into this realm is mediated by its spiritual escort, and one could say that the spirit is reborn in the spirit realm, where there is great celebration over its return. Relatives on earth, however, continue to grieve over the loss of their loved one. The spirit having completed its arduous assignment in the course of its human life, has earned its rest, but is denied this by the intensity of earthly grief. The agonized relatives are attempting, as it were, to keep the deceased alive. As a result, the spirit has no choice but to communicate with one or more of them by means of an audible voice, and implore them to resign themselves to this parting and allow the spirit to rest in peace.

Voices of ego-spirits

For every spirit, the initial phase of growth is the ego-phase. The purpose of this time is to learn to stand on one's own two feet, which is the essential foundation for all future learning. During this period of training, however, there is always the danger of the spirit acquiring some disability, such as jealousy. An ego-spirit is one which simply cannot tolerate the knowledge that there are other spirits inhabiting a much higher plane. It will do everything in its power to dislodge any higher spirit from its chosen human body: in other words, an ego-spirit will seize a body that does not properly belong to it in order to manifest itself, and render the rightful occupant inactive. This is what is meant by possession. Such situations can be extremely unpleasant, and are often exacerbated by the effects of mistaken psychological diagnosis: when medication is administered, there may be disastrous consequences both for the body and for its natural inhabitant.

The result of possession is often that the victim is no longer able to react and function according to his or her own will; deprived of their normal ruler, the vocal cords speak to us in an unfamiliar voice. Examples from my own experience include a fifth-year grammar school pupil who gave the teacher answers entirely unrelated to the lesson in progress. A more serious case involved a child, living in a quiet neighbourhood, who suddenly threw open the window and poured out a torrent of obscenities, and proceeded to insult her parents in the same terms. In this instance, the police had to be called to take the girl away. It will be clear from these examples that ego-spirits are mischievous and malicious, and all too eager to be heard.

Ouija board voices

The Ouija board is a far more dangerous game than is often appreciated, and I would like to clarify the possible consequences by outlining how it works, with particular regard to voices. Harmful effects are not, of course, inevitable, but the outcome of such games is impossible to predict. Those who view the Ouija board as a family game are seriously misguided in seeking an opening into the spirit realm, uninvited and unequipped. When this is accomplished, with the assistance of ego-spirits and their powers, the resting-place of all manner of spirits is disturbed, and unknown evils may be unwittingly unleashed.

When a spirit (other than an ego-spirit) is summoned and then refuses, for some reason, to depart, it will persist in molesting those who have called it up. It will do this by means of a sound resembling a human voice, but one which is audible only to those concerned, and will plague them day and night, for it knows no boundaries. Such a spirit feels itself to be superior to its summoners, and comes armed with demands which must be satisfied. It is hard to understand why such a purely negative voice should exist. The effects upon the hearer's family can be extremely upsetting, with those hearing the voice, and indeed conversing with it, being unable to offer any plausible explanation to those being talked about - who cannot, of course, hear anything. It will be readily appreciated that family life can quickly become very uncomfortable when one of its members spends all day and all night talking or cursing, apparently to him or herself. Indeed, entire families have been broken up by the consequences of playing this game.

Deathbed voices

Deathbed experiences in this field will often combine hearing voices with visions of the spirits of long-dead friends and relatives. The dying person may call out names very distinctly, and laugh delightedly; the face may suddenly come alive, and the eyes light up. Those witnessing this are likely to find it incomprehensible, and often remark that the dying person is delirious and raving. It is notable, though, that the delirium often ceases, and the person then addresses those present once again: the spirit allows the power of reason to function in the mundane realm again, and to focus exclusively on the earth and its inhabitants.

This process, in which the spirit is alternately attuned to the other side and revived on the earthly plane, may be repeated several times: the consciousness is allowed glimpses of the world awaiting the spirit once it has discarded its earthly form. It is unfortunate that the dying person who is granted such insights is so often assumed to be demented or hallucinating under the effects of medication. This is especially sad when we realize that there is a welcoming committee of departed loved ones waiting at the portals of the spirit realm.

Conclusion

As we have seen, there are various ways of hearing voices, including many that I have not touched on here. Many people are grateful for the support they get from their voices, and their lives would be less happy and fulfilling without them. All voice-hearers, though, face the same crucial problem: that of proof. Even when a psychic or sensitive is able to confirm that voices exist, it remains impossible to prove this to other people, given the lack of absolute research evidence. Because of this, voice-hearers find themselves under a great deal of pressure, and are often dismissed or regarded as mad. Let us hope that the pioneering work being carried out with voice-hearers will some day bear fruit, so that people will finally realize that the immortal spirit within us all is the most important factor on earth.

8. GROWING OUT OF PSYCHIATRIC CARE

Introduction
Marius Romme

In this chapter, five English people and one Dutch person with extensive histories of psychiatric care relate their experiences of hearing voices and learning to cope with them. These six individuals represent a striking selection of those people who have found their own ways of coping with voices and other unusual experiences. All, at some time, have been regular psychiatric clients over long periods, and have spent a considerable amount of time as in-patients. All have been diagnosed at least once as schizophrenic, and from a psychiatric point of view might still be regarded as severely ill. However, in spite of the fact that they continue, to this day, to hear voices or to have other exceptional experiences, all have succeeded in finding ways of functioning effectively within their social spheres. All six would acknowledge that they still suffer occasional difficulties in which they need support from others. Indeed, their success in creating independent lives for themselves is due at least in part to their good fortune in having partners, family or friends who were ready to face and accept the presence of their voices and other unusual perceptions.

All six have found it essential to identify with their voices in order to control them and keep them from undue interference in acquiring a social position and fulfillment in their tasks. Sadly, this has obliged them to distance themselves - in some cases completely - from psychiatry, which is not prepared to allow the voice-hearer to identify with his or her voices. The orthodox attitude to the phenomenon fails to examine the actual experience, and consequently too little attention is given to the resolution of social or relationship problems which may be associated with that experience.

These six people have shown extraordinary courage and energy in the struggle to regain control of their own lives. Meeting and working with them has been a great pleasure for us, and we would like to thank them warmly for their enthusiastic co-operation in this project.

Eighth Contributor (M. L.)

A 40-year old black woman, mother of three children, and a grandmother, who first heard voices at the age of 12, but started to hear them regularly in 1984 after racial difficulties at work. During the following two years she was hospitalized twice, and was also divorced. Mrs M. L. is a Rastafarian; she describes this as a way of living, although others call it a religion.

I have been sexually abused, I think when I was three years old, by a much older cousin. He must have been about 12. To me he seemed very big. At that time my family was living in Dominica. We moved to England when I was seven years old, which was to me more than a culture shock. In the streets, old people - whom I had learned to respect - said to me 'Dirty nigger' or 'Go home monkey'. I was shocked. My parents did not allow me to play outside. As they gained more confidence they allowed me to go outside. But by then I did not have anyone to play with. That was terrible as well.

I was sexually abused again when I was nine. We lived in a shared house. The man upstairs lived with his family. He did not only abuse me, but I had seen him doing it with his daughters as well. He gave me the warning 'Don't tell your parents', and I did not. As soon as he moved out, I told my mother and she went to the police. But they told her that I had to give evidence in court. It would be difficult to give evidence, and it would probably be said that I had provoked his behaviour.

When I was 12, we moved to a flat in a very old building. It was Halloween night. (As far as I am concerned, Halloween is there to make fears respectable.) That night I heard a terrible laugh coming from the garden. It sounded like witches laughing. The garden must have been at least 50 feet long, and the voices were coming from the corner of the garden. I prayed to God; I prayed so hard to God that night to make him stop that noise. My first experience of hearing voices in my head was God answering back to let me know that it was my fear, and that I had to stop being afraid in the dark.

At the age of 12, I met my ex-husband. He was my first real boyfriend. When I was 16 I got pregnant twice, and both times I lost the baby. My mother decided that I was not going to have babies. She told me to use the douche, and I obeyed. The second time, I lost a lot of blood and I went to the stairs to call my mother. I fainted and banged my head upon the doorpost. As I fainted, I saw my father running up the stairs, and felt him pick me up. I blacked out.

That night my spirit left my body. I thought I was dead, to be quite honest. When I was halfway between heaven and earth, I asked JAH (Emperor Haile Selassie) 'Will I come to you?'. I saw a big bubble, and curled myself in it as a baby. I fitted in that capsule like a piece in a jigsaw, and asked if I did not have to go back. But JAH said 'You will have to go back, because you will have twins.' I said 'Oh JAH, for them I will go back', and floated back to my body. Then I dreamed of my grave and saw two babies curled up in a car. Then I decided to go back. I awoke and said to my mother that I was going to have twins. She thought I had delirium.

The twins were born when I was 18. When I got pregnant, I still was not married. But this time I wanted the babies, and did not listen to my mother. I married when I was 20, and I wanted another baby. We then quarrelled quite a bit, but still I wanted another baby. I asked God for my daughter Sam, and asked that my husband would agree.

When Sam was three years old, I got into trouble at my work. I am a child care worker. One of the nurses tried to prove that I was aggressive, and the rest of the staff backed her up. I had the idea I was talking to a brick wall. And they had the idea that it was all my fault. When I talked, they thought I was too emotional. When I did not talk, they disagreed as well. (This made me very angry.) Therefore I felt I needed a place of my own.

I needed to get away from my husband. Not that he was horrible, but I was in too much pain. The reason why I went away in the first place was that I had too much anger in me. It was a question of either letting it out and taking the consequences, or fighting to keep it in. And I chose to fight to keep it in, in the right and proper way, and that took time.

Gaining more control

I started to work again, but after a year I had the same kind of trouble. Racial problems. I started to defend myself. I had to stop working because at my work they wanted me to reply to a letter of grievance (this caused the first breakdown). In the meantime, I got divorced.

When I started to get ill, I said to myself, This time you have to get through all of it. Time was pressing. I knew I had to get better because of the letter of grievance that I had to respond to so I could start working again. My wise cousin helped me with it. I listened to his advice. At my work, the letter was accepted and understood. They decided to organize a racial awareness course, for which all workers got one week free to attend. After the racial awareness course I went to work again. Things changed, and I felt more accepted by my colleagues.

I wanted to be on my own, because I did not want the children to see me go through another period of sickness. They had suffered badly enough. There was another reason. Although my mother meant well, I had the idea I had to prove to her that I was not as ill as everybody thought I was. I wanted to be on my own. I had never lived on my own. I had no furniture, just my bed.

I went to hospital twice. My mother sent for an ambulance. Once, she was very worried because I did not let her in. I was reading her mind and I thought that she was going to give an injection to kill me.

This second period of illness was longer than the first one. From January till November I was very bad. I smashed windows, and was sectioned for 28 days. I was hearing voices all over the place. I still heard my thoughts outside my head. I was put on medication, but I did not get any psychological help. A psychiatrist talked to me, but I did not trust him. However, medication got me to a level where I did not feel afraid. That got me to a state where I could sort things out without upsetting myself. The worst thing was that I now heard constant breaking of glass.

In my mind, I ran to Ethiopia to tell everything to the Emperor, but he said 'I know'. He gave me a nursery book. When I looked at it, it was black with white pages. I said 'There is nothing in it', and he said 'You have to write in it yourself. You have to write your own story'.

This happened some time ago. I still hear voices. I still hear God's voice. It is not a spoken word. It is an intuition. My voices give me good instructions like: 'Take care when you cross the road'. My voice said: 'No, you can do it on your own as well.' Hearing voices outside my head is my illness. Normally I hear my thoughts inside my head. When I am ill I hear my thoughts outside my head. I am still on medication. I take one tablet every two or three weeks.

When I got ill, the conflict both times was that I live in a country that does not accept black people. Do you realize that a lot of our black history is left out, hidden? The Moors came from Africa, and the Egyptians. They all came from Africa. All white people talk about is slavery. That is how they think of us. My problem was that I could not be myself living in a country that does not accept black people. But through the voices I found myself - my identity, which has everything to do with my racial history and my own past. The memory of my abuse stayed. I have learned to cut that memory off. I know now that in a situation that is harmful, I shut myself out. I also know that the memory of that situation stays.

How I have come through my particular fire? Because I trusted completely in JAHOVIAH! All my thoughts are inside my head now.

Ninth Contributor (A. G.)

A 36-year old woman with a four-year old child, who started to hear voices when her relationship did not work out as she hoped. She has been in hospital five times, and now takes medication on a regular basis. Since the birth of her son, she feels more in control of her life.

My experience of hearing voices began in 1980, when I was 25 years old. I had actually been experimenting with telepathy. I got the idea in my head that perhaps I could make people do things by thinking of them. Soon after this I started hearing voices. I thought that the neighbours were talking about me. I was sitting in my room and generally overhearing voices through the wall. I had the idea I was literally overhearing someone. I did not realize I was hearing voices in my head; I thought they were real voices. I did not know anything about mental health problems. I just thought that people did not like me, and they were saying things about me behind my back.

At that time I was very depressed, very paranoid, I could not concentrate at work because I felt everyone was against me. I think it had to do with my relationship. It was not working out. I had been living with a student in Cambridge for four years. This man pulled me down. He was making comments about my clothes, criticizing me a lot. I thought that if it did not work out with him, I would never meet anybody else. I would be on my own for ever. I was even thinking that when I was 80 I would be on my own and not have any children. So I decided I would try and stick it out with him.

When I went to see my company's doctor he referred me to my General Practitioner, who passed me on to a psychiatrist. I did not tell him I was hearing voices, because I did not want to discuss what the voices had been saying about me, in case they were real people's voices. So I just said I was depressed and crying a lot, which I was.

Following friends' advice, I went to my parents' house in Bolton for the weekend. I had a sort of physical breakdown, which I thought might have been due to the Prothiaden tablets which the psychiatrist had given me. I lost complete control over my senses. I thought I was dying, and I had an overwhelming sense of guilt. I kept thinking I had killed someone, although I did not know who. My parents got a doctor for me because I asked for one. By Tuesday I was admitted to hospital. No one explained to me where I was going, and I did not realize it was a psychiatric ward. I hated my stay in that very old building in which the ward was housed. I kept thinking I was in some sort of training camp. I thought the Government had put me away for doing something wrong. I did have a feeling I was involved in some conspiracy and had to do something. Some sort of mission.

This first period of admission is a bit hazy. I cannot really remember much, except that I was always trying to escape and run away. After three weeks I was discharged and attended the day centre. Still I had not the slightest clue about mental illness. I did not know that hearing voices was a symptom of schizophrenia. I was on quite large doses of medication. I still thought I was being treated for my depression.

After seven months at the day centre, I took a job on a campsite in France. However I again started overhearing people talking about me. I could hear the voices of two people I knew saying: 'Do the right thing.' I thought they wanted me to destroy myself in order to save England from nuclear attack, so I set fire to myself. Following this suicide attempt I came back to England for skin grafts and a further spell of three months on a hospital mental ward.

Whilst I was in hospital this time, I was put on a large dose of chlorpromazine, and spent most of the day involved in weird dreams which I would tell to the psychiatrist. She did not understand English very well, so she probably wondered what on earth was the matter with me. Whilst on chlorpromazine in hospital, I even had visual hallucinations, which is something I have never had except in hospital. They eventually changed my medication to Depixol, and I started to come out of the psychotic state the chlorpromazine put me in.

After my discharge, I again attended the day centre, but I found it very hard to get out of bed, especially on the days I was not going to the day centre. Then I did a course at Salford Technical College, and after this I worked for a year at a sportswear firm. At that moment, I had a normal life again, but now I had the stigma of being an ex-patient to cope with. Half the problem of being mentally ill is coping with the fact itself; never mind what you actually go through in the illness. I tried to make sure that I kept in touch with my friends despite the fact that I had been ill, and most of them have coped with it very well.

Apart from a couple of weeks in hospital, I remained quite well up to the age of 31. At this time I met someone to whom I was very attracted. Let's call him Tom. Following a friendship of several months, during which we had no physical contact apart from kisses on the cheek, I fell in love with him. I wrote a lot of letters to him, and when I heard he was not reading them, I left Bolton and became pregnant through a brief affair in the south of England. I went to live at my brother's in the south for a time. I was hearing Tom's voice in my head and thought it was he who got me pregnant.

There again the voices, Tom's among them, were saying terrible things about Tom and other people. Because I couldn't cope, I tried to overdose myself. I was admitted again for a couple of weeks, but because I was pregnant they kept the drugs to a minimum.

Throughout my pregnancy I always wanted to find Tom. I was hearing voices all day long. I thought I was in telepathic communication with Tom. He seemed to be telling me everything that was happening in his life in my head. The things he would tell me would sometimes make me shout out loud in reply to the voices in my head, even if someone was in the room with me.

Gaining more control

After my son was born, my life really changed. I had to pull myself together to do all the necessary things to look after my baby. Although I could still hear voices, I started to pay them less attention. I thought if I could not look after my baby he would be taken off me and probably put up for adoption, and I would have lost him for ever.

After a voluntary stay of four months in hospital (voluntary in the sense that I didn't have to go there; but not voluntary in reality, because prior to that, my child was in care, and I would never have seen him again if I hadn't opted to go into hospital), we eventually came home together on 17 October 1988. He is still with me now, and my medication is only 20mg of Depixol every four weeks at the moment.

I hear voices by using my ears, but they are inside my head, not outside. It is an effort to listen to them now. I don't hear them if I am doing something else like listening to television. It is company, in a way. I think I am just used to tuning into them, like switching on a radio. I suppose they help me think things through a bit. It is like people doing your reasoning for you in your head. Often they are soothing and helpful, but sometimes I have to wait for this comfort before I can switch off and go to sleep. They usually just give comment rather than criticism. Even when they say something like 'Do the right thing', it is up to me to choose to do it. They have never said something like 'Go and see if your son is alright'.

The nearest explanation I have for the voices is telepathy. That is the only explanation I could easily live with, rather than with madness. Telepathy with living human beings or with dead ones. Sometimes I hear my dead grandmother's voice. She has the same humour she had when alive.

Sometimes the voices say what is going to happen. They are not always right. I had a strange experience the other day. I heard a friend of mine and her husband talking about having a baby, and two days later she actually rang me up to tell me she was going to have a baby.

Sometimes the voices can say disturbing things about me, criticizing me in unpleasant ways and making me feel that people are saying unpleasant things about me behind my back. Things that are not true, such as questioning my sexuality or my morals.

Recently, I have been hearing Tom's voice again in my head, and he says things like he will come back to me or write or ring me up. But he never does. I believe the root of my problem has still not been tackled, namely my love for, and subsequent rejection by, Tom. Once, when I mentioned exactly what I felt about Tom, my social worker immediately said 'You're not getting ill again, are you?'

I believe even now that a psychiatric condition often presents a problem which the patient is unable to deal with in the normal way, and which shows itself through abnormal behaviour. I think psychiatrists should try and do more to unearth these problems, and help the patient to solve them for themselves. Then I believe a cure for mental health problems would quickly follow.

As each month passes and my medication dosage gets gradually lower, I get more confident in my ability to cope with hearing voices. I only hope that psychiatrists will learn to be more forbearing in their prescription of drugs, and will try and keep them to a minimum even when a patient is in hospital.

Tenth Contributor (A. B.)

A 34-year old single man with a child. He is self-employed, making and selling jewellery and teaching t'ai chi at colleges and adult education centres.

After High School, I did not want to go to work, so I went to college to study social geography. When I finished, there was nothing I really wanted to do. I started to do casual work like carrying carpets around. When I did this five days a week, I thought I might as well get a proper job. So I started working for a newspaper in Oxford.

I realized I did not like my life, and travelled abroad. When I came back, I went to my brother in Manchester, and I stayed. I found a job as a sort of detached health worker. At that time, I was seeing things quite negatively, and was confused about my direction in life. I did not see myself as very successful. I was a little bit at odds with what I was doing.

After nine months I started to hear voices. When this exceptional experience happened the first time, I remember being in a room and feeling entered by a strange energy. I made connections with a force towards death, a force towards entities. I suddenly understood a whole new dimension to things. Some things that I had read from different sources suddenly related to this new experience. I felt so good. I felt fortunate to experience this.

The first time I got psychotic, I was sectioned. They told my mother I was diagnosed paranoid schizophrenic. I was 24 years old. Within a few days, I started to hear voices. Hearing voices was for me only one of a whole range of phenomena that I experienced during what psychiatry would call psychotic episodes. They have affected me over the last ten years. These phenomena include hearing voices (experienced as thoughts, seemingly projected into my mind from an external source), delusions and paranoid delusions of every kind, visual hallucinations, heightened states of awareness, depression, and so on. Although these experiences are not mutually exclusive, I shall deal with each in turn.

Hearing voices

These inner voices were seemingly from external sources. Often it was an unknown source, but sometimes I would believe they came from (or would be told by the voices that they came from) a known source. Sources included a variety of people, living and dead (an Australian aborigine, an American Indian, people of various religious denominations, occult figures, animals, plants, aliens, ancestors, mythological characters, Beelzebub, spirits in heaven and hell, other patients in the hospital, occasional people that I'd meet). The majority of these voices were benign. Sometimes communication would occur and I could converse, sometimes not.

One voice, of unknown origin, is around most of the time and stays with me constantly. This voice punctuates my thoughts with comments and advice, such as 'Yes, No, Maybe, Good, Bad, Wonderful, Be careful, Right, Wrong', and so on. I do not care to accept any advice, and often do the thing it tells me not to, with no dire consequences. Sometimes I can communicate with this voice, though this often proves difficult and frustrating. Sometimes it amuses me. Quite often it will say 'Don't worry. It will be alright', which can be consoling, though sometimes this is said when the situation is so intense that I can't help doubting its sincerity.

Occasionally, voices are dark and evil, and the experience can be frightening, particularly when I feel the presence of the voice's owner. Another thing is that I am able to let the voices speak through me, and this can be fairly alarming if they say scary things. Very occasionally, the urge to let these voices speak through me has been so strong that I could not help but allow it, and have had to cover my mouth to hide my moving lips from passers-by. In some instances, this has been the only way to hear them anyway. I had a really strange experience like this around the time of the Gulf war, when a voice, expressed in a fairly nasty-sounding tone and seeming to be a broadcast from some malevolent source, went on about how it was time for blood, and how it (or they) were looking forward to it. If anyone had heard this, they would have been pretty freaked out by it. Another way of communicating has been by the asking of questions and receiving yes/no answers by allowing my head to be nodded by whatever it is I was communicating with. This can also prove to be a little frightening, because it seems to involve some sort of possession. Some of this experience has been involuntary, though I've been quite interested in what the voices might have to say, and have investigated the phenomenon in this way.

Hallucinations

Hallucinations can be good or bad. The world can be transformed into heaven or hell at the drop of a hat. The most common type that I experience involves people suddenly taking on ghoulish characteristics. This seems to happen mostly when a lot of people are around. In the centre of town, for example. These can be fairly strange and scary experiences, though they occur so frequently that one gets used to them happening. I can easily ignore them, knowing that they will end. The plus side to them is certain moments of vividness that can turn a walk through a park, or wherever, into a walk through paradise.

Both kind of hallucinations are altered states of perception. They occur spontaneously and frequently during psychotic episodes. Then I hear and see things that do not exist, but at that moment they are real to me. I know now that they are not real. For example, one day I found a record in my room. On the record sleeve were pictures of some friends of mine as a group. In my head, I was convinced that they had made an album. I picked up and played it. I did not dream it, I played it. On another occasion I found a letter, and when I checked it out, it never existed. I check things out now, but I am more careful not to upset people or make them suspicious. So I might say to someone: 'I dreamt that I saw someone standing next to the door'. Then I observe the reaction. If the person I talk to thinks it is a nice dream, I don't talk about it any more. If he says there is someone next to the door, I know it is real.

Delusions and paranoid delusions

There have been many different ones. Sometimes I think that it would be impossible for me to fall for a new one. I have passed through so many that it seems unlikely that a variety I haven't experienced could exist. However, the creative principle knows no bounds, and some new delusion, carefully worked out to be seemingly plausible, comes knocking on my door.

When you are in the deluded state, the delusion is the reality. So you take it seriously; no matter how absurd on reflection, it transforms your world. Delusions can be good, in the sense that the world is magical, stimulating, and suggests an optimistic ending; or bad in that the world becomes a dark and dangerous place. Some of the delusions are really good stuff. They give me inspiration. I have some interest in being creative, so I make some pictures at this time while I am in that state.

The most serious kind is to do with being spied upon, persecuted, accused, and threatened by terrible things happening to me. These delusions can cause great panic. Some have a very strong plausibility factor and are very difficult to shake off. They survive as frameworks, often very complex, in the subconscious. Given a new piece of evidence that seems to fit the jigsaw, they can suddenly appear fully intact and completely overwhelm me for a time.

Physical phenomena

When I get psychotic, on the physical side I experience an increased sense of physical well-being, have an incredible feeling of strong internal energy (which has a reality), and respond to invisible forces. I feel so healthy and full of energy that I imagine myself capable of amazing feats of strength and agility. This wasn't so far from the truth. I was able to do things I previously could not do. I could survive with very little sleep. The most incredible physical phenomenon, however, was the responsiveness to invisible external forces (of course this was more likely a response to internal forces, but that was not how it seemed).

I investigated these phenomena as far as I could, and this led to some bizarre and mysterious happenings. I discovered that by giving up my own will to move, I would be moved. I called this 'Following'. Sometimes this would have me performing some strange dance, rather like t'ai chi, which I later took up. On other occasions, I would go through some postures similar to yoga. One recurring pattern of movements, which became a sort of ritual, would have me first bending over to touch my toes, then bending over backwards, arching my back. Next, my arms would rise out to the sides and I would twist first to one side and then to the other, so that the hands would describe a complete circle. Finally I would sink into a squat. In this position, I would then summon (I forget why it was that I thought I could do this) various animal spirits. The animal spirits would enter into me and I would move as if I shared some of their characteristics.

By far the most interesting 'Following' experiences, though, were the ones that took me for walks. Of these, the most notable one lasted a whole night, and took me on quite a journey, covering perhaps 15 or so miles. It started when, being alone in a room, I decided I'd try a bit of 'Following'. I soon found myself walking in a circle around the room. I then started spinning like a dervish, going faster and faster. It seemed to me that I was going very fast indeed. I came to a sudden stop, and stood relatively motionless while the room kept spinning around me. When I stopped spinning, I was obliged to leave the room and go for a walk. I was very interested to see where this would lead, and remember imagining possible destinations. After some hours, by which time I was convinced I was going to London, I turned off the main road and eventually came to a small village. The village had a small triangular green surrounded by a low spiked fence. I found myself walking around this fence. I came to a halt, and turned to face the fence. I then arched over backwards, and thought that I might be about to make contact with something, and that this must be the ultimate destination. Then suddenly, and very quickly, I was thrown forwards from the posture, so that my head came up and then down in front of me. I stopped abruptly and found my lips just kissing one of the spikes. This alarmed me somewhat, and I stopped 'Following'.

Fear and vulnerability

My experiences occur spontaneously, and are overwhelming at first. They can be accompanied by moods ranging from ecstasy to great fear. The worst obstacle still is fear and vulnerability. The vulnerability is more difficult, because during my experience I am living in a more abstract world. There is no passion to my psychoses, but they are influenced by what is going on in reality. Sometimes they are so intense that you forget about the material circumstances anyway. When I go through that, I do not give a damn about it. My psychoses are influenced by the world around me, and I am more vulnerable to other people's influences.

Gaining more control

In the beginning, I had no idea how to deal with my experiences at all. Later, I got more control during the experience (unless in crisis), and learned to cope with most phenomena. As I said before, hearing voices is for me only one of a whole range of phenomena that I experience, and that have affected me over the last ten years. For example, acting on delusions can lead to one involving other people, which is usually bad news, and fairly odd behaviour. I can draw people into my delusions and upset them seriously. I even might upset people to the point where they beat me up.

Over the years, I realized there is a pattern to it, and that this pattern is very much like hills and valleys. In the early phase, I spend a lot of time in the valley. Let's say I experience things one hour a day; I've 23 left for myself. Then it starts to change to two hours, three hours a day. By the time I am at the top, there is only one hour during which I am without the experiences. But as long as I have got an hour to reflect, I can keep some distance. I have never taken any medication. When I am at the top of the hill, there is no time at all for myself, but I am more excited and I start exploring everything.

Over the years, one of the most important things for me is to stay out of psychiatric care. I don't want medication. So when I am psychotic, I avoid my family circle. I do not want to have my experiences in front of my parents, because maybe then they will lock me up. My friends are concerned about me, but they know me by now.

When you are hallucinating, that does not mean that you cannot go out and buy your clothes. And even if you are deluded, you still have to eat. In some way, daily life goes on.

When I hear a voice now, I can sort of dismiss it. It is just second nature to me. Although there are times when they still totally overwhelm me, I know there is a point where it lessens. There is also always a point where I can still make a decision. Like the last time I decided I did not want to smoke marihuana, because the delusion the day before was so strong, it was too real. I was afraid that if I started to smoke I would go straight into that. I learned to be very careful about saying things, as well. In the beginning, when I had spiritual contact I felt the need to communicate about it. Now I tend to communicate more in anecdotes or little stories, and I find people interested rather than frightened.

Sometimes you cannot avoid involving others. Often they want to be involved. They come in, and they are interested. There is a problem when you are having a delusion and you feel you are going to tell somebody about it, because you want someone to say 'This is not going on'. So I learned to say I am having this crazy thought, and then tell them what is going on. Then I see what reaction I get. Sometimes I feel that if somebody would say 'Yes, it is true', they would shock me out of my head, because I hoped I was imagining it.

Often you can feed your own paranoia, because if you say to someone, 'This or that is happening', they think 'Why does he think that?' Then they tell somebody else what they think you said, and they alter it a bit. And then you hear from someone else a story which makes you wonder how that could be happening. It is difficult to explain. People exaggerate, and so it builds up out of your influence.

Another barrier to coping, or to getting one's feet back on the ground, is the addictive nature of larger-than-life experiences. It's a type of drug, something that people would pay money for. Delusions of grandeur, the ego clinging to an exaggerated sense of self. Having said that, though, the negative delusions are not something to wish on oneself, and really, there is no way of stopping these things from happening. One could, though, perhaps do more to prevent or at least not facilitate them. Staying awake too long, drinking and smoking too much, living on a diet of beer and coffee - these things lead to exhaustion, and create more confusion.

Perhaps though, like the alcoholic, we take the good with the bad. Some of what is discovered in these states is of value. People who are unwilling explorers of the subconscious (or whatever) are in a position to bring something back. Some explorations lead to dead-ends. Others might uncover ideas, priceless jewels, new ways of looking at things, creative tools, and so on.

Thinking like this positively empowers me. If this is going to happen to me, then I am going to see as much good in it as I can. Given all the knocks I've had, the embarrassments I've suffered, the losses I've incurred because of this thing that happens to me, I could be full of regrets. However, I consider myself the luckiest of individuals, and am most pleased with this mind. I, at least, am an explorer of these great jungles of illusion. My life is an adventure, not necessarily safe or comfortable, but at least an adventure. What I am is not dependent on how I am seen by others. I reject all labels. Also, more often than not, when I meet those who would like to pigeon-hole me, I see only little people with small minds, and cannot really take them very seriously. My current situation is quite stable, and I believe that I will be able to handle the next episode or crisis point, should it occur.

Eleventh Contributor (L. P.)

A 26-year old woman whose medical diagnoses have included schizophrenia. Over a period of five years she was in and out of hospital. She is now the chairwoman of Survivors Speak Out.

I always had a lot of spiritual activity in my life. That has always been quite important to me. I need spiritual contact. I remember when I was about ten years old, I had a year of continual dreams, like a serial. I could tune into it each night. In this dream I was indestructible, and the person who was persecuting me was also indestructible. Between the two of us, it was a question of who could terrify the other more. I always took the same physical forms - that of a crucifix or of a metal box.

Around that same time, I began to feel a spiritual presence outside my bedroom door. Fortunately, it felt as if there was something in the door stopping it from passing through and getting in. But I knew that if this spirit could get in, it was going to be harmful to me. I would just feel it pressing on the door. I could actually see the door sometimes bending under the pressure. It stayed there for seven years, day and night. I didn't think anybody would believe me, so I never told anybody about it for those seven years.

When I was 17, I came into contact with a spiritual healer. I met him literally by chance. I did not seek him out. He was a friend of a friend who had noticed that I was very distressed; increasingly distressed from the age of about 14. This friend suggested that the spiritual healer might give me a hand. When I saw the man, I told him about the spirit outside the door. He said 'Why don't you talk to it?', so I did. I talked to the spirit, and it went away. Then one day I woke up and felt as though my own spirit had died. This was devastating. I felt like an empty vessel. I thought that if my spirit had died, my body might as well follow. So I tried to kill myself.

When I recovered, everything took a new shape. I noticed that another spirit had got into my body to take the place of my own. I felt that this entity was very evil and bad; my body felt contaminated. It was as if there was something rotting inside me. I wanted to get rid of it, so I went to a priest and had an exorcism performed on me. As with the spiritual healer, a friend of a friend said: 'Well, I know this priest. Why don't you go to see him?', and I did. I told him about the entity in me, and he performed the exorcism. I didn't realize he happened to be the Church of England's top exorcist. I was okay for a while, but then the entity came back. I now know why it came back. I have a hole in my aura, and it is located in my chest. I know the exact point. I have learned to recognize when that hole opens. So now, when it opens, it is very simple to cover it with my hands, or my partner covers it. If I do this, entities cannot get in. I can stop them. It is so simple.

Back to when I was 19. So I had that bad entity inside me, but I also had another spirit beside me that would be following me around. It was a male spirit, and he told me his name was Fred. He told me that he was the devil's advocate, and I could always feel him beside me by my right shoulder.

Over the next couple of years, everything was quite a blur. It is hard to remember some of what was happening during that time. I don't know if Fred had any connection with the entity inside me. Very rarely did he order to me to do things. His comments about me were persecutory, continually putting me down. Fred didn't tell me why he had come, but he would just tell me that I was shit, fat, ugly or stupid. He would tell me what he thought of me, and the single words would drop into my head. It was almost like my head was a cup and you could drop an object into it. That object would bang at the bottom.

I didn't talk about him to anyone for quite a while. At times he would do something which was absolutely terrifying. He would send out snakes to attack me, and this was when I became very freaked out. It was at times like this that I would become so-called catatonic because I was just terrified. He would send the snakes out in a specific pattern. He would let me know by saying: 'I send them. They are coming'. Fred would also tell me their colour. Then I would sit down and think: 'Oh shit, what am I going to do?'. Then I would hear the thumping of the snakes' heads against the door. They would come in from under the bottom. Sometimes I would literally see them whizzing up and down the room. I could not see them in a way that I can see this chair and this table. It's hard to explain how I could see them, because it is not that kind of literal vision. It was more like I know their dimension, their shape and their size. It is a different type of vision.

Sometimes there would just be a couple of little ones, and they would get into my drink. When I started to swallow, I would realize there was a snake in my stomach. They would bite my inside and then dissolve. Sometimes they would go over my legs, and occasionally one would bite my neck or wrist and would just stay there. Then I would be immobilized, terrified and unable to speak. I would sometimes see the snake go into the gas fire and be burned. I could smell it burning. The noise is overwhelming; their actual hissing. When there were a lot of them, the sound would be deafening. While all this was happening, it was very difficult to tell other people what was going on. So I felt helpless, because I really did not know what to do.

I started to have other kinds of sounds and visual experiences with colour. I could walk down the road, and everything red would jump out at me. A red traffic light, somebody's socks or jumper, would jump out at me, and they would say 'Contaminated'. Only that single word, 'Contaminated'. Or green would jump out at me and say 'You are alive'. The green was the first positive experience I had ever had. I walked down the road and felt euphoric. You know Marks & Spencer? On the front of the building, the wording is in green. Those letters changed to: 'You are alive'. And I felt just wonderful by this experience; very happy. Sometimes things would alternate between the red and the green. I almost wished for the green to come on.

And sometimes I watched my body grow. I can see it happen in minutes. It normally starts with my hands, and then goes through the rest of my body. It always feels like I am mutating. I do not hear any voices with it, but it is quite distressing.

I would like to tell you about one important experience I had with the snakes. It is the first premonition I had with them. One night, a snake came which gave me a pretty hard time. It forced its way into my mouth and went into my body, but then it came out through my birth canal. I knew it had something to do with my sister, who was pregnant. When I rang up my Mum to ask what had happened, she told me that my sister had given birth to a baby with a slight facial difference. She had a harelip. I knew there was something wrong before I rang my Mum. I knew it was something to do with my sister, because of the snake coming out of my birth canal. It was a horrifying experience, but incredible that it was actually telling me something. It is the one and only time a snake has ever actually told me something.

Over the years, I have also been able to pick up global distress. And I am not alone in this - other voice-hearers experience this. We can sometimes pick up if something bad has happened. You just have a bad feeling, then you might see on the news that maybe a plane has crashed, or someone has been hurt.

Psychiatry

I came into contact with psychiatry at 17. I was talking to them about eating and throwing up, so I started off with an eating disorder label. When I started to talk about an exorcist, they were not too sure. It didn't quite fit in with how they had got me categorized. Then I made the mistake of telling my consultant about Fred and the snakes, and he said: 'Oh, this is very interesting, I know what you are talking about', and he labelled me as schizophrenic. He informed my parents, but I didn't realize this at that time. I remember him saying: 'You have got an underlying illness', but I did not understand what he meant.

For five years, until I was 21, my life was in such a mess. During that time I was going in and out of hospital. As an in-patient, out-patient, and through casualty, as I was continually harming myself. Fred was there most of the time. The evil spirit was still in the place of my spirit. I felt as if I was dead. How could I be alive if I did not have my own spirit in my body? I did not exist. I started self-harming because I felt powerless. It was a reaction to the treatment I was receiving. I would cut myself up as a way of expressing my pain and anger. Also out of sheer frustration, as a way of dealing with all the things that went on, including Fred and the snakes. I was never instructed by the spirit or Fred to do it. That was something I did of my own free will.

Around this time, I would also hear a female voice screaming. The sound was by my ears; outside my head. It was like two female heads screaming in. Now, I think that was a metaphor for my own screaming.

At times, I could not cry or scream. Certainly in a hospital you can't do that, but even outside of the hospital I felt I couldn't do it. So I think I would hear my own screaming and I would cut myself instead of crying. Because when the blood ran away, it felt like tears. The injury was doing the crying for me.

Obviously, psychiatry wasn't very helpful. When I became frozen and rigid when the perceptual differences were very intense, they would just prod my body. I was subjected to behaviour modification and drugs. It was very difficult being told what to do and having no control in my life. But I would try to behave in the way that was expected of me. As I was being treated like a child, then I would behave like a child. It was expected of me, so I would live up to their expectations.

When I came out of hospital and went to the day hospital, they tried to blackmail me into taking injections of tranquillizers. Then I said: 'NO'. It was the first time I actually took a stand. The first time I was assertive. Then I made the decision to escape psychiatry.

When I came into contact with other survivors, it was the turning point of my life. That was when I could start to look at what the hell had been going on. It was not until I got out of psychiatry, was not drugged, was not controlled, that I could look at what had happened. When I came into contact with other survivors, I had a chance to talk about the anger, and have those feelings validated. I felt safe to talk about my experiences without fear of being judged or told that I was stupid or sick. It was such a relief. I then gained a couple of friends who accepted me as I was. If I could feel the snakes coming in, I did not have to rush off. I could stay.

I think that when my understanding grew of what was happening, that was when Fred left me. It was not as if one day I woke up and realized Fred was not there. Very gradually, his presence became less and less. The snakes have always stayed. Fred does not send them out, so I don't know why they still try to trouble me, but how I deal with it now is very different.

Gaining more control

At first, I would not be able to say what was happening till it had finished. But gradually, when it started I alerted someone; I could actually say 'The snakes are in the room' to another person. One of my friends would even talk to the snakes and say 'Go away, leave Louise alone'. It helped that somebody believed me. Somebody was taking me seriously and doing something. It did not necessarily help the snakes to disappear, but I didn't feel totally alone. It does not help to tell me they are not real, because they are. There is no point in denying what is happening to me.

What has been quite liberating is that my partner is particularly good in helping me deal with the snakes. If there is one attached to my body, I can actually say to him: 'There is one on my hand'. I can tell him how big it is, and he will help to pull it off me; physically pull the snake off and throw it right out of the front door. He can dispose of it for me. I am not yet able to do that for myself.

However, my ability to deal with the snakes is developing. It is very rare that I am completely incapacitated. If I am, it is only for a few hours. I know that they will go away eventually, and it helps when I am assertive with them. The other week, they were all over the bed and I said: 'Just fuck off, go away'. When I get angry with them they will go away, even if it takes all night. Last year, when I was at a conference, the whole foyer was covered with snakes. I was walking around, stepping in between them, and totally freaked out. I had a couple of friends who stayed with me all night. They did not have to do anything. I could not talk about the snakes until the morning. My friends stayed all night, which stopped anyone thinking 'This woman looks strange, let's call the doctor or the ambulance'. They protected me from that. I worked through the snakes. It took me all night, but I did it. I came through it.

So how I deal with them depends on how stressed I am, what is going on in my life at that time. If I am stressed, then I will not be so good. If I am feeling strong, then I may be able to get them away by just telling them to go away. But I now feel I have more power. I know that they can come at any time and bite me, and the bites hurt, but I know that they will go away at some point. In time, I hope to get to the point where they don't even get physically on to me, where I can send them away before they get that far. I know I will get to that point.

My own spirit has come back. It is hard to pinpoint the exact time when it returned. But it was definitely at some point when I was escaping psychiatry. My spirit periodically leaves me, but that is not so much of a catastrophe any more. I do not feel the need to kill myself every time my spirit leaves me. I feel very depressed if it is not with me, but I know at some point it will return.

I learnt a lot from my partner, because he has had much experience with voices and entities himself. It is so easy to talk to him about it: that makes a major difference. I have taken ownership of my experiences and found my own meaning.

Twelfth Contributor (A. L.)

A. L. is 42, and has been hearing voices since the age of ten. He has now begun to develop a range of strategies that help him cope. He is presently the Development Co-ordinator for Lambeth Forum for Mental Health.

I can remember hearing voices from a very early age, but it was always associated with seeing a floating face that always seemed to be smirking, but this has now gone. However, I was about ten when the voices became aggressive and difficult to handle. Throughout my childhood and early adolescence, I was sexually abused by a member of my family. The voices were ever-present during this time, and I can recall them teasing, bullying and talking to me. I remember that I lived buried inside myself, and although I went to school, I seemed to be outside the mainstream of activity. I had a friend called Trevor who knew about the voices, and he said that it scared him, but he did not reject me, and we were very close. However, the voices began to dominate me to the extent that I was distracted by them, and I spent hours talking back to them.

At the age of 14, I was taken to see a child psychiatrist, and I was admitted to a large hospital which had established a special unit for children. However, the reality was that I was admitted to an adult male ward. Here, my voices went on the rampage. I was diagnosed as schizophrenic and given Modecate injections. This actually removed my ability to cope with the voices; my emotions were flattened, and my mind could not help me engage the voices.

I was transferred from one hospital to another. At no time was I asked what I thought and felt, and as soon as I said that I heard voices, I was either told to pull my socks up or given different cocktails of chemicals. It seems to me that psychiatry has the nasty habit of turning ordinary experiences into extraordinary ones. It steals your experience, blurs it, twists it, and then hands it back to you, and you are expected to be grateful. At no time did anyone ask me about my life at home. It seemed that instead of being cared for, I was just managed. I was just one of many in a warehouse of human souls. The sexual abuse I experienced has left physical, emotional, spiritual and psychological scars, and I believe that these four elements are connected to my four voices.

In fact, my voices were not the problem. It has been society's attitude towards them and how it has responded. By trying to bury them, or exorcize them by medication and ECT, they have reinforced the cycle of abuse and suppression. Whatever treatments or therapeutic interventions were given to me, I still had the voices. The psychiatric system would only be happy if I denied my experience. This process of denial means that you have to become a model patient and play the game by their rules. You have to bury any awkward feelings, emotions or thoughts so that you become well-adjusted and so that you will not rebel.

Breaking the silence

Only once in 15 years of psychiatric intervention, and at the age of 36, was I able to find someone who was willing to listen. This proved a turning point for me, and from this I was able to break out of being a victim and start owning my experience. This nurse actually found time to listen to my experiences and feelings. She always made me feel welcome, and would make arrangements so we would not be disturbed. She would switch off her bleeper and take her phone off the hook, and sometimes, as there were people outside her room, she would close the blinds. These actions made me feel at ease. She would sit to one side of me instead of across a desk. She told me that what we said was confidential, but that there were some exceptions, so I could decide what to reveal. Slowly, as trust grew between us, I was able to tell her about the abuse, but also about the voices. Sometimes when I was describing what happened to me, she would tell me that it was hurting her and she needed a break. At last, I had found someone who recognized the pain I was feeling. She helped me realize that my voices were a part of me, and had a purpose and validity. Over a six-month period, I was able to develop a basic strategy for coping. The most important thing she did was that she was honest - honest in her motivations and in her responses to what I told her.

I would like to say that maybe other mental health/social work professionals could learn something from her approach:

- be honest about your motivation and the reasons for your intervention;
- establish ground rules at the start;
- provide a safe environment, and keep it safe;
- don't force the agenda - provide people with a breathing space so they can decide what to bring and what not to bring;
- be honest about your own feelings - this is not rejection, but a sign that you are also alive;
- let the person decide what the goals should be and say if they want changes.

Voices: survival and coping

Thanks to the support this worker gave, I have been able to develop a range of coping mechanisms. One of these is that I give them a specific time each day when they can flow and I can engage with them. However, to allow this to happen, I must prepare myself; some things done in advance also help, like establishing a regular sleeping pattern. Even when I promise the voices a particular time, they still carry on, but they do not overwhelm me. One of the things that I have had to learn is to allow myself to be in touch with my emotions, and sometimes I get afraid of my feelings and the voices.

Over the last four years, I have been able to identify trigger events or situations that start the voices off. Sometimes I become more aware of the depth and shade of colours; their brightness seems to be intensive. This phase lasts about 20 to 25 minutes, and then out of a sea of sound comes the voice. Sometimes I feel scared, as the voice becomes more dominant.

I have four distinct voices in my life, and I have noticed that their tone and pitch have changed as I have got older. Each voice seems to have different triggers; however, some world events start them all off. For example, during the Gulf war, I found it difficult to sleep or even concentrate during the day, as the voices screamed abuse at me for three whole days on the trot without respite.

Here are my voices... and their triggers

- Voice one: the Silver Voice. This voice is softly spoken and usually whispers, often fragmented phrases and comments about the people I meet or have relationships with. Triggers: talking to people over the telephone; becomes dominant if I have to travel to new places or meet new people; often talks when I touch someone for the first time, eg shaking hands.
- Voices two and three: the Two Brothers. These two voices speak to each other, as well as to me, in a rhythmic pattern. They are very aggressive and abusive and talk to me about the other voices. These two voices are the most difficult to cope with. Triggers: these voices often seem to be dominant after any sexual activity; sometimes they are triggered when I touch old or antique objects such as furniture, jewellery and mirrors.
- Voice four: the Mechanical Voice. This voice usually comes in the night, and is dominant and active when it is dark. It usually repeats the same set of phrases - it often tells me that other beings, usually animals, can hear all the voices, and that cats hear the best. Funny as it may seem, this is the voice I am most scared of, but I have built up a mechanism of coping by allowing myself to be scared, and this makes the voice fade away. Triggers: darkness; the full moon; cats sitting on me; lying awake in bed when everyone is asleep.

In order to be able to function and be responsive to the world, I have had to take control and be fairly disciplined. One of the things I don't do is to try and block them out by playing music and listening through headphones. When I have done this in the past, they have waited until I was in a social situation where I could not retreat, and then all started on me, making me feel dizzy and totally disorientated. Some therapists promote this as a way forward, but I personally feel that it is a form of denial of the experience, a way of saying that it has no value or significance. I totally reject this attitude.

I have found it easier to live with the voices now that I have developed a balance of energies, and also allowed myself to feel uncertainty and anxiety, and also fear at times; to own my experience, to respect myself and to be in as much control as possible. As I have said I have found a number of things that make it easier to cope with the voices. However, each voice needs to be handled differently.

Training the voices: getting them balanced with my life

- **The Silver Voice.** I often found that drawing pictures or even speaking out loud what the voice is saying helps to reduce its power (each session lasts about ten minutes).
- **The Two Brothers.** These are the most emotionally demanding. If they start, I have to find a place of sanctuary and let them go (lasts up to three hours).
- **The Mechanical Voice.** I usually talk back to this voice, asking it questions that I hope it will find difficult to answer. By allowing myself to be afraid, I am able to question the voice by asking, for instance: 'You cannot hurt me, can you?' By teasing the voice, I prove that I am stronger. Sometimes, if I don't respond, it will get very abusive and say strange things, but only lasts for about ten minutes per hour throughout the night.

I have found that in order to live my life, I have had to take control and reject the notion of seeing myself as a victim. You may find that by talking about them with others, your voice may play you up for a few days, doing all it can to distress you and disrupt your daily routine - don't give in. Once you have established a pattern, and you keep to it, then the voices will become less powerful. Here are some tips that may be helpful:

- Create a space or a time when you will engage with the voices. Create a specific time each day, and over a period, reduce the time you allow for them to be in contact.
- Don't try and block out the voices, but instead try and find out if they have any common thread. When and where do they come? Can you identify any triggers?
- It may help if you learn some basic relaxation techniques. These will

prove helpful when your emotions become knotted by the voices' constant barrage. Use them when the voices start.
- Own your experience: live it and breathe it, and pass through it in your own time and at your own pace.

Writing this has not been easy. The voices have told me that once this is read by others who hear voices, my voices will become stronger and return to me. This does scare me a bit, but I am alive. I am pleased that we are coming together to share our experiences and explanations, but we have to be careful not to lose control, and that any movement does not end up synthesizing our experiences and turn them into stereotypes. I am pleased that there are people helping, but any support or assistance must be on our terms, because at the end of the day we are the ones who have to live with and cope with the voices. We don't have to enter a competition against each other, because each of our experiences is unique and valid.

From a sea of sound, from the soup of emotions
   a power is stirred
       and
  the world is full
       of
       voices
       voices that whisper
           voices
  that laugh
           voices
  that crush me in the
         darkness
            of day
            but I
            have a song
            in my heart
            that says that
            they can live
            in peace beside
            me.

Thirteenth Contributor (P. H.)

This is the story of a woman whom I (Marius Romme) had begun to treat in 1983. She was then 26 years old, and had been hearing voices since the age of 14 or 15. She came to me because the voices gave her orders, for example forbidding her to do certain things or to meet people, and they dominated her completely. She had been hospitalized several times and diagnosed as suffering from schizophrenia. Neuroleptics failed to still the voices, although they did reduce the anxiety they caused. Unfortunately, the medication also reduced her mental alertness, and so she chose not to take it over long periods, and avoided long stays in hospital. The voices, however, continued to isolate her more and more by forbidding her to do the things she had always loved to do, and sometimes even ordered her to injure herself. During the first conference for voice-hearers in 1987, she told her story as follows.

As far as I can remember, I was seven or eight when I first heard voices. At that time, they were friendly, told me stories, gave advice, and protected me from unpleasant situations, for instance quarrels. But when I was 15, they also became malicious and began to give me orders. At first, these orders were rather harmless, for example to do certain things in a given order when I got up in the morning. Over the course of the years, they became more coercive and troublesome. They started to forbid friendships, or destroy them by making the other person seem totally ridiculous. Often I was not allowed to answer the telephone or open the door if the bell rang, or go visiting somewhere. They had comments about everything, and their remarks were usually negative. They disturbed me when I was studying, reading, and in conversation. For years, I did not tell anyone about them, because they forbade that too. If I did not obey them, they made so much noise that I could not hear what was going on around me. At such times, they often let themselves be seen, and frightened me. If things got really out of hand, they made me hurt myself.

I used to think they were all-knowing and all-powerful gods who managed and determined everything on earth. I sometimes tried to fool the voices, but they were too clever for that. Sometimes I tried to ally myself with them, even brought them offerings, but the voices would not be suppressed. Because I thought that the voices were connected with the situation at home, I ran away. I started treatment in the juvenile section of the Department of Social Psychiatry, but I did not get rid of the voices.

For a brief period, I thought I had become insane, but I soon discarded that idea. The voices are too real to be called a hallucination. Four years ago, I encountered Professor Romme. When I went into therapy with him, it took me all of the first year to convince him that it was not a clinical disorder, that the voices were outside myself. We tried to discover whether there was a connection between certain feelings and the voices, but that connection was, at most, that the voices could reinforce a particular mood. For example, if I do not feel very well, the voices may get so wound up that they make a mountain out of a molehill. So we attempted some training. I learned from Professor Romme to create the conditions in which I have more control over myself and am less easily impressed by the voices. I have not got rid of the voices, but the talks with Professor Romme did help me. This man keeps me thinking clearly; he forces me to use my brain. I have learned to see connections between what the voices say and my own feelings, and to structure my days. I keep the evening free for the voices, so that I will be less bothered by them during the day, and can therefore function better. I have also learned to use neuroleptic agents (psychiatric drugs) properly. The use of such medicines is something I resisted for a long time, because they dull your thinking and feeling. I now take them in a low dosage and am less troubled by the side-effects, and if the voices seem to be gaining dominance over me, I increase the dose temporarily.

Since telling my family about the voices, which helped them to understand my behaviour better, I have had a great deal of support from them. This year I had a bad time again, and I went to live with my mother. That went well. The pressure of not being able to take care of myself any longer was relieved. And it also helped that my mother was very optimistic. She said: 'So far it has always passed, so it will pass this time, too'. I don't know where the voices come from and what they mean, but I do know that they belong to me and will stay. Although I can cope with them better now than a few years ago, I still find it difficult to live with them.

9. HEARING VOICES: PSYCHIATRIC AND PSYCHOLOGICAL PERSPECTIVES

Introduction
Marius Romme

However difficult it may be to estimate the numbers of those who hear voices, it is clear that a great many of them come into contact, at some stage, with the world of psychiatry. For this reason, we include here a selection of frames of reference which are either used in or have developed with clear regard to psychiatry.

There are other grounds, too, for the incorporation of these perspectives: a number of them offer possible strategies for learning to cope with hearing voices, although regrettably this does not apply to them all. The various sections of this chapter overlap in many areas, and are not mutually exclusive; broadly speaking, each examines and emphasizes a different aspect of the same body of theory.

In Classical Psychiatry, we find the familiar assumption that voices are symptomatic of illness and brain dysfunction, and of schizophrenia in particular. This approach, of course, pays little or no attention to the voices themselves, and implies treatment consisting of suppression with neuroleptics.

Functional Analysis focuses on what the voices say. It outlines approaches to dialogues about the voices and how these can be used to discover the significance of their messages within the context of the hearer's life history.

Dissociation interprets voice-hearing as the outcome of a psychological mechanism brought into play to cope with threatening situations, particularly in early childhood. This, it is said, results in the splitting off of certain emotions and memories from the personality, which then reappear in the form of voices.

The childhood experience of sexual or other abuse is discussed in Trauma: this presents the results of research which appears to show a correlation between such abuse and the later appearance of auditory hallucinations.

In Cognitive Psychology, the phenomenon of hearing voices is approached as a special interpretation of perceptions, in other words as a particular way of processing information which may be especially uncomfortable or difficult to assimilate.

Social Psychiatry considers voices as a metaphorical expression of the hearer's life situation and history. In this model, the person's interactions within relationships and the wider social context are reflected or echoed by the voices.

Family Interactions and Psychosis examines the contribution of the domestic environment to both the onset and the management of voices. The emotional atmosphere and dynamics within a given family can, it seems, be a crucial factor for better or worse in coping with the voices.

Psychosis offers Brian Davey's reflections on various approaches to mental and emotional disturbance, and includes his own remarkable account of his struggles with psychosis. Brian has studied psychological and psychoanalytical theory in depth, and provides a refreshingly personal theory grounded in experience.

In Carl Jung on Extrasensory Perception, the notion of the collective unconscious is explored as a possible source of voices. Jung, a psychiatrist who himself heard voices, believed they might be expressions of contact, at the deepest level, with an unconscious realm of spiritual life shared by us all. This idea offers one possible explanation for the common experience of voices as not-me.

Jaynes and Consciousness considers the role of evolution in the development of consciousness. The originator of this theory, the psychologist Julian Jaynes, believes that there was once a time when hearing voices was a routine human experience, and that the phenomenon today represents an evolutionary residue. This is a more personal perspective than most of those represented in this chapter, in that it is seldom drawn upon within the psychiatric field - nor, indeed, is it particularly current elsewhere. However, we have included an account of this approach (written by Patsy Hage, herself a hearer of voices) because we have seen how reassuring it can be for many voice-hearers seeking ways of understanding their experiences.

It is notable that the hearers of voices seldom find psychiatric frames of reference sympathetic or faithful to their personal experience. This in itself makes it imperative that there should be the freest possible exchange of experience and theory between professionals and hearers. For the time being, however, there appears to be a chasm between experience and theory - between subjectivity and objectivity - which makes effective co-operation and mutual assistance extremely difficult. The crucial issue, then, is not which camp has right on its side, but how this chasm may be reduced or bridged. This chapter may, we hope, suggest some possible approaches to this essential task.

Classical Psychiatry
Alec Jenner

To see something which is not there, or hear something which has not been spoken, would appear, at the very least, to be to make a mistake. In psychiatry, these two types of experience are respectively known as visual and auditory hallucinations. For the classical psychiatrist, they reveal that there is something wrong with the perceiver, given that he or she cannot rely on his or her senses, at least in some circumstances. The assumption here is that when we are well, we are capable of distinguishing ourselves and our thoughts from what is happening around us: we know the difference between hearing something and imagining something. The failure to make this distinction is said to illustrate a loosening of the ego-boundaries (some psychiatrists use the even more technical expression 'failure of the diacresis').

However, a simple failure of our eyes and ears is not sufficient explanation for the perception, for example, of speech in our own language. If there is a physical explanation, it must involve some parts of the brain deceiving us by failing to work properly - parts which have already learnt our language. Classical psychiatrists know that there are many situations in life in which our imagination can run riot: when we are frightened or alone, have had too much to drink, when we are suspicious that others are talking about us, when we are dropping off to sleep or waking up. To the psychiatrist, experiences at times like these are not truly significant hallucinations.

Psychiatrists tend to be at pains to distinguish the hallucinations of the wide-awake from those of the drowsy, feverish, senile, brain-damaged, and physically ill. There are some hallucinations that occur when one is wide awake, and these are considered to be signs of a severe psychological illness, of what is known as psychosis. There is no consensus about the nature of so-called functional psychoses, but they are generally believed to be due to certain illnesses to which one is susceptible because of an inherited defect of the brain. These are illnesses in which one has lost contact with reality. What, precisely, it may be that tips the balance is more debatable; this may involve combinations of birth defects, viral infections or difficult life-events, particularly within the family.

In essence, there are two recognized kinds of functional psychosis. In manic-depressive illness, it is thought that the individual's moods swing to and fro because a controlling mechanism is out of order. Hallucinations can then occur at the extremes of mood, and are seen as consequences of those moods. Schizophrenia, however, is the so-called illness in which the hearing of voices is most centrally involved. To some extent, we can think of this condition as a loss of the more usual associations of thoughts and ideas: some see it as a confusion of circuitry within the brain, like tangled wiring inside a television set. To begin with, psychiatrists observed that people with schizophrenia tended to deteriorate progressively, while those with manic depression usually oscillated between mania (elation and hyperactivity) and depression. Although there is some truth in this observation, it is only approximately valid: some of the downhill course does seem to have been due to the nature of the institutions to which people were sent.

Whatever the difficulties, psychiatrists must struggle to classify the types of mental state they are expected to treat. Perhaps they are mistaken to believe that there are separate illnesses, or even if there are, to believe we have the right classification. However, the struggle to produce a science of psychiatry has led to studies of what correlates with what. Indeed, it was the man in the street, not the psychiatrists, who first identified mental problems in need of explanation.

Historically, the Heidelberg Clinic in Germany was especially important in the attempt to describe illnesses and their signs and symptoms. In particular, it was claimed that the hearing of voices speaking in the third person, whilst the hearer was wide awake, was diagnostic of schizophrenia. ('I am' is in the first person, 'you are' is in the second, and 'he or she is' is in the third.) This diagnosis was said to be further confirmed when the voices appeared to belong to groups of people talking together about the hearer, especially if they made derogatory comments. Most modern psychiatrists would still classify as schizophrenic anyone reporting such experiences. Some may find it strange that this preoccupation with diagnostics can mean that the doctor is less interested in what the voices say than in the way they say it. This is because psychiatrists struggle to distinguish between what they call form and content: the form, in this case, is the hearing of voices speaking in the third person, while the content consists of what they are saying. If we hear people speaking to us, the form is that of a perception if they are, in fact, talking; if they are not, then the form is that of a hallucination. In both cases, the content is the same, but the forms are different (the reverse, of course, can also apply). For the purposes of diagnosis, then, form is more important than content. The attempt to make a diagnosis is always central to medicine: this, as often as not, is what one goes to the doctor for.

Proper treatment can only come after a correct diagnosis. It must be kept clearly in mind that psychiatry is a branch of medicine, and so its language is medical. The question of what ought and ought not to fall within the domain of medicine raises various other issues outside the scope of this section.

I am trying here to help the client understand the psychiatrist's frame of mind and what he or she is doing; why he or she asks this question or that; which part of the answer will be given most importance, and which is more likely to be disregarded. The psychiatrist is scanning the conversation for - amongst other things - reference to schizophrenic hallucinations such as those voices in the third person.

What it is to be human is, of course, extremely complex, and much of the science behind psychological medicine involves an attempt to understand how the brain - a physical object - produces thoughts, imagination, and experiences. Given that it does so, it is clear that when the physical mechanisms go wrong, then so must the thoughts. While it would be crude to suggest that there can be no crooked thought without a crooked molecule, this can characterize one possible attitude to mental illnesses. We can see this at a simple level in patients who have had strokes: a lot of blood in the left side of the brain (of a right-handed person) damages the ability to find the right words to speak, even if the patient understands quite well what is said. This offers an illustration of how the mind is affected by the functions of parts of the brain.

Another reason for choosing the above example is to make a point about the different functions of the left and right sides of the brain. In most people, the left side is developed for such things as language, logic, theory and mathematics; the right has more to do with art, imagination and the spatial relationships between objects. There has been considerable research in an attempt to refine these ideas, but it is difficult to be categorical - not least because there is much individual variation; speech, for example, is not always developed on the left, even in right-handed people. Even so, every new insight into brain function has been studied for possible clues to the nature of schizophrenia.

There is evidence that damage or malfunction in certain parts of the brain - especially in the so-called temporal lobes - does tend to produce characteristic psychological effects (particularly in people with epilepsy), including hallucinations. People with right-side defects do tend to be highly emotional, while those with left-side defects tend to have a strong sense of personal destiny, and to be philosophically curious and morally scrupulous. Such interesting glimpses into the relations between brain functions, thought and experiences might well be influencing a psychiatrist when interviewing a patient. Could this person, he or she might wonder, have temporal lobe epilepsy, a physical condition of the brain with a psychological manifestation? If so, this may be rather more significant than the patient's life situation.

Schizophrenia is as real a word in the English language as is witch or any other. However, it is often overlooked that words do not always represent specific things; some represent collections of things, as in the case, for example, of a word like animals. Without words, of course, we are limited in our ability to think, but with them, too, we can still be misled. Schizophrenia is essentially an umbrella term used to describe states in which people hear voices in a certain way, and have delusions not easily understood in terms of their racial, religious or other backgrounds. Such experiences and beliefs can often respond to particular antipsychotic drugs, though inevitably at the cost of certain side-effects (notably unwanted bodily movements).

When an individual's life with another is made painful or even impossible by these voices and ideas, psychiatrists rightly feel justified in doing what they can to improve the situation. Where there is no distress to the self or others, however, just hearing voices does not warrant interference, especially if this is not an early sign of more serious developments.

Functional Analysis
Jan van Laarhoven

Modern technology has made it ever easier for us to communicate with one another over long distances. Sometimes this involves a dialogue, as on the telephone, and sometimes a one-way message, as with radio and television. It would appear to be a law of nature that, as the scope of communication expands, people feel the need to limit its range. The need for privacy, peace and quiet, and a self-contained personal living space is rapidly becoming the norm, although the realization of this ideal is often hampered by lack of financial means, overpopulation or simply the intrusions of those around us.

In the case of those people who hear voices, we are dealing with a form of communication which is seldom either voluntary or desirable. Initially, at least, the voices are generally experienced as coming from outside and intrusive; they present a one-sided conversation which, at this point, makes it impossible to enter into any proper dialogue with them. It goes without saying that this loss of control over one's privacy can cause a great deal of anxiety, regardless of whether the content of what is said is frightening or not.

Some hearers manage to find their own way to resources which can help them to cope successfully with these voices. Similarly, those who have actively sought voice experiences, along with others who regard their voices as positive phenomena, will probably not be found in psychiatric care. Psychiatrists are consulted by those who, in one way or another, are troubled by the fact that they hear voices, or find their contact with them problematic. This should not tempt us to jump to any hasty conclusions, however: our goal is not to force the voices into complete silence, even if that were possible. The important thing is to help the patient to increase his or her control over the voices, thus making the most of a potentially disadvantageous situation. My contribution to this book is to indicate a number of resources which may be helpful in this respect; to suggest some tools which may serve to develop a dialogue about and with the voices in order to detect - in co-operation with the patient - the significance and function of the voices in the hearer's life.

When a patient enlists the help of a therapist, that patient's psychiatric case history will be drawn up. This is done in order to establish whether depression, anxiety disorder or psychosis (ie the chaotic result of an attempt to process certain information) may be involved; one or another of these may warrant the use of psychotropic drugs or some other form of treatment. A physical case history, and sometimes a physical examination, is also important for the detection of any possible physical disorder.

In investigating the personality, the therapist will pay close attention to any traumatic events in the patient's life history, especially to (long-term) sexual or other abuse in early childhood (see the section on Trauma elsewhere in this chapter).

One way of interpreting the hearing of voices is as a dissociative disorder; that is, a form of organization whereby the mind is split into a number of parts which are more separate than usual. In the course of any examination, the therapist must also be prepared for other signs of dissociative disorder, such as altered time perception (even loss of time), the use of the royal 'We', the denial of clearly-observed behaviour, and feelings of depersonalization and unreality. Should there be any great fluctuations evident in previous psychiatric symptoms or diagnoses drawn up by others, this is even stronger suggestion that we are dealing with a dissociative disorder (see the section on Dissociation in this chapter).

Sometimes the function performed by the voices, in terms of the patient's mental housekeeping, is immediately clear; indeed, the patient him or herself is occasionally able to explain this function to the therapist during the very first session. However, it is more likely that the patient does not think in terms of function, or cannot discover the function him or herself. Dissociative disorders do not, after all, arise without cause: they often have a protective function. Consequently, even if the therapist has a clear idea about the significance or function of the voices, he or she will not automatically confront the patient with this idea. The following questions are important in arriving at a clearer idea of the function of voices:

Circumstances
  - When, and under what circumstances, did the voices first occur?
  - Are the voices the same as they were the first time? If not, what has changed?
  - Do the voices occur at set times?
  - Do they occur at set places?
  - Do they occur when the patient is in certain company?
  - Do they occur during certain activities?
  - Do they occur when the patient is in a certain mood?

Identity
  - Do the voices identify themselves?
  - Are they the voices of people or spirits?
  - Are they male or female?
  - Are they the voices of well-known or of unknown people?

Internal organization
  - How many voices are there in total?
  - Are the voices aware of one another's existence?
  - Do the voices form an organized system among themselves?
  - Did all the voices start at the same time, or is one more recent than others?
  - Are all the voices equally developed as people or spirits?

Control
  - Does the patient experience the voices as coming from inside him/herself, or as coming from outside?
  - Is he/she dependent on the voices?
  - Can he/she call up the voices by choice?
  - Does he/she feel the voices coming, and if so, what happens? Can he/she talk to the voices?
  - Do they obey his/her requests to be silent?
  - Can he/she shut him/herself off from the voices?

- Do the voices sometimes take over his/her entire mind?
- Are they responsive to his/her arguments?
- Can the patient refuse their commands?

Content

- Generally speaking, does the patient experience the voices as positive or negative?
- Do all the voices have the same emotional significance, or do they vary?
- Do the voices have a specific aim?
- Are the voices clear, or do they speak in vague terms?
- Do the voices warn against specific activities?
- Do the voices incite the patient to undertake specific activities, and if so, do these activities have a specific character?

Role

- Do the voices know something, or can they do something, that the patient does not know or cannot do?
- Can the patient do something, or does he or she know something, that the voices cannot do or do not know?
- What has changed in the patient's life since the voices appeared?
- What would change in the patient's life if the voices were to disappear?

On the basis of the answers given to these questions, we try to discover a pattern in the voices, thereby exploring their function and significance in the patient's life. If possible, the therapist will try - with the patient's help - to make this function more explicit. Together they will then attempt to establish whether this function is acceptable to the entire person. This is followed by an examination of the relative success of the strategies adopted by the voices; ultimately, this leads to the question of whether there are no easier or better ways of achieving these ends.

How do these questions help us to clarify the voices' function? Well, there are a number of frames of reference open to us, and generally speaking we can only discover a pattern if we know the corresponding frame of reference. With a variety of frameworks at our disposal, we can be more flexible in our interventions. This means that the patient should not be addressed solely in terms of the therapist's own perspective: on the contrary, one should adhere as closely as possible to the patient's experience and language. However, a particular framework may serve as a guideline and a support for the interventions which are contemplated for the benefit of the patient. Let us consider a number of the commonest functions in combination with the most important frames of reference. The perspectives described below are by no means mutually exclusive; it is, on the whole, sensible to allow interventions to stem from a variety of frameworks.

Freud's theory of the unconscious

For these purposes, we shall presume the existence of both consciousness and the unconscious. Some modern supporters of this model believe that the unconscious is situated in the right hemisphere of the brain, which makes only a part of the information present available to the left - verbal - half. If this information does not correspond with what the left half of the brain thinks, it is experienced as ego-dystonic (not-me), and sometimes heard in the form of voices. In hypnosis, we attempt to make direct contact with the right half of the brain by bypassing or diverting the left half of the brain. If this contact can be made, it is possible to exert some influence.

The nature of the information-organization in the right half of the brain (primary process, pre-verbal or pre-logical) means that it is best influenced in the same manner, for example by means of metaphors, non-verbal sounds, movements and so forth. It is also possible for the right half of the brain to understand fairly simple sentences; the passive capacity for understanding is greater than the active. This model might be considered if the voices also have a low degree of verbal organization. A freer exchange of information between left and right can be stimulated under anxiety-reducing circumstances, such as a structuring therapy.

Freud's theory of the id, ego and super-ego

This model is built on the assumption that the personality is composed of an id, an ego and a super-ego. Generally speaking, the deliberations of the ego are experienced as ego-syntonic (me), and are acceptable to the patient (although exceptions to this rule are seen in many dissociative disorders). Consequently, there is usually no need for the ego to express itself in the form of a voice. Voices might stem from the id if certain primitive drives are not accepted by the super-ego; they might, for example, be experienced as advice from the devil. Accusatory voices can be seen as stemming from a stern super-ego expressing criticism towards the drives of the id - criticism too harsh for the ego to share in; these could be experienced as coming from a judgmental God. Advisory voices in a more constructive tone can be expected from both the ego and the ideal-ego (which, together with the conscience, goes to from the super-ego).

Example

A 16-year old girl has masturbated since the age of three. One day, her mother came into the room without warning and caught her in the act; her mother blushed with embarrassment, turned round and left the room without a word. Since that day, the girl has heard her mother's voice, and that of an unknown woman, providing a commentary to her masturbation and telling her that she will be burnt alive while the rest of the world watches. During therapy, the girl is given factual information on normal sexual development, and reads the Hite Report. She resolves to pass this information on to the voices that night, but at that very moment the voices disappear, never to return. The girl also gives her mother a relevant book to read; her mother, in turn, tells her a little about her own sexual development, which had a strong religious bias.

In conversations with voices from the id, it is appropriate to use moral or practical arguments. With voices from the super-ego, one uses arguments of compassion and forgiveness, supported if necessary by reference to the Bible (eg the Good Samaritan) or by offering a more realistic description of a parent perceived as a punishing presence ('do you really think that your father has never done that kind of thing himself?', etc.).

It strikes me as worthwhile to aim at maintaining a certain distance between the structural components; the most important thing is to strive for good mutual communication, and to give each component a balanced share in the matter.

Dissociative organization

The basis for this perspective is the assumption that the personality accommodates a collection of more or less separate sub-personalities, each with a more or less developed learning process of its own. The more closely these sub-personalities are connected with one another, the more their host feels whole. The more separate they are from one another, the greater the effort required for internal dialogue, and the more sub-personalities are to be experienced as not-me. The likelihood of a dissociated organization of the personality is determined both by inherent predisposition and by the need to cordon off any traumatic experiences (see the section on Trauma in this chapter).

In general, treatment is directed towards better communication between the dissociated parts; in other words, towards a better equilibrium between the diverse constituents, and a strengthening of the principal sub-personality. My own preference is to call a meeting in which each part can have a say, giving one part less and another part more time to speak; in these exercises the chairman usually needs intensive support from the therapist. Other metaphors can also be used too: the members of an orchestra, a business, a family, and so on.

Social perspectives

Here, the voices represent a substitute for desired companionship. If a patient feels generally lonely, one can help him or her to examine whether there might be opportunities in his or her daily life to extend the scope for interpersonal contact. One might think here of joining clubs or societies, or looking for a partner through the services of a dating agency or marriage bureau.

Example

A 34-year old Moroccan man is increasingly losing his grip on the world around him. He considers 90% of the population to be dishonest, and is afraid that he will turn aggressive, as he has before, and do irreparable damage to people and property. When he is under stress, he sees little people all around him, who talk to him in his own language, offer him sympathy and calm him down. He finds this dimension more attractive than the normal world. He does not think he is mad, but he is frightened of going mad.

Instances like this must be carefully distinguished from the well-known phenomenon, amongst children, of the make-believe playmate (person, animal or fairy-tale character), with which only the child is capable of communicating. These imaginary companionships are not, in themselves, abnormal; only if the child cuts itself off from the real world is treatment called for. If a given patient recognizes the voices heard as belonging to someone with whom he or she would like to have a closer relationship in real life, then it becomes a question of reality-testing. Unfortunately, the third party is all too often unwilling to become involved in this, but if such co-operation can be won, it is helpful to arrange a discussion during therapy in which the other person is actually present. Even then, however, the patient sometimes attributes a greater reality to the voices than to the real-life person: he or she might say, for example, that the person is holding back in front of the therapist, and not telling the whole truth.

Example

Seven years ago, a 29-year old woman had a brief affair with an artist. She still keeps his self-portrait as a memento, and when she holds this picture in her hands she has paranormal contact with the artist. The face in the painting moves, and she can talk to him. By this method, he assures her that he will marry her one day, and that his other girlfriends mean nothing to him. The young woman has given up her education, and is unemployed. The artist, in person, agrees to talk to the woman and the therapist together, and tries to convince the woman that her expectations are unreal. She then damages the self-portrait, although she later tries to restore it.

Recently, she has had her doubts about whether the marriage will go ahead; she is now considering taking holy orders and joining a convent. God speaks to her, too: he tells her he is eager to take her as his bride if she is suitably cleansed of sinful desires. She is not prepared to take neuroleptics or lithium.

Grief

In the immediate aftermath of the death of a partner, close friend or relative, it is not unusual for people to actually hear the deceased speaking. It is remarkable how often the voice gives or is asked for advice; comforting and cheering words are frequently the pattern. In cases like these, I see no need to interfere. It is a different matter, of course, when the deceased turns into a tormentor, constantly returning to unfinished business which may have been secret or taboo before death. The therapist can help by encouraging the patient to see this type of conversation through to the end, once and for all, instead of breaking off at the same point every time.

Example

A 64-year old woman asks for help. Her husband died of a heart attack seven months ago, after what she considers to have been a good marriage. However, she had never dared to tell him that their only son, the second of their four children, was by another man, the result of a fleeting romance in The Hague. For the last four months, she has been plagued every night by a voice singing: 'In The Hague lives an Earl, and his son's name is Jantje', followed by terrible laughter. She recognizes this as her husband's voice.

After conferring with the therapist, the woman writes three letters to her husband. In the first, she confesses to the affair; in the second, she describes all the good times they shared in their marriage; and in the third, she outlines the plans she has made for the rest of her life. She buries these letters in the garden, under the bench where they always used to sit together. After this, she never hears her husband's voice again.

Surviving relatives may sometimes hear voices talking about who is to blame for the death; this is particularly common in cases where it is a child who has died. The child may cry pitifully from the other world, and beg for the protection which the parent was unable to give in life. The therapist's task is to put the situation into a realistic perspective; rituals of mourning can be useful in these instances, particularly at the end of therapy.

It is also quite common for the voice of the deceased to be heard when the surviving relative is preparing to enter into a new relationship. Here, the therapist can help by working through any points of ambivalence. If the relationship in life was basically good, the deceased will certainly give his or her blessing if he or she is convinced that the new relationship has a future.

Self-aggrandizement

In some cases, an important mission is received directly from God or from some famous historical personage. On the whole, these orders are not viable in practice: often they are such that there would be damaging repercussions if the patient were actually to embark on the task.

If these ideas of grandeur are brusquely dismissed, there is a fair chance that the patient will feel misunderstood, alienated and insulted; feelings of inferiority generally lie just under the surface of self-aggrandizement. It seems to me that the way to tackle these situations is to analyze the aims of the order-giver in conjunction with the patient, and by conferring with the voices to arrive at a morally acceptable - and feasible - interim aim, and then try to accomplish this.

Example

A 29-year old man recently gave up his university degree course in history. He found he could no longer concentrate or make contact with his fellow students, and went back to live with his parents, where he spends a lot of his time on the home computer. He hears a voice telling him that he is the reincarnation of Mussolini, and that it is his task to unite Europe. In addition to training his reflexes with Space Invaders, he also writes off for information on different weapons' systems, and is trying to get accepted for commando training.

Working on the hypothesis that he is looking for a super-solution to his own inner chaos and disorganized social life, the therapeutic approach is to work step by step towards social reintegration. As a result, both he and his parents have more realistic demands and expectations, and the voices are becoming less intrusive.

Self-injury

When voices order the hearer to harm him or herself - in extreme cases, to commit suicide - the patient is usually conscious of a basic, underlying mood of depression, which is sometimes accompanied by delusions of guilt or nihilistic convictions. The feelings of depression may also be entirely dissociated. The therapist's task is to provide firm support for the healthy part of the personality, which may itself be represented in a voice that can be encouraged. Negotiation with the destructive voices is more productive than any attempts to ignore them. Anti-depressive medicines, possibly combined with a neuroleptic, may assist these negotiations.

Example
A 23-year old woman has suffered from depression since the age of 15, and was 17 when she made her first suicide attempt; since then, more have followed. For a long time, she would refuse to say more than a few words, and it later transpired that her voices had forbidden her to speak. She has lost 16 kilos in weight since the voices began telling her that any food she eats will turn into worms. Her grandfather, to whom she had been close, died when she was 13; at his funeral, she felt as if she was being sucked down into the grave. She said that her grandfather had been buried on top of her grandmother, and she now hears both their voices at night, asking her to come and lie between them. In therapy, she is encouraged to test the voices critically: if their advice is well-meant, then they can have no objection to clarifying their motives. She is also given the support of a depot neuroleptic.

Self-injury commands can also arise from other conflicts. The voices may say that such a deed is necessary to preserve the family or some individual relative from greater evil. This is sometimes encountered in children whose parents are about to divorce. In cases like these, the best option is to arrange sessions with the entire family.

These situations can also be understood in the light of other perspectives outlined in this chapter: for example, orders from the super-ego to suppress impulses from the id.

Metaphysical aspects
There are many variations in the metaphysical or mystical perspectives that may arise for the hearer of voices. He or she may, for example, have been chosen as a special protégé to whom special powers are granted and rewards promised; on the other hand, there may be particular trials and ordeals to be undergone. Such individuals are likely to seek advice and guidance from those who are versed in the metaphysical system concerned. In my view, it is essential for the secular therapist to ensure that the patient does not, in this pursuit, neglect his or her health, daily tasks or social contacts. It is also important to be aware of the pitfalls of a psychasthenic personality structure as described by the French

psychiatrist and psychologist Pierre Janet (see the next section of this chapter on The Dissociated Personality).

As I have tried to show, the viable options for effective help or support for the hearer of voices depend largely on the functions of those voices. There are, nevertheless, a number of general guidelines that can be recommended to the voice-hearer:

- These voices are usually rather vague. It is often fruitful to initiate a dialogue and ask the voices for clarification.
- Initially, the voices tend to arise at awkward moments; if they are positive voices, we can schedule set times for them to be heard.
- If there is more than one voice, it is important to bring them all into contact with one another. If there are to be discussions, these can take place entirely among the voices; it is not always necessary for you to join in yourself.
- If the voices repeat themselves, start writing down what they say; next time they appear, tell them that you already know what they have to say.
- Do not attach too much importance to what a particular voice has to say; each voice represents only one point of view.
- Try to get to the bottom of the symbolic significance of the voices, and pursue this line as far as you can.
- If you dislike the voices or their contents, treat them as you would any annoying noise. Teach yourself to drown them out by: turning down the volume; making loud noises yourself; using a personal stereo; switching on another source of noise; finding some form of distraction, in particular physical activity.

The aim, in my view, should be to take greater control over your voices, so that you are no longer at their beck and call; in fact, the voices should be at your service. I would advise you not to rely solely on the voices themselves during this process, nor indeed on books, but to ask for assistance from professionals or survivors in this field. Finally, in all dealings with these voices, common sense is the best possible guide.

The Dissociated Personality
Onno van der Hart

Introduction
We all relate to our surroundings in two fundamental ways. We do some things which are essentially repetitions of what we have learnt in the past, and others which are new and creative attempts to adapt actively to changing circumstances. As a rule, of course, our behaviour is a combination of both. Most of the actions characteristic of us are very

familiar to us; the more these come to be performed automatically, the more they form a part of our personality.

It is also true that some people perform actions more or less automatically which are not, in essence, characteristic of them, and experience thoughts and feelings for which they are not themselves responsible. These actions, thoughts and feelings are not, as it were, functional to them personally. In such cases, a part of the psyche functions more or less independently of the personality as a whole, but is nevertheless likely to influence how one functions as an individual. This phenomenon, the principle feature of which is dissociation, has had a great deal of attention devoted to it in recent years.

Dissociation

In 1889, the French psychiatrist and psychologist Pierre Janet (1859-1947) defined dissociation as the loss of systems of ideas from the control - and often the knowledge, in everyday awareness - of the person concerned. These systems lead a life of their own at a subconscious level, and can interfere with everyday awareness or simply alternate with it. The simplest example of their operation is perhaps the hypnotic suggestion which is acted upon in an automatic manner; the most complex might be the formation of multiple personality disorder, whereby an individual's personality disintegrates into a number of separate identities which may co-exist and surface independently of one another. Janet considered the tendency (or capacity) to dissociate to be a pathological symptom; modern psychologists such as Hilgard and Erika Fromm, who have rediscovered Janet's dissociation theory, believe it to be a phenomenon of normalcy - in other words, that anyone is capable of manifesting this tendency to varying degrees. Modern research indicates that those who have been especially traumatized in their youth will, as a rule, develop this capacity to a greater degree than those who have not: there does appear to be a relationship between trauma and the tendency to dissociate.

Trauma and dissociation

The term 'trauma' was originally applied to physical injury, and indeed this usage is still retained. In the 19th century, the expression 'psychological trauma' was introduced as a metaphor for the reactions of bewilderment and fear produced by a shocking event. We can describe someone as having psychological trauma (or psycho-trauma) when he or she has directly experienced a shocking event, has been a witness to it, or has heard about it, and has reacted with intense feelings of powerlessness and fear. Such events might include serious road accidents, robbery, rape, the sexual abuse of children or the sudden death of a family member. Many victims of incest in particular have been shown to dissociate while undergoing their traumatic experience; some, for example, subsequently report in therapy that for the duration of the abuse they floated to the ceiling and watched what happened from there. The natural feelings of fear, rage, grief, etc., as well as the physical sensations of pain and tension, do not form part of their experience as it occurs: they are dissociated.

A fuller dissociation occurs when the abused child succeeds, mentally, in disappearing completely from the scene of the ordeal. Thus, he or she might fantasize about flying out of the window, hiding behind the wallpaper, or taking refuge on a cloud, and that which has not been consciously experienced of the trauma cannot be remembered. This phenomenon is described as 'amnesia of the trauma'. There is, however, probably at least one other (dissociated) part of the personality that has wholly or partly experienced the event, and is therefore fully aware of what has happened. Hypnosis offers the possibility of investigating this.

Traumatic memories

An experience which is dissociated does not become an integrated part of the personality; the memory of it is not stored in the memory bank in the usual way. Instead, the traumatic perception remains deposited in the bank as an emotionally-charged state, which can be reactivated through circumstances (triggers) which correspond in some way or another with some aspect of the original, shocking event. The woman raped at knife-point, for example, may recall the incident while chopping vegetables in the kitchen, and react with the same anxiety and panic she felt - but dissociated - during the rape itself.

Traumatic memories, then, are not memories in the usual sense of the word, where the person in question can recall and recount an experience at will; they have no social function (they do not involve anyone else in the present), nor any adaptive value with regard to the circumstances of the original trauma. They represent not a narrative memory, but rather dissociated experiential states. When some element of the dissociated experience is reactivated, the experiential state itself is automatically and vividly summoned.

The phenomenon of reactivated traumatic memories explains why so many traumatized people can react so violently to situations which, for most other people, hold little tension or are entirely neutral. Many psychiatric patients show symptoms which are the result of early traumatization; they are often heavily burdened by their buried perception of the trauma, and by its related dissociative phenomena, all of which is likely to be unrecognizable by those around them, including, for example, their social workers. This may be one of the reasons why behaviour and perceptions coupled with reactivated trauma are sometimes labelled as psychosis, and related phenomena such as hearing voices earn the diagnosis of schizophrenia. The dysfunctions of multiple personality disorder - which are often considerably more diverse - are overlooked.

Trauma: A Study of Child Abuse and Hallucinations
Bernadine Ensink

Introduction
Many works have been published in recent years on the psychological impact of child sexual abuse. Early studies tended to take the form of personal documents, such as 'Kiss Daddy Goodnight' by Louise Armstrong (1978) and 'Conspiracy of Silence' by Sandra Butler (1978). These were soon followed by influential articles and books written by therapists treating women with histories of sexual abuse as children: (Herman, 1983; Gelina, 1981, 1983; Goodwin, 1982; Summit, 1983). However, neither personal accounts nor clinical observations allowed reliable generalizations on the impact of such abuse until somewhat later, after a period of extremely rapid growth in related research. By 1986 - just ten years after the publication of the first personal account - Browne and Finkelhor were in a position to review the results of 14 research projects in the field, all employing sound research methodology; since then, almost as many again have been conducted.

Almost 100 women took part in our own study. These women were all abused in childhood, predominantly sexually, by their father or stepfather for a period of four or more years.

This investigation is based on the premise that the correlations between child (sexual) abuse and particular psychiatric symptoms have already been firmly established. There are, for example, several studies showing that women who were sexually abused as children are more likely to attempt suicide than those who were not; others have found a relationship between abuse and dissociative disturbances. Research into dissociative disturbances has also linked auditory hallucinations with childhood traumatization. Our own central question in this study was this: do the various characteristics of child (sexual) abuse correlate with specific psychiatric symptoms in adult life? From the body of symptoms ascribed to child sexual abuse, we chose those belonging to four problem areas: dissociative disturbances in consciousness; hallucinations; self-injury; and suicidal tendencies.

Here, we will concentrate on the relationship between the characteristics of child sexual abuse and auditory hallucinations in particular. For the purposes of our study, child sexual abuse is defined by the following criteria:

- – sexual events include bodily contact with primary or secondary genital zones;
- – they are experienced by girls of 15 years or younger;
- – sexual acts are committed by members or friends of the family who are at least five years older than the girl.

Hallucinations are defined as any percept-like experience which

- – occurs in the absence of an appropriate stimulus;
- – has the full force or impact of the corresponding actual perception; and
- – is not amenable to direct, voluntary control by the experiencer (Slade and Bentall, 1988).

We distinguish several types of hallucinatory phenomena: flashbacks with a hallucinatory character, visual hallucinations, and auditory hallucinations.

N=97	Hallucinatory experiences	
	n	%
hallucinatory flashbacks	33	34
visual hallucinations	41	42
auditory hallucinations a)	37	43

Flashbacks with a hallucinatory character

What is meant by hallucinatory flashbacks is perhaps best illustrated by an example. Ilse (B37) was sexually abused and badly beaten by her father. She speaks of one of her present problems:

The most horrible thing is that I can't see my husband. If I'm in the bathroom, and he comes in, I have to leave - I don't see my husband coming in, but my father. I see my father coming into the bathroom. I get really sick of it.

Ilse is experiencing perceptual distortion: the actual event (seeing her husband) triggers a flashback and is perceived in a transformed way.

Others report such flashbacks to be so intrusive that they lose their grip on their adult identity and really feel like a child again. Jenny (B40) was sexually abused by her father between the ages of six and twenty-seven. In therapy, she tried to recall more emotional details of the childhood incidents.

Then something happened that really scared me. I felt I became a child again, with the same trapped in a tunnel feeling - the feeling that I could not escape from the situation. I really did not know how to escape. It was hard to convince myself that I had in fact escaped from that situation a long time ago.

Some women experience phases during which they relive childhood memories so intensely that they need others to help them with reality discrimination. All those who reported hallucinatory flashbacks said that these experiences were brief.

Visual hallucinations

These were reported by 42% of our sample. Several types of visual hallucinations were experienced:
- daymares experienced as hallucinations;
- daytime somnambulistic periods as vivid as hallucinations;
- autoscopic hallucinations (visions of oneself);
- visual hallucinations clearly related to sexual abuse.

In our study, eight women reported hallucinatory experiences related in various ways, and to a greater or lesser degree, to sexual abuse. Koos (B42) was sexually abused by her father as a child, and was raped in adulthood.

I was admitted to hospital after I was raped. During that time I refused to eat - I saw semen in my food and in my drinks, I saw semen everywhere.

Daymares as visual hallucinations

Five women reported daymares with contents similar to their nightmares. Hilly (B32):

I often have this terrible dream that my father comes to kill me. When I wake up from one of these nightmares and find my friend sleeping beside me, I can't get rid of the feeling that my friend wants to kill me. During

*the daytime, I often feel as if someone has caught me by the throat, or
that monsters are jumping on me. This is much more horrible than what
my father did to me. Generally I wake up, because I scream - very loudly,
it seems to me - but nobody hears me. In reality, my screams are not
loud, and I am sure there have been times when I have only dreamt them.*

Somnambulism with visual hallucinations

Eight women reported somnambulistic periods during the day, in which
they experienced terrifying hallucinations so vivid that they found
themselves screaming and struggling. Els (B18) told us:

*On one occasion I saw my husband come in. He put his hands around my
throat and tried to kill me, and I felt my life slipping away from me. At
that moment, I began to resist, punching, kicking and fighting. After an
incredible fight, I threw him to the floor, and he ran out of the room.
After this experience, I always checked to make sure I had locked the
door properly before going to sleep. It felt as if I had been fighting with
my father, as if the fight had really happened.*

Els now doubts whether any of this actually happened. She had
experienced it very vividly, but in a dream-like way. She concludes:

*I think the experience is similar to those of people who have been in
concentration camps.*

Autoscopic hallucinations

Elsbeth (B20):

*Sometimes when I am wandering around the house I meet myself
everywhere. When I open a door, I will see myself standing behind that
door. I really panic when this happens.*

Grada (B23):

*During the time that my husband was having an affair, I had strange
experiences. I actually saw myself sitting next to me. The one that was
sitting next to me wanted to commit suicide, but I didn't.*

Lydia (B49):

*In my dreams, and also during flashbacks, I have encountered myself as a
child. I took the child-me by the hand and talked to myself: 'I will take
care of you'.*

Auditory hallucinations partly related to child sexual abuse

Twenty seven women in our sample reported hearing voices, and eight of these described auditory hallucinations at least partly related to childhood (sexual) abuse. Four others told us that they do not remember the experience directly, but hear voices informing them about their childhood.

Hanna (B31) was sexually abused by her father up until the age of about 11. He raped her violently, and threatened to kill her. She said she feels as if she only has a few memories of herself; most memories are of a small child, in the third person. She explains that in childhood she used to talk to herself to keep these dreadful memories at bay. When Hanna gets flashbacks, the small child says, 'You know this happened'.

She (the small child) tells me what happened, and then I say: 'These things you tell me are horrible'.

The child's voice sometimes speaks of other matters, too. Hanna also has periods during which she hears many voices, amongst which she recognizes that of her mother.

Hallucinations: hysterical or dissociative versus psychotic or schizophrenic

Within psychiatry there have always been various approaches to the problem of connecting particular symptoms with psychiatric diagnoses, and several different criteria have been specified for distinguishing dissociative or hysterical hallucinations from those associated with other psychiatric diagnoses. Most of the experiences reported in our study (23 out of 27) satisfied the Schneiderian criteria specified for identifying schizophrenic auditory hallucinations. (In 1959 Schneider formulated a set of 11 criteria to distinguish between simple and complex auditory hallucinations. These included categories such as voices communicating, voices arguing and hearing thoughts aloud. Mellor (1970) later re-defined these criteria more strictly.)

Auditory hallucinations were described as being located inside the head by 18 of the 27 subjects, outside by four, and both inside and outside by five. Those reporting these hallucinations were not noticeably influenced sub-culturally; none was a member of any sect, and few were particularly interested in paranormal phenomena. In all eight cases where women had dialogues with their voices, these were instigated by a therapist. Only a small number of women reported hallucinations in the immediate aftermath of dramatic life-events, and these were always short-lived. Most of those with auditory hallucinations said they had heard voices for many years.

Correlation of childhood abuse and auditory hallucinations

Childhood trauma may be related to hallucinations by several different kinds of psychological processes. Several theories have been put forward in this respect, the best-known undoubtedly being the seduction theory proposed by Freud in his early works. (For more information about this and other perspectives, we refer the reader to Ensink's book 'Confusing Realities', 1992.) We tested some of these theories against our results.

Some of the main findings of our research are summarized below. In order to keep matters relatively simple, we formulated a cumulative trauma scoring system, whereby each woman was scored for her experiences with child sexual abuse, with physical aggression from the perpetrator, and for abuses suffered by other members of her family - usually the mother. These various types of trauma were then scored for three different age periods:
- infancy (0-6 years);
- childhood (7-12 years);
- adolescence (13 years and over).

The cumulative trauma-scores were subsequently correlated with the presence or absence of auditory hallucinations. We found that:
- the trauma experienced in early life by women with auditory hallucinations was greater, and more severe, than that endured by those without;
- women with auditory hallucinations experienced more frequent sexual and physical aggression from their fathers before the age of seven than those without;
- women with auditory hallucinations experienced more frequent emotional neglect by their mother, from an early age, than those without.

We must, of course, be wary in our interpretations of retrospective accounts of abusive situations before the age of seven: the only conclusion that can safely be drawn from these is that the women concerned cannot remember a time when their fathers or mothers did not abuse or neglect them.

A young child has to learn the difference between reality and imagination. There is evidence that parental incest is usually associated with a distortion of reality on the part of the parent(s) (Summit, 1983); if the child's parents are incapable of making this distinction, then the child may have serious difficulty in learning it. It is clear, furthermore, that a child who is abused by one or both parents from an early age may find certain advantages in not learning the difference between reality and imagination: a full appreciation of the distinction could be too devastating for the child.

One final, important finding is that the repression of emotions makes perhaps the greatest contribution to the incidence of auditory hallucinations. This suggests that not recognizing feelings as belonging to the self makes it more likely that emotions and associated thoughts and images will be attributed to ego-dystonic sources. This attribution process seems to be especially important in the relationship between auditory hallucinations and cumulative childhood trauma.

Cognitive Models
Richard Bentall

There have been considerable advances over the last few decades in the understanding of the human mind. The branch of psychology which has, perhaps, been most responsible for these developments is known as cognitive psychology; this is concerned with how individuals acquire and apply knowledge about the world (cognition = knowledge). The theoretical models of mental processes developed by cognitive psychologists have, in turn, been used successfully to understand unusual mental phenomena. In this section, I will briefly outline what is meant by the cognitive approach in psychology, and show how it has led to advances in our understanding of hallucinatory experiences such as hearing voices.

Cognitive psychology
Cognitive psychology is concerned with how information is perceived, stored and utilized by intelligent organisms (mainly human beings, but cognitive psychologists have sometimes turned their attention to other species, or even to intelligent machines). Historically, this branch of study has owed a great deal to computer science, as computers seem to provide a model of how intelligence might work. (See Johnson-Laird, 1987, for an introduction to cognitive psychology for the lay reader which emphasizes the role of the computer in the simulation of psychological theories.)

The extent to which the mind is exactly analogous to the computer remains controversial. On the one hand the mind, like the computer, seems to follow rules when processing information about the world. On the other hand, the architecture or construction of the mind seems to be radically different from that of the average desk-top computer. Pursuing the analogy for a moment, it has been argued that if we are to understand the human mind, the problem must be tackled at three levels. First of all, we need to understand the functions of the mind (what it is capable of doing and what it is not capable of doing). Secondly, the rules or algorithms used by the mind to achieve these functions (analogous to the programmes run by a computer) must be discovered. Finally, the machinery employed by the brain to execute or implement these rules can then be studied. The first two of these levels are the province of cognitive psychology, whereas the last is that of neurophysiology.

Traditionally, cognitive psychologists have studied cold cognitive processes such as perception and memory. More recently, however, they have also become interested in the hot processes involved in emotion and self-understanding. Not surprisingly, cognitive psychology has been used to investigate a variety of psychiatric problems. Although much of this work has focused on anxiety and depression, recent work has turned its attention to psychotic experiences such as hallucinations and delusions.

In carrying out this kind of research, the task of the cognitive psychologist is to find out how, if at all, the processing of information by people with psychiatric problems differs from that of people without such problems. Experiences such as hallucinations lend themselves to the cognitive approach because it seems likely that they reflect abnormalities in the way the mind is processing information about the world. In the case of hallucinations, it might be argued, something is happening in the mind which causes the individual to believe that something is out there, when in fact there is nothing in the world to correspond with the perceived experience.

Some facts about hallucinations

Any psychological account of hallucinations must be able to account for a number of facts.

- As the work of Marius Romme and Sandra Escher has shown, hallucinations are experienced not only by people labelled as mentally ill, but also by a surprising number of people who lead relatively happy lives and who do not consider themselves to be psychiatrically disturbed in any way.
- Hallucinations are much more common in some societies than in others; for example, it is relatively common for native Hawaiians to report seeing dead ancestors. This observation suggests that people's beliefs and expectations may influence whether or not they have hallucinatory experiences. Interestingly, there are also cultural differences in the kinds of hallucinations reported by psychiatric patients. For example, visual hallucinations are much more often reported by patients in the developing nations than by those in the Western or developed nations.
- Related to this is the fact that it is possible to provoke hallucinations in a small proportion of otherwise ordinary people by the use of

suggestions. For example, if a group of average people are told to close their eyes and listen to the record White Christmas, approximately 5% will say that they have heard the record even if it has not, in fact, been played. This, too, indicates that beliefs and expectations play an important role in hallucinatory experiences.

- Auditory hallucinations tend to occur more often in certain kinds of conditions, particularly those of sensory deprivation (or near-silence) or when there is a lot of unpatterned stimulation (for example, machine noises).

- A fact which will surprise few readers is that hallucinations are often experienced during periods of stress. People who do not experience voices at other times may hear them during periods of exhaustion or following severe stresses such as the death of a loved one. Psychiatric patients often report that their voices get worse when they become stressed, or when something bad happens to them. Consistent with this observation, it has been found that the onset of voices in psychiatric patients is often preceded by physiological responses (for example, changes in skin conductance) which usually occur in response to stressful stimuli.

- Finally, a less obvious fact concerns the role of the speech muscles during auditory hallucinations. When a person hears voices, these muscles become more active, as indicated by increased electrical activity. Such subvocalizations, as they are known to psychologists (movements of the speech muscles which are too small to see, and which generate no sound), occur during normal verbal thought, and reflect the fact that thinking in words involves a kind of inner speech. (Readers will be aware that this type of speech is not always completely internalized, so that we sometimes speak aloud to ourselves, particularly when alone.)

The psychology of hallucinations

Various theories have been put forward to account for these observations, but all are very similar. Put simply, they all suggest that hallucinations occur when mental events are mistaken for events in the real world. According to this view, the person who hears a voice is thinking in words but mistaking those thoughts for something that is being said by someone else. In many ways, this idea is very similar to Carl Jung's account of hallucinations, which is outlined elsewhere in this book.

A number of psychologists have attempted to carry out experiments to test this theory. For example, in one of the studies carried out by myself and my colleagues at Liverpool University, psychiatric patients - some of whom heard voices, and some of whom did not - were asked to listen to 100 five-second bursts of white noise (a hissing sound like that of an untuned radio). There was a voice present in the background in 50 of these bursts, and the volunteers were asked to say, after each burst, how strongly - on a five-point scale - they believed it to have contained a voice. (0 = sure that the voice was not present, 3 = completely unsure, 5 = sure the voice was present.) By a fairly complex mathematical analysis of the volunteers' responses, it was possible to derive two measures: a measure of sensitivity, which indicated how good the volunteers' hearing was; and a measure which indicated their general bias or tendency towards believing that a voice had in fact been present. The results indicated that the hearing of the hallucinating patients was just as sensitive as that of the non-hallucinating, but that the hallucinating patients had a greater tendency to believe that a voice was present under conditions of uncertainty. This finding suggests that those who hear voices will, when experiencing an event which could either be a thought or something they have heard, tend to assume that it is something they have actually heard. Interestingly, very similar results were found when hallucinating non-patients were compared with non-hallucinating non-patients.

This theory accounts for a number of the observations which have been made about hallucinatory experiences. For example, it is not surprising that hallucinations are accompanied by electrical activity in the speech muscles, given that such activity accompanies ordinary verbal thought. Nor is it surprising that hallucinations occur more in conditions of silence or unpatterned stimulation, as it is in precisely these conditions that it is most difficult to tell the difference between the internal voice and external stimuli.

What the theory leaves unanswered is the question of why some people tend to mistake inner thoughts for external stimuli. Obviously, the brain must have a system for distinguishing between self-generated thoughts and events in the world. This system is not, however, always accurate: scientists, for example, sometimes mistake ideas they have heard from others for ideas they have thought up themselves, and in our dreams we all mistake imagination for reality.

Chris Frith has suggested that the system responsible for distinguishing between self-generated and real-world events - which he calls 'the monitor' - is anatomically located within a part of the brain called the hippocampus. However, there is little direct evidence that this part of the brain is functioning abnormally in people who hear voices. Another possibility is that those who hear voices, in comparison with people who do not, use different rules to distinguish between internal and external events. (In other words, to pursue the computer analogy one step further, hallucinations may be caused by software rather than hardware.) The fact that hallucinations are influenced by suggestions and cultural beliefs provides some support for this latter hypothesis.

It is interesting in this context to note that voices often play a particular role in the lives of those who hear them. Sometimes they represent a malevolent force (perhaps the bad part of the self, which is difficult to accept), but sometimes, too, they are companions or sources of comfort. In either case, it is almost always true that voices are supported by a complex set of beliefs and expectations.

Cognitive psychology, illness and treatment

I hope the above account gives some idea of how recent advances in psychology have led to a better understanding of what happens in the mind of someone who hears a voice or sees a vision. From this account, it might be thought that the cognitive approach is consistent with the traditional psychiatric approach, which sees hallucinations as always being evidence of illness. Certainly, many cognitive psychologists who study unusual experiences such as hallucinations do think within the framework of the medical model, and see their work as contributing to a general advance in psychiatric knowledge. However, I do not share this assumption.

It seems to me that the decision about what counts as illness and what counts as sanity is essentially a moral one. For example, one can imagine a morally gloomy society in which happiness is seen as a form of insanity. A cognitive psychologist, working in such a society and seeking to understand what goes on in the mind of someone who is happy, would take exactly the same approach, and would use very similar experimental methods, as those used when cognitive psychologists in our own society study people who hear voices. For example, if one wanted to understand happiness, one might look for features of information-processing which would account for the happy person's unrealistically optimistic view of the world and which are not found in unhappy people.

The task of cognitive psychology is to investigate the mental processes associated with particular kinds of experiences and behaviours. It is up to others to determine whether those experiences and behaviours should be regarded as pathological or not. My own experience of people who hear voices is that they are often very intelligent, sensitive and creative individuals who are struggling to make sense of a world which is often confusing and sometimes frightening. In this regard, they have much in common with those cognitive psychologists, like myself, who are trying to make hallucinatory experiences more intelligible to others.

One advantage of the cognitive perspective is that it leads to testable theories. For example, the experiment I described above provides some direct evidence in support of the view that voices are misattributed thoughts. Another advantage of cognitive research into hallucinations is that it might lead to new methods of helping the hearers of voices. The idea that those who have hallucinations are mistaking their own thoughts for real-world events raises the question of whether it might not be possible to help hallucinators take possession of those parts of themselves which they see as alien. One strategy for achieving this end, known as focusing, is described in a separate section in chapter 10.

Social Psychiatry
Marius Romme

Ever since the mental health movement came into being (around 1880), there has been a school of thought known as social psychiatry. Social psychiatry studies the relationship between societal conditions and mental health problems: it considers the individual's thoughts, emotions, perceptions and behaviour in relation to the conditions in which the person lives and functions.

Biological and psychodynamic psychiatry approach mental health problems from different angles. Biological psychiatry is concerned with the relationship between human behaviour and the physiology of the brain; in psychodynamic psychiatry, we examine the relationship between mental health problems and the attempt to cope with emotions. The living conditions that influence mental health are many and various, from one's working environment to the freedom (or otherwise) of expressing one's sexual identity, and any number of these can be instrumental in the onset of hearing voices. External influences which disturb the balance between the individual and his or her surroundings may give rise to feelings of extreme powerlessness, and these can often lead to psychological disturbance. In this section, we will consider a few important examples of such influences:

- intolerable or unsatisfying situations;
- recent trauma;
- conflicting aspirations;
- threats;
- childhood trauma;
- emotional denial in childhood.

Intolerable or unsatisfying situations

When voices have been triggered by intolerable circumstances, they tend to make comments which reflect how the hearer is treated by others. They report, directly or indirectly - very often in the form of metaphors - what is going on in a relationship.

I met a 67-year old woman who heard voices which. chided her as adults do children: 'Be careful you don't fall over, Button your coat up', and so on. When she entered my study, she was accompanied by her two daughters, and I noticed that one was holding her arm, as though the woman was unable to walk without assistance. The other daughter gently guided her into a chair and began to unbutton her coat. The patient, meanwhile, looked distinctly uncomfortable. The daughters began to tell me about their mother's problems, as if she could not speak for herself, but after a while I managed to get the woman to tell her own story.

She told me that she had started to hear voices when her husband stopped working: he had usurped all her functions in the home, and she had gradually taken on the role of a child. When I referred to this as a possible key to the meaning of the voices, all three were astonished. However, when we explored this a little further, they began to recognize the relationship between what the voices said and how the family treated the mother.

In this example, the connection between the voices and the outside world is straightforward: the voices are echoing exactly what the people around the hearer are telling her. The connection can be a good deal less obvious when the voices translate situations into metaphor. For example, we came across a man of 24 who heard voices imposing all sorts of regulations upon his life. This young man calls his voices 'fascist forces'. In fact, the instructions they give him reflect his experience of how he is treated in hospital and at home. When he first started living on his own, he found it difficult to make independent decisions, and used the voices to maintain order in his life. Unfortunately, in so doing, he became dependent on them, and they gradually eroded his autonomy and became a permanent fixture.

Voices may also be associated with stressful events such as divorce or losing a job. Such voices generally express criticism about recent stressful events and changes in the hearer's life situation, and the hearer may end up feeling as powerless with regard to the voices as they do with regard to the external stress factors themselves. In such cases, therapy initially focuses on ways of altering the stressful elements of the material situation.

Recent trauma

The commonest form of severe trauma is the death of a loved one. In the immediate aftermath of this kind of loss, many people continue to hear the voice of the one who has died. As described in chapters 6 and 8, the hearing of such voices often persists for a long time afterwards. This appears to be particularly likely in the most painful cases, for example when a child or partner has died in circumstances such as suicide.

It is perhaps less well-known that voices may also appear in the wake of other, less obviously traumatic experiences such as the loss of a job. Alexis, aged 26, was a very hard-working secretary who, for many years, worked in the same company for the same boss. Lately she had seen the business beginning to fail, and had put a lot of energy into helping to revive its fortunes. Then, on top of everything else, she found herself the victim of malicious gossip amongst her colleagues, and this resulted in her dismissal from her post. She was left with very strong feelings of injustice and powerlessness.

In the months following her dismissal, she had the impression that people were talking about her when she went into a particular cafe. She became more and more preoccupied with this, and began to hear voices regularly. These voices told malicious lies about her, and little by little began to appear in other situations, too - at home and at family gatherings. Eventually this became completely intolerable, but Alexis did not understand the connections between her situation and her reactions to it until much later, after more than a year of voluntary psychiatric treatment. This went on for two years before she had the courage to apply for another job. She got the job she wanted, and as a result of this positive experience the voices gradually faded away.

In a case like this, treatment consists not of warfare against the voices, but rather the development of a more independent personality capable of achieving equality in relationships.

Conflicting aspirations

Given the complex nature of our world, it is not easy for everyone to realize his or her desires. When an individual's personal goals are not being achieved, we sometimes come across voices that serve to help the hearer to find his or her way.

In chapter 8 there is the story of an orphaned black woman who heard the voice of Haile Selassie advising her on how to deal with the racism she was suffering. He instructed her to write her own history, that is to say, to learn to be herself. At a simpler level, of course, voices may also have a wish-fulfilment role: they can, for example, offer companionship to someone who is lonely. One of our patients takes his voices to a café and drinks coffee with them. Another, who lives alone, asks the voice of a successful close friend for advice when he has to make decisions. We have also come across more complex and difficult situations where people's voices are helping them either to realize some ideal or to suppress unwanted sexual drives and identities, such a exhibitionism or homosexuality.

Threats

Voices can be part of a survival strategy for life-threatening situations. Torture, for example, is recognized by Amnesty International as a trigger for voice-hearing. Psychosis provoked by an impossible dilemma may have the same result; William Styron's book 'Sophie's Choice' provides a graphic example of this: a German officer forces Sophie to choose between the life of her son and that of her daughter by handing one of them over to be killed in the gas chamber.

This is a very dramatic example, but we have come across similar dilemmas in less extreme forms. In one case, a teenage girl's father was dying of cancer and asked her to give him a fatal dose of pills to end his suffering. Her mother was outraged and refused to allow this, saying that it would be murder. Should the girl listen to her father or to her mother? In yet another case, a girl submitted to the sexual advances of her father after he threatened to take her younger sister instead if she did not co-operate.

In all such cases, one of the biggest problems is that the person caught in the dilemma feels personally responsible for the repercussions of any choice. If they can be persuaded to accept that their actions were imposed upon them by someone else, it may be possible to free them of the emotional consequences.

Childhood trauma

Voices do not always conform to our conventional ideas of time and space. We have encountered people who hear voices associated with childhood traumas; these present fragments from the past, but the information they contain is so distorted that it is not always apparent to the hearer that they are echoes of past experiences. As we know from the literature, therapy for this kind of problem is complicated when the relationship between the voices and the traumatic situation is not clear to the individual. The voices may function as a safeguard against frightening memories, and so it may be that neither the hearer nor the voices themselves are open to therapy: they may be afraid of losing one another and the safety they have created. This situation is excellently depicted in the film 'Shattered', based on the experience of Trudy Chase.

In one scene, Trudy is frightened by the thought that her therapist might destroy her safeguards in his attempt to integrate her voices; she asks him, 'Who are you going to kill first?' For her, the integration of the voices within the ego was tantamount to killing them. Clearly, the priority of any therapy must be the understanding of the voices content and function.

Emotional denial

Voices may also be a consequence of emotional denial or abuse, as is described so well by Brian Davey later in this chapter:

If someone has been brought up in an over-critical and over-controlled relationship, then almost by definition they will not be their own person. The young person has not been allowed to take his or her own decisions on the basis of their own feelings. The expression of their own feelings about things has not been tolerated...What such parents want is well-behaved compliance. All feelings such as anger, fear and perhaps even joy which a child needs to learn to cope with and use to make its own responses, its own choices, are not allowed. The expression of anger may be seen as an unacceptable challenge to parental authority for example and may be described as being naughty or wicked. However, feelings of any kind are inevitable in life. Even if hate is perceived as unacceptable, a person might still be confronted with this feeling in daily life. A way in which such hate may be denied is to expel that hate part of the personality from the inner stream of consciousness that is defined as me. Instead of being integrated, it will be experienced... as an interruption from outside.

Those psychiatrists and others who insist that such voices do not exist are missing the point. It is wrong to deny them, or to try and eclipse them by the use of headphones, music and videos. As we have shown, these voices represent real influences, and they have something to say; sometimes the message may be unwelcome and uncomfortable, sometimes wise and instructive. The proper therapeutic approach is not to deny their validity, but rather to find out more about them and examine the origins of the real problems.

Conclusion

Social psychiatry explores human behaviour and perception in relation to the individual's living conditions, both past and present. Of particular interest are those social relationships and interactions in which it is difficult or impossible for the patient to be him or herself, or to continue to accept such relationships.

By exploring, in collaboration with the client, what the voices say, the therapist can help to identify those relationships and circumstances which have given rise to problems. The hearing of voices is not itself caused by the situation concerned, but what the voices say reproduces the situation metaphorically. Cause-and-effect approaches are therefore less helpful than exploration of the messages' contents in relation to the life-situation of the hearer.

Family Interactions and Psychosis
Nick Tarrier

We are all sensitive to the influences of our environment, but it has long been thought that those who suffer from schizophrenia are especially so. Environments that are over- or under-stimulating are believed to be especially stressful, and may result in experiences involving hallucinations, delusions and confusion. One environment in which most of us spend a considerable amount of time is the family home, and it is therefore no surprise that the domestic emotional climate should be of particular importance to our well-being.

Expressed Emotion
In the 1950s, a group of sociologists and social psychiatrists in London became interested in what happened to people once they were discharged from psychiatric hospital. To their surprise, they found that those with diagnoses of schizophrenia who went to live with their families did worse than those who lived alone or went to live in a hostel: those who returned to their families were re-admitted to hospital much more frequently than those who lived elsewhere. This prompted a series of research studies investigating the effects of environment on the progress of those designated as schizophrenic. Researchers in the field, notably the social psychologist Christine Vaughn and the social psychiatrist Julian Leff, developed a measure called 'Expressed Emotion', with which they were able to assess the amount of stress in the home.

'Expressed Emotion', or EE as it is frequently called, is measured by means of an interview with someone who knows the sufferer well. This is usually a close relative, but in recent times the test has also come to be used with nursing staff and with sufferers themselves. It is possible to assess the type and degree of emotional content displayed by the interviewee in terms of their criticism, hostility, over-involvement, warmth and positive comments. From the scores in these various categories, it can be determined whether a given household is high or low in EE. At least 20 large-scale research studies have now been carried out all over the world examining the relationship between high and low EE households and schizophrenic relapses. Almost all of these studies show a greater rate of relapse in sufferers living in high EE households, and most of them reveal a highly significant differential.

Some people have interpreted the EE concept as blaming the relatives for causing schizophrenia, or suggesting that they themselves are somehow abnormal, but this is clearly incorrect. EE represents a level of stress operating within the home environment which is not necessarily abnormal in any way; it is simply that sufferers from schizophrenia are highly sensitive to even small degrees of stress. If anything, in fact, low EE households could almost be considered abnormal because of their low levels of stress.

Therapeutic developments

EE research has been extremely valuable in suggesting ways for sufferers, their families, and healthcare professionals to work together more effectively in learning to live with and overcome the difficulties and distress created by the disorder.

A number of large studies have now been carried out, mainly in the USA and the UK, to examine and test these new methods based on EE research. These methods have been given various names by different researchers: psychosocial intervention (London), family management (California, USA), psychoeducation (Pittsburgh, USA), and family intervention (Manchester, UK). Briefly, these studies have looked at specialized help that has been made available to families including: information about schizophrenia and its treatment; problem-focused advice; and the teaching of skills to manage difficult, confrontational and stressful situations. These resources have been found to offer enormous advantages over and above the traditional mental health services. Such family intervention programmes (to use the Manchester term) have radically reduced rates of relapse and re-admission to hospital; they have also improved the levels of function for sufferers, allowing them to become more independent. Furthermore, there is evidence that relatives have benefited, and that the family as whole has functioned better in terms of coping with stress and resolving problems; economic analysis has also yielded evidence that these interventions result in financial savings to the health services.

Because these programmes adopt a collaborative problem-solving approach, they have been welcomed by sufferers and relatives alike, and are generally perceived as being beneficial. It is not the case that family intervention programmes keep people out of hospital simply by increasing their medication doses; in fact, there is some evidence from the Californian study that sufferers who participate in family management programmes actually receive lower doses of medication. This is presumably because both they and their families are better able to cope with stress. Further evidence for this is offered by the Manchester study, which shows that the programme participants experienced more stressful life-events than those who were not receiving family intervention. This is important, because it has been shown before that the experience of such life-events - such as being made redundant, or an illness in the family - can be sources of acute stress, which frequently results in relapse and hospitalization for schizophrenia sufferers. The fact that sufferers involved in the intervention programme experienced more potentially stressful situations but very few relapses indicates that they were successfully acquiring the skills to help them to cope with any stress in their immediate environment.

As people become more independent, of course, they are likely to encounter more stress simply as a consequence of becoming more active and autonomous. The danger here is clear: increased levels of functioning are accompanied by exposure to higher levels of stress, and this could result in relapse. It appears, however, that family interventions allow increased functioning while equipping the sufferer with the necessary skills to deal with any increase in stress.

We have also learned some lessons about what types of programme are not effective, because there have been other studies carried out in Germany and Australia which have failed to show positive results. These intervention programmes have differed in a number of ways from the successful ones we have already considered, and this makes it possible to identify what works and what does not. The less successful programmes have been: those that have adopted a psychodynamic approach; those that have separated sufferers from relatives during the therapeutic session, or left the sufferer out completely; those that have been of short duration only (usually less than three months); those that have failed to liaise properly with the mainstream mental health services; and those that have not adopted a problem-focused, collaborative approach.

The aspects most crucial to the success of these family intervention programmes, then, are the collaboration between sufferer, relatives and professionals in identifying and meeting needs, and the playing of an active role by the sufferer and his or her family in resolving their own difficulties.

Psychosis
Brian Davey

The last time I was psychotic I had the experience that I would describe as hearing background voices. Restrospectively I would now say that I was hearing the background noise that we usually filter out of our conscious awareness, and that I was projecting my own internal concerns onto this noise. My internal concerns gave an apparent structure to this noise so that it sounded as if I was hearing conversations that were relevant to me.

When you are psychotic your inner concerns are so dominant that they structure your interpretation of your incoming perceptions. The relationship between one's internal world of thoughts and feelings and the external world is dominated by the internal world. This internal world of extreme feelings and strange thoughts seems to be utterly bizarre and not to match the external reality at all. I believe, however, that it is possible to make sense of this strange internal world. The way to do this is to see oneself as reliving the concerns, responses and feelings of the earliest stages of one's life - when one was a baby, infant and small child; to put it in the jargon, one has regressed. But one has regressed to the concerns, feelings and responses one made in conditions of fear and powerlessness of that time, to feelings of horror or, and I shall explain this later, to one's 'slave feelings'.

To understand psychosis in this way it is necessary to develop a theoretical framework which explains the role of our feelings and emotions, how these need to be understood as distinct from our thinking, which is different again from our actions. Our emotional responses to situations, how we think about situations and the active responses we make are the three dimensions of our personalities which evolve out of our earliest experiences and relationships.

At the most basic level as a species the function of our feelings is to motivate us to actions which maintain and sustain us. Tiredness motivates rest, hunger eating and thirst drinking. Feelings and emotions as physical states which we experience in our bodies also have social and interpersonal functions. Affection and love motivate and sustain bonding and co-operative behaviour, anger and fear both signal and energize our protective responses. Many emotions are in fact blends or mixtures of others. For example envy is a feeling of desire mixed with anger or hate because it is blocked from realization.

Emotions motivate us to act. Remove the 'e' from emotion and we have 'motion'. Pleasurable feelings move us to try to recreate sources of pleasure or to seek them out. So to speak they move us towards situations that are positive and associated with creativity and enjoyment.

Painful feelings we wish to avoid, not recreate, move away from or resist. We label them as negative.

So positive or negative feelings move us to act. However as babies and small children we cannot act other than signal directly our feelings to those who can act for us and on whom we are dependent. Long before we can think with words (or the other symbols of communication) and long before we can act for ourselves we are directly dependent on finding a matching response to the direct expression of our feelings in the feelings of our mother and father and older siblings. Our infantile state is one of helplessness and vulnerability.

As infants we survive because others respond to the expression of our raw feelings. But what if they do not? What if they ignore the expression of our feelings or respond to the cry of helplessness with eyes that speak resentment and hate? What if, worse still, they abuse their greater power and generate new feelings of fear?

The answer at first is that the infant feels horror and terror. Such terror, such horror is what underlies the horrors of regression. Later the baby or small child will develop a numbed, extreme emotional detachment, a sort of zombification. Psychiatrists call this 'poverty of affect' when it is relived in later life. Terror states that immobilize, horror states and the experience of oneself as always having to be for the convenience of others, for others' use, are the emotional states of psychosis. I call them 'slave feelings' because they are associated with the powerlessness a baby or small child feels if it cannot find the appropriate matching response to the expression of its feelings or if it finds it always has to do what the big people want, irrespective of its feelings.

The point about such early experiences of powerlessness is that they create the foundations of the personality and form our basic responses to situations in later life. They become part of our learned responses. This is not the kind of learning we are supposed to do in school, but the more fundamental kind of learning associated with how we respond in conditions of highly charged emotion.

An absolutely central thing we learn at this time is whether we matter or not. If parents do not respond to the direct expression of our feelings we learn that our feelings do not matter and that therefore we do not matter. If our distress is never comforted and perhaps we are only recognized when we achieve, we are liable to be always attention-seeking, always seeking a reassurance that we never had at the beginning, by showing off our various accomplishments. We will continually struggle in this way to recreate some self-esteem because this self-esteem will have been undermined when our feelings were ignored or when we were abused in infancy.

If we are loved for ourselves then all our feelings will be respected, recognized and taken into consideration or responded to. We will then continue to have access to the positive and negative feelings. This is important because we will then feel secure in making choices. We will seek out those situations which give us pleasure and affection. We will move away from or resist those situations which upset or frighten us. We will, in short, grow up our own person. We will have the property right over our own lives. Love at the beginning of our lives - as appropriate, protective and affectionate responses to our feelings - is the prerequisite for our later independence. If we do not find this we will develop protective and defensive responses to situations, cut off from our feelings, be dependent on others for our choices, struggle to maintain self-esteem and be vulnerable to breakdown.

Our structures of thought will reflect the nature of our early experiences. In this respect thinking is the use of the symbols of human communication, chiefly words, to form an inner picture of the world and our place in it, that guides our responses and interpretations. We are likely to grow up with systems of interpretation that reflect or are maybe mirror rejections of our parents' thinking. Perhaps if we grow up unloved and we seek an understanding for this we take for our explanation their account that we are bad. They say this because we ignored or rejected their demands on us. In our thinking we construct strategies that will enable us to survive.

Breakdown is the collapse of our defences, it is the return of feelings we learned to cut off from or not notice; it is a return to the starting point, the horrors and fear and powerlessness we felt at the beginning.

In the 'Psychotherapy of Schizophrenia' Karon and van den Bos points out that virtually every soldier put in conditions where death seems almost certain, where he has to lie in one place for a long time and urinate and defecate on himself, virtually every such soldier, on being rescued, breaks down into the classic symptoms of schizophrenia. In most cases, however, this schizophrenic form of psychosis can be recovered from. What I suspect matters is whether the original experiences of the personality were sufficiently positive for a recovery. But if we are stressed with negative feelings for long enough breakdown is inevitable. For the function of our feelings is to motivate us to change our circumstances, to change our lives, to move away from, or remove the source of the stress. If we cannot, if we are powerless, breakdown is inevitable. In madness we return to the original experiences of powerlessness. If in our original experiences of powerlessness there was no one there to support and comfort us then we find nothing but an incoherent awareness of endless terror and horror. The experience seems as if it will be endless, for the baby has, as yet, no notion of time, no notion that it has a future in the adult world.

The early states of mind are those in which ego boundaries are unclear and unformed. One of the very first distinctions that we make is the difference between ourselves and the rest of the world. This isn't at first clear. Most psychotic symptoms can be thought of as odd ways of thinking about the interrelationship between self and the rest of the social and material world. In severe psychosis, in deep regression, a person will be reliving a state of mind prior to the differentiation between self and not self.

As an infant, when we rock, our cot rocks with us. When we wriggle our legs it is the blankets that we see move. Being taken out of our cot and blankets, if we have been in them so long, may seem strange, as if we have been separated from something we thought was part of ourselves and now we see as separate. At this stage we have no way of knowing what relates to us individually and what does not. For all we can know the face in the TV screen, using words we do not yet understand, may indeed be talking uniquely to us. The voices we hear in the background of our lives, our parents or brothers and sisters in other rooms, may indeed be talking about us. We are only aware that these voices have vast importance. Depending on our experience these distant voices may carry promises of pleasure or terror and we listen intently to their emotional tone, without understanding their immediate meaning.

Above all the psychotic experience is one of powerlessness. Leff and Vaughn's work gives some idea of the sort of process that may be involved. As is well-known they have found empirical evidence that if people return, after a schizophrenic breakdown, to relationships that they describe as 'High Expressed Emotion' (High EE) then the chance of relapse is likely to be high. But this may well also explain initial breakdowns.

In my interpretation, High EE relationships are those where the emotions of the people (usually parents) living with the patient are at odds. Whether these are in the form of hostile criticism or in the form of exaggerated praise and expressions of love attached to required and expected behaviour, the effect is that the patient is having their life controlled, and their decisions taken for them. The relationship is over-involved and over-controlled.

In terms of the analysis I have given it would explain the stereotypical young schizophrenic breakdown quite well. If someone has been brought up in an over-critical and over-controlled relationship, then almost by definition they will not be their own person. The young person has not been allowed to take his or her own decisions on the basis of their own feelings. The expression of their own feelings about things will not have been tolerated. What such parents want is well-behaved compliance. All feelings such as anger, fear and perhaps even joy, which a child needs to learn to cope with and use to make its own responses, its own choices, are not allowed. The expression of anger may be seen as an unacceptable challenge to parental authority, for example, and may be described as being naughty or wicked. However feelings of any kind are inevitable in life. Even if hate is perceived as unacceptable a person might still be confronted with this feeling in daily life. A way in which such hate may be denied is to expel that hate part of the personality from the inner stream of consciousness that is defined as 'me'. Instead of being integrated, it will be experienced as an interruption from outside.

In such families a young person will also be without the benefit of having observed and being familiar with emotional interactions in his/her parental role models. There is an aloofness and emotional distance necessary to maintain any authoritarian relationship. In these circumstances the emotional relationship between the two parents will be a closed book that is no business of the child. The child will be unprepared, without any models for emotional relationships.

The child cannot become independent without its own feelings to guide it to its own choices. So the young person will feel lonely and will increasingly become aware he cannot enter emotional relationships. His emotional wings have been broken. Such a person will thus be unable to fly out of the family nest. It will not be clear to either the young person or to the family what has gone wrong.

It will be very difficult to both parties to find words to express what has happened. One of the problems, even found in psychiatric literature, is that if something has gone wrong between people, and we want to explain it, many people will simply ask the question 'Who is responsible?, Who is to blame?' This mode of thinking will be particularly prevalent in the kind of families we have been describing for the question 'Who is to blame' is closely related to the question 'Who should be punished?' It is the taken for granted mind-set of all authoritarian social relationships; it is the way of thinking, the language found in top-down 'Do as you are told', command structures...

The family may think something like this: John, who is behaving so bizarrely, is a quite well-behaved studious boy; he has always been rather shy but up to now has been a credit to his family. In fact the life crisis for John is how the hell he can be himself other than being loud, lazy and a disgrace to the family whose definitions he alternately wants to reject but then accepts again as he realizes the extent of his dependence. He would love to be wildly gregarious, but he hasn't a clue how to be. John may be able to manage leaving home, but lives in a university hall doing nothing but work and unable to form supportive real emotional relationships. His mind focuses on the first year exams to keep out anxiety. These are what his parents want him to do well at. They promise the job which is so important for his transition to adult life. He lives in terror that, on his own for the first time, he will fail the big exam - this important symbolic transition in growing up. He wishes he had his GCE in talking to girls.

Whatever the final straw that breaks the camel's back (eg exam failure), the young person will eventually be overwhelmed by a life crisis which will inevitably throw up emotions the power and intensity of which he will not have faced since before he learned to live within the parental emotional straitjacket ie pre-verbal infancy. These powerful emotions may not be remembered. In earlier childhood times when they were experienced they may have been made to seem shameful and invalid.

The young schizophrenic person can think only on a limited conceptual plane bound by the parental expectations of conformity to safety, propriety and respectability. The framework of the controlling parents will rule out the validity of a variety of positive or negative emotions as criteria for action.

Psychotic feelings are so confusing since the discouse of the family takes place in a way that automatically invalidates these feelings. They either seem to come from nowhere or must be from the 'badness' in the person or 'their madness residing in faulty chemistry and family genes'.

In a full scale regression the young person will start reliving childhood ideas and fears and may revert to early attempted childhood fantasy defences against these reawakened unacceptable feelings and fears. The attempt to interpret the world through the vague and frightened mind-set of an infant is what I think is meant by 'confusional states'. Unlike more fixed delusions they are often more fluid thought processes.

I think psychotherapists who develop a specific skill for working with psychotic people can eventually learn to home in on the interpretation of these strange regressive mind states. The quickest therapeutic method will often be to explain to the sufferer in retrospect of these experiences, in simple language, and with many examples, how these mental processes work and then seek to involve the patient in doing their own interpretations of their past experiences of these mind states. In my other writings on psychosis I have given a number of examples.

An example of the replay of this infantile thinking was a fantasy I had that kindling fire was the key aspect in a sort of ritual that established sexual relationships. Retrospectively I am sure this strange idea arose as the infant interpretation of the trauma of being punished for playing with matches. Matches and fire must have seemed to my infant mind in some way to symbolize adult power and being grown up. Another feature in this was that the punishment came from my father who was also a competitor for my mother's affections and attentions. If you put the two bits together the idea has a sort of infant logic to it... I remember vividly how the sight of a box of Ship brand matches triggered the words in my head which reoccurred over and again 'He's got to learn', 'He's got to learn'. My terrified psychotic mind wondered what I had to learn and why this idea repeated itself. Retrospectively it seems obvious that the Ship brand matches in my regressed state triggered the memory of my father saying I had got to learn not to play with matches... the prevalent anxiety was the memory of the fear of this punishment.

Certainly I now do not find interpretations of my own even quite bizarre psychotic experiences all that difficult. The trick is to guess at the meaning of the strange ideas by imagining the infantile emotional situation. One must try to reconstruct the inner mental situation of an infant who cannot know most of what is later learned in life. The interpretative activity of an infant needs to be thought of in the context of the host of things from the natural and social world which, as external perceptions are cues and stimuli acting upon that infant mind. The regressed psychotic mind is an infant-adult mind.

Carl Jung on Extrasensory Perception
R. J. van Helsdingen

Towards the end of his life, Jung was able to speak more freely about his personal views and experiences concerning hallucinations. According to his autobiography, 'Memories, Dreams, Reflections', he had been interested in this subject since he first began writing scientific literature. He writes:

My first book, in 1905, was on the psychology of dementia praecox [schizophrenia]. My aim was to show that delusions and hallucinations were not just specific symptoms of mental disease, but also had a human meaning.

So what is a hallucination? A hallucination is a sensory perception which is not confirmed by anyone else. However, this alone is not sufficient definition: if I happen to see or hear something to which no one else is witness, it may still be an accurate observation. More problematic still is the difficulty of defining normality. The person who claims to hear voices is not necessarily abnormal or mentally disturbed: Joan of Arc, for example, heard God's voice calling upon her to save France, which is what she succeeded in doing. Extensive archives have survived from that time, including the interrogations of the committee that sentenced her. These reveal that everything she said was completely lucid and reasonable, except that she insisted that God had been speaking to her in person. Interestingly, most French people today tend to believe this story.

When we perceive something, we believe that our perception relates to something outside of us, although the perception itself lies within us. Any sensory impression has to be embodied in a framework of memories before perception as such can take place: when we see or hear something for the first time, this can become a perception only after it has been placed in that framework. For example, I know for certain that the ball-point pen in my hand has a certain form and shape, that it exists in space and that I am using it now. My pen is present in the outer world of space and time (in the now), but it is only thanks to my own inner world, my awareness of space and time, that I am able to make this observation. It is this world that enables me to perceive; any perception of the outer world involves a large part of our inner world. When we perceive something, for example with our eyes or ears, we believe it to be completely apart from us, but our inner world is intimately involved in the process of perception.

Whenever our level of consciousness decreases, the personal, subjective aspect becomes more prominent. When I daydream, my consciousness decreases in proportion to the growth in my subjective world of perception; I observe the world about me less clearly, and emotional factors and memories begin to play a part. For extremely introverted people, to whom the internal world of emotions and thoughts is more significant than whatever is happening in the outer world, internal images and voices are often clearer than parallel external stimuli. Jung writes:

Since my experience in the baptistry in Ravenna, I know with certainty that something interior can seem to be exterior.
Here, what struck me first was the mild blue light that filled the room; yet I did not wonder about this at all. I did not try to account for its source, or to wonder if this light without any visible source did not trouble me. I was somewhat amazed, because in place of the windows I remembered having seen on my first visit, there were now four great mosaic frescoes of incredible beauty which, it seemed, I had entirely forgotten. I was vexed to find my memory so unreliable. The mosaic on the south side

represented the baptism in the Jordan; the second picture, on the north,
was of the passage of the Children of Israel through the Red Sea; the
third, on the east, soon faded from my memory.
When I was back home, I asked an acquaintance who was going to
Ravenna to obtain the pictures for me. He could not locate them, for he
discovered that the mosaic I had described did not exist.

Jung had been seeing the frescoes in his mind's eye only. His religious mood had led him to see pictures that were not there: in other words, he had been having visual hallucinations.

Jung also experienced auditory hallucinations in the form of voices on many occasions, especially in times of particular introversion. He would occasionally retreat to a remote (self-built) country residence on Lake Zurich, and there, in deep solitude, he would sometimes hear voices around the house at night. He would get out of bed to check whether anyone was there, see nothing, and go back to sleep. This experience was repeated several times. Later on, Jung felt he knew almost for certain that these had been the voices of the so-called Salig Lut, the deceased souls, who were part of the German god Wotan's army; belief in Wotan had not completely died out in this area.

Jung experienced a very difficult period in his life when his mental health was poor. During this time, he heard a woman's voice on several occasions, telling him that he was an artist and should take up painting. He acted upon this advice for a while, until he realized that this voice was not well-meaning, and that it was seeking to mislead him. Jung writes:

Actually, the patient whose voice had been speaking inside me exerted a
fatal influence on men. She had succeeded in talking a colleague of mine
into believing that he was a neglected artist; he believed this, and he
perished. The cause of his failure? He did not have a strong sense of his
own self-esteem, but gained esteem from being acknowledged by others.
This is hazardous. It made him insecure and open to the insinuations of
the anima; what she is saying often has a seductive power, and it is
unfathomably cunning.
Particularly at this time, when I was working on fantasies, I needed a
point of support in this world, and I must say my family and my
professional work were that for me. It was most essential for me to have
a normal life in the real world as a counterpoise to that strange inner
world. My family and my profession remained the base to which I could
always return, assuring me that I was an actually existing, ordinary
person.

After freeing himself from this plight, Jung got in touch with the voice of a sage, whom he recognized as Philemon from Greek mythology. This voice was a benevolent presence for him, gave him sound advice and replied to his questions. In mythology, Philemon was a poor man who, together with his wife Baucis, had shown warm hospitality to the supreme god Zeus when he visited them in the shape of an ordinary, humble human being. Everyone else in the region had turned Zeus away in this human guise, and in punishment he destroyed them in a flood, saving only Philemon and Baucis. To Jung, Philemon was a wise old man who clarified a great deal for him. Indeed, Jung's most profound, gnostic work, 'The Seven Sermons to the Dead' (Septem Sermones ad Mortuos), was dictated to him by Philemon. Jung writes:

Philemon and other figures in my fantasies brought home to me the crucial insight that there are things in the psyche which I myself do not produce, but which produce themselves and have their own life. Philemon represented a force that was not myself. In my fantasies, I held conversations with him in which he said things which I had not consciously thought. For I observed clearly that it was he who spoke, not I. He said I treated thoughts as though I generated them myself, but in his view thoughts were like animals in the forest, or people in a room, or birds in the air, and added:

If you should see people in a room, you would not think that you had made those people, or that you were responsible for them. It was he who taught me psychic objectivity, the reality of the psyche. Through him, the distinction was clarified between myself and the object of my thought. He confronted me in an objective manner, and I understood that there is something in me which can say things that I do not know and do not intend, things which may even be directed against me.
However, it was obvious to me from the outset that I would be able to find a connection with the world around me, with people, only if I did my utmost to show that the contents of the mental reality are real; and then again, not just as being my own personal experiences, but as collective experiences which can also occur to others. That is what I have attempted to prove in my later scientific work.

A certain set of feelings, a so-called emotional complex, can become overwhelming to the extent that it breaks away from the psyche and takes the form of a person. This, says Jung, is why the voices people hear are always personifications of parts of their own souls; and it is precisely because they are such personifications that the hearers do not recognize the voices as parts of themselves - they believe that the voices come from other people. This, on the other hand, is a possibility not ruled out by Jung. According to him, each of us is in touch with the unconscious spiritual life of all other people at the deepest level of our psyche; this includes those who have already lived and died, as well as those who are yet to be born. Jung termed this shared spiritual realm the collective unconscious, a dimension connecting the whole of humanity which also allows for contact with other people by means other than sensory perception. This theory accommodates the possibility of hearing the voices of people we cannot see, or who died a long time ago.

In the light of all this, it is quite conceivable that emotional complexes represent a part of the collective unconscious, and this makes it possible for me to believe in the reality of hearing the voices of other people, even if no one else hears them. The likelihood of the phenomenon is greatly enhanced by such factors as extreme introversion, a decreased level of consciousness and a strong attachment to the person whose voice is heard. For example, a widow who had loved her husband very dearly would hear his voice at times when she was faced with difficult decisions. In another case, a young man who had been strongly attached to his father would go to his grave from time to time to talk with him and ask his advice. None of this is necessarily indicative of mental disturbance.

Those who are easily susceptible to feelings of guilt sometimes hear critical, accusatory or abusive voices. They often believe the voices to be coming from outside, and neglect the role played by their own internal world in their creation.

References

Jung, C. G. (1969) Memories, Dreams, Reflections; Pantheon Books, Random House, New York

Jaynes and Consciousness
Patsy Hage

In his book 'The Origin of Consciousness in the Breakdown of the Bicameral Mind', Julian Jaynes outlines a theory about the relationship between the evolution of consciousness and the phenomenon of hearing voices. I have no room here to give more than a very brief summary of Jaynes's thesis, but the essence of it is the remarkable claim that, until around 1300 BC, the hearing of voices was common to all humanity, and that the experience was all but eliminated by what we now know as consciousness. Those few people who still hear voices today, he says, are the carriers of an evolutionary residue from this ancient time.

First of all, Jaynes examines the concept of consciousness, and offers his own definition in terms of what it is not:

- The seeming continuity of consciousness is really an illusion arising from the artificial division of time. We are conscious for less of the time than we think, because we cannot be conscious of the time during which we are not conscious.
- Consciousness is not the reproduction of experiences. Conscious memory is not a storing up of sensory images, but the retrieval of something of which we have previously been conscious.
- Consciousness is not necessary for conceptualization. No one has ever been conscious of a tree. We experience a particular tree and the function of language is to let a word stand for a concept.
- Consciousness is not necessary for learning: conditioning does not require consciousness. The acquisition of behavioural traits takes place automatically. Consciousness plays a role in formulating a problem in a certain way, but is not necessary for its solution.
- Consciousness is not necessary for thinking. Thinking about something is never conscious. We do our thinking before we know what we are going to think about. The important part of the process is the initial instruction, which allows everything to take place automatically.
- Consciousness is not necessary for reasoning. Reasoning consists of a wide range of natural thought processes in everyday life. We need logic because most reasoning is not conscious.

We tend to locate the conscious inside our heads: we create a space there for it, even though we know that there is no space in our heads. Aristotle located consciousness somewhere above the heart. In fact, one might just as well locate it in the room next door, given that it has no location at all in the sense that we imagine.

Jaynes's conclusion, based on these observations, is that it is possible to conceive of a civilization without consciousness. He also says that we cannot understand consciousness because we have no metaphor for it, and metaphors are essential to understanding. We use space as an adjunct to consciousness: for example, we allow time to move from left to right. We are conscious of the parts of a whole, as when we are conscious of a clown rather than the whole circus. We use the metaphor 'I' to do everything in our imagination instead of employing metaphors on a conscious level. Consciousness is a metaphor of our actual behaviour. In essence, then, consciousness works with the help of analogy and a constructed space: with an analogous 'I' that can observe that space and metaphorically move within it.

These, in brief, are the main planks of Jaynes's argument. The central point is his assertion that it is plainly possible to have a society that functions well without consciousness. This, he says, is well depicted in the 'Iliad', a book dating from before the existence of consciousness as we know it: the time, that is, when everyone heard voices. Apparently, there are no words used in the 'Iliad' relating to consciousness or mental acts; in the religion of the ancient Greeks, the gods take the place of consciousness. As Agamemnon says: 'The gods always have their way'. The 'Iliad' represents what Jaynes labels the bicameral mind: the human spirit at work in two distinct rooms or spaces. These parts are both unconscious. The larger part was occupied by the gods who spoke to the people, and by their voices. The individual - the follower - filled the other space and performed ceremonial acts. Will-power, planning and initiative did not exist at a conscious level; actions and decisions were carried out at the level of the gods, and the individual obeyed their commands, because he or she could not consciously see what must be undertaken. The entire 'Iliad', then, depicts not the character but the deeds of human beings - deeds performed in the service of the gods.

There is nothing in the 'Iliad' to suggest the possibility of holding a discussion with oneself or having personal responsibility. These identifying marks of consciousness come into being at a later stage of human development, as a product of culture - when man becomes his own god, as it were. As the bicameral mind disappears, consciousness dawns.

There is a remarkable resemblance between the way the gods speak in the 'Iliad' and the ways in which many of us experience the hearing of voices. They converse, threaten, curse, criticize, consult, warn, console, mock, command, predict. They shout, whine and sneer. They may come in anything from a whisper to a scream. Often they have a special peculiarity, such as speaking very slowly or rhythmically.

The gods in the 'Iliad' were always obeyed. Similarly, many of us obey our voices, and Jaynes suggests some possible explanations for this obedience to either voices or gods. When you want to understand someone who is speaking to you, then you must mentally take on their identity and put yourself in their place. When what is addressed to you is a command, this identification becomes obedience. You can only avoid this obedience when there is a real distance between you and the speaker, and when you are critical of the speaker. The gods who speak in the 'Iliad' were in closer contact with the individual concerned than he or she with his or her own 'I'. In particular, the gods were obeyed because the individual had no critical attitude towards them: gods were always omniscient and omnipotent, and could not be subordinated.

At this point in his book, Jaynes offers a highly technical discussion of the functions of the two brain hemispheres. All that needs to be noted here is his suggestion that the right hemisphere has the capacity for hearing voices, and that both hemispheres can function independently of one another - exactly as in the god-man relationship in bicameral times. The brain can be influenced by its surroundings, and so be culturally modified from a bicameral nature to a state of consciousness.

Jaynes traces the history of voice-hearing in human evolution. Language, he says, initially comes into being in the form of involuntary cries of reaction to threats; these are soon put into use within a given group by its leader, for the purpose of warning of encroaching danger. Next, special catch-words evolve and are used by the leader to assign tasks to group members. Because these tasks become increasingly more complex, the individual self develops accordingly, and people begin to have hallucinations of the leader's voice giving orders.

With the development of a community of several 100 people comes a king, whose voice is heard throughout the whole community. When such a king dies, his people continue to hear his voice, and he is elevated to the status of a god. In this manner, humanity has created its own gods. Temples and statues are built to take the place of the tombs of dead kings. Cities grow, and a bicameral mind - with its capacity to hear voices - is necessary for the maintenance of social control. The Egyptians treated their most prominent dead as if they were still alive, because the community still heard their voices. Temples or shrines to gods have been found dating from 7000 BC. In Turkey, pictures from 1250 BC have been found representing a number of gods lined up in long rows; this graphically illustrates how closely the gods were grouped together.

Jaynes examines a number of ancient cultures in order to demonstrate that many societies were governed through their gods, which were heard as voices. But because these societies were constantly growing larger and more complex, and because their peoples became involved in trade (through which they came into contact with other cultures and other gods), it became more and more difficult for the gods to remain united. Humanity found itself with too many disparate gods in conflict with one another, and in the period between 2100 BC and 1300 BC such social systems no longer functioned entirely in accordance with the hearing of voices: consciousness began to develop, and to take over the tasks of the gods. It is quite clear that between the end of this period and the present day, there have been only a few people who have heard voices - for example, those visiting the Greek oracles, and the prophets of the Bible.

My own conclusion, as a result of reading Jaynes's work, is that the origin of consciousness does indeed lie in the breakdown of the bicameral mind: in the disappearance, that is, of the collective hearing of voices.

Those of us who still hear voices are therefore probably living in the wrong century.

References

Jaynes, J. (1976) The Origin of Consciousness in the Breakdown of the Bicameral Mind; Houghton Mifflin, Boston

10. TAKING CONTROL

Introduction
Marius Romme

In this chapter we will examine various techniques used by the hearers of voices and/or their therapists in order to gain more control over their relationship with the voices. Note that I do not speak of curing people of their voices. This is a word we have deliberately avoided throughout this book: we assume that hearing voices is a human experience which may have great meaning in an individual's life, and that it should not, therefore, be viewed only as a phenomenon of illness.

There are, of course, exceptions to every rule: in this case, these might include voices heard in epilepsy or during one of the polar phases of a manic-depressive psychosis. For those with a psychiatric diagnosis of schizophrenia, however, the hearing of voices is frequently quite a different matter. The voices are significant, and often give meaning or direction to the hearer's life. The term 'cure' cannot properly be applied to these voices; it is more a question of learning to manage them, of giving them a specific time and place in the context of life as a whole. In order to minimize the disruption to everyday functioning, it is essential to gain as much personal control as possible. The techniques described in this chapter can be very helpful in this respect.

We have listed these strategies in order of the degree of personal contribution required of the voice-hearer. Thus, the Diary section comes first because it demands the greatest input (nearly 100%); the chapter ends with Medication, in which the individual's contribution is generally the smallest, depending on the degree to which others allow him or her to become involved. We will discuss the following techniques:

- **Diary.** In this section, we have accounts from four people who hear voices. They explain why they started keeping a diary, and how this helped them.
- **Self-help.** Here, we examine the possible benefits of attending self-help groups. One organizer, a woman who herself hears voices, explains how these groups work, why people participate in them, what kind of ground is covered in them, and so on.
- **Focusing.** Two psychologists describe a method which they have developed and applied to people hearing voices. This method involves gaining greater insight into actual perceptions as well as their interpretation.

- **Anxiety management.** A psychiatrist describes a number of techniques that he has used with the hearers of voices. These are designed to lower anxiety levels and so make it possible to take greater control of the situation.
- **Dialogue.** This section gives the detailed account of one psychologist's experiment in establishing dialogues with the voices heard by one of her clients, with the aim of giving the woman concerned a greater degree of control over the voices.
- **Rehabilitation.** The hearer of voices is inevitably influenced to a large extent by the nature of his or her immediate environment. Society often reacts negatively to those who admit to hearing voices, and for this reason careful attention must be paid to any rehabilitation process. Here, a psychiatrist suggests ways of approaching this.
- **Medication.** Voice-hearers receiving psychiatric treatment are frequently prescribed various forms of medication. In this section, a psychiatrist explains the different types of drugs involved, and the circumstances under which they are prescribed.

Diary
Sandra Escher

The hearing of voices is a complex phenomenon, but for me, one of its most significant features is the reflection it may offer of the hearer's habitual ways of attempting to cope with his or her own emotions and those of others. This can reveal a subtle emotional drama that is something like listening to a radio play, and one that may provide valuable personal insights. However, the experience is also capable of triggering extremely negative feelings, reducing the hearer to panic and powerlessness. By communicating with others about the voices and their repercussions, the voice-hearer can often find ways of taking more effective control over the situation. Certainly, in our many interviews and discussions with voice-hearers, we found communication to be one of the most important and successful means of finding some order within an otherwise chaotic experience. Those who can manage this enjoy greater self-confidence, and become more closely in touch with their surroundings.

Some people, though, find it too painful or difficult to speak openly about these problems; in these instances in particular, it can be very helpful to keep a diary. Before it is possible to share thoughts and problems usefully, and communicate the nature of a very personal situation, it is clearly necessary to be able to describe and explain your experiences and ideas: to formulate what it is that the voices say, how this is triggered by your emotions, and why. A diary can be a very helpful tool in this process. One of its greatest merits as a therapeutic aid is that it is infinitely patient and totally uncritical!

In order to sketch out the possible functions and benefits of keeping such a diary, I interviewed four women, all of whom were voice-hearers and ex-psychiatric patients. I asked them for detailed information about their own experiences with diaries, with particular reference to the following points:

– under what circumstances the diary was begun;
– how the voices reacted to the diary;
– whether keeping a diary helped to impose order upon chaos and reinforce the sense of self;
– whether the diarists were able to show their diaries to those close to them;
– what the diary means to the person concerned.

The results of this small survey offer a good insight into the possible meaning and uses of keeping a diary, which were quite varied among these four women.

Mrs A.

Now 34 years old, Mrs A. first started keeping a diary about her voices after being assigned a new therapist. During her first visits, she could hardly bring herself to talk to him, and decided on her own initiative to begin a diary, so that she would be able to formulate more clearly what she wanted to say.

I wanted to talk, but everything stuck in my throat, so I started giving him my diary as soon as I arrived. He would then ask me questions about what I had written, which I found I was able to answer.

Initially, I would write about things after they had happened, but at a certain point I started writing at the actual time that the voices were bothering me. The diary then turned into a very confused account, although this did not give me any extra anxiety, and nor did the voices forbid me to keep the diary. I never wrote down what the voices said. Instead, I usually wrote about my powerlessness against the voices.

Mrs A. talked about this powerlessness with her therapist, and together they tried to find solutions to the situations in which this arose. One example she gave was going to parties with her boyfriend: she would often have to leave halfway through the evening because of her voices, and this caused problems with her boyfriend. In conversation with her therapist, she came up with the idea that if she made a firm agreement with her boyfriend beforehand as to when she would leave the party, this problem would probably disappear. This, in fact, is what happened: the voices did not trouble her when she kept to her agreement.

When I asked her whether keeping a diary had strengthened her sense of self, she replied:

That's a hard question to answer. I'm well aware that when I write I cannot distinguish between my emotions and my own self. Is that frightening? I never re-read what I have written. And if you don't go back over it, it's not threatening.

Three years ago, she used her diary to let her mother know what had happened and was still happening to her. With such an emotion-filled document, of course, it is important to warn anyone who is allowed to read it about the nature of the contents. Her mother was enormously shocked, and wept - something she rarely did - but then responded by saying she now understood her daughter's behaviour much better. Since then, their relationship has been much closer.

Mrs A. no longer keeps a diary. From talking to her and seeing how well she now manages socially, I doubt that she will have any further need of it; she can now express and explain her needs very clearly.

Mrs B.

Mrs B. is now 26 years old. When she first started in therapy, she wanted to confide in her therapist but found herself unable to do so. On her therapist's advice, she began keeping a diary, and says this is now her only means of making contact with her therapist. She told me:

I find it difficult, in therapy, to do an hour of obligatory emotions.

She finds, on the other hand, that she is able to express her emotions freely in her diary, even to the extent of venting anger towards her therapist. Mrs B. now writes mainly as a way of opening herself up.

When I write, I have to concentrate, and then everything flows of its own accord. It is also enormously important to me to be able to discharge my feelings this way.

When I asked what her voices made of her diary, she replied:

This has tended to vary. At first, the voices did not interfere when I was writing, and I imagined that they stayed away while I did my diary. But then the more I reflected about things, the more the voices interfered. Sometimes they are really difficult, and forbid me to write. In the early days, I would obey, and stop; later on, though, I started to stick at it regardless. When the voices disturb me now, I carry on writing.

Mrs A. had told me that she tended to lose herself in her writing. When I asked Mrs B. whether she found the same, she told me:

Yes, I do lose myself somewhat. This was especially true in the early days. There was a time when I would put pen to paper and just let rip, and I literally wouldn't know what I was writing. I write from the inside of my emotions. This doesn't feel threatening, but I'd rather not re-read what I write. Only my therapist should do that.

Mrs B. has found her diary a source of growth and strength. She commented:

Recently I have come to understand what the voices mean, and my diary has played an important role in this respect.

Mrs C.

Mrs C. is 43 years old, and has kept a diary since the age of 12. She started writing out of loneliness when her parents sent her to a foster home. A year earlier, she had been through a horrible ordeal in which she was almost raped: a gang of youths had held her down in front of her younger sister and pulled off her clothes. She never dared to mention this at home.

When she first started keeping a diary, she invented imaginary little friends, as many children do. Somewhat later, she began to hear voices, and to identify with the imaginary friends. For example, when she wrote to or about one of these by the name of Ann, she herself became Ann. Writing became an addiction, something with which she could occupy herself for hours at a time. At first, she was unaware of anything untoward in this, and could not do without writing.

I write to discharge my emotions. I let myself go in my writing, and this refreshes me. I have to let my feelings out, otherwise I feel as though I will explode. It's true that you can lose yourself and no longer be in the here and now, but you can also find yourself, in the midst of writing.

Three years ago, Mrs C. underwent a brief course of hypnotherapy, and this helped her to recognize that she had several personalities, each with its own distinctive character traits. There were, for example, the wicked person, the lovable person, the desperate person and the grief-stricken person. She gave each of these a name of its own, and allowed them room in her diary to talk to each other. Here, she would put questions to them, such as, 'Why are you so sad?'

Through this dialogue, I found myself again.

Keeping a diary is a sort of catharsis for Mrs C. In this arena, she is able to express violent emotions which she acknowledges as her own but which would be unpleasant and disruptive if communicated directly to others. When she feels herself on the brink of psychosis, she starts writing, and finds that this helps her. She says she is strict about time-keeping, and now writes for no more than an hour at a time.

I have to keep to my time limits, if you know what I mean.

Mrs C. has also noticed that keeping to these limits in writing her diary has kept troublesome voices at bay.

Mrs D.

Now 30 years old, Mrs D. was first admitted to psychiatric hospital about ten years ago. Twenty-four hours after admission, she started hearing voices. After about six months, however, she found herself well enough to leave hospital, and her therapist gave her the task of keeping a daily diary about what she did around her flat and how she was feeling. The idea of this was to help her impose some order upon her emotional chaos.

Mrs D. is a perfectionist. She is anxious to perform the therapist's task as meticulously as possible, and when she is not satisfied with what she has written she rips it up and rewrites it. From the very start, then, she has tried very hard to set down as perfectly as possible what she wants to express. This is in considerable contrast to our other diarists: she is the only one who resists writing in her diary until she has thought over what she will say.

When I am too emotional, I can neither think nor write.

By a long process of trial and error, Mrs D. has mastered the technical art of writing down her personal feelings precisely.

When I take up a pen and paper, something happens to me. Something I have experienced and dealt with is expressed in such a way that it is as fixed as a snapshot. In this way, I can deal with my emotions better, and be detached from them.

Perhaps for this very reason, she does not feel threatened by re-reading her diary. She also told me that the voices never interfere with her writing. Writing has been a source of positive growth for Mrs D.

Through keeping a diary, I have learned that my emotions are somehow connected to the situations I find myself in.

Conclusion

From all my interviews and discussions with voice-hearers about the diaries they have kept, I can only conclude that the practice appears to be a positive experience. By and large, it seems to be a far less threatening or disturbing process than I anticipated. The writers seem to be able to exert control over any threatening information that may be forthcoming, and to create voice-free interludes where necessary.

The diary is a striking means of entering into communication about voices. As time goes on, according to individual temperament, it can provide a stimulus for finding a clearer overview of one's own emotions and how these are reflected in various situations. This, in turn, leads to greater insight into the nature and meaning of the voices.

Where a diary is intended to be used as a tool for communication with others, it is important that those to whom it is to be entrusted should satisfy a number of conditions. In particular, they must be eminently reliable and sensitive to the emotions of others.

For anyone who does not feel quite ready to jump in at the deep end by using a diary as part of a fairly intense therapeutic transaction, there remains the question of how you can help yourself by using this tool for your own private purposes. There is no easy answer to this, but the following points appear to be important:

- consider ways of concealing your diary in order to be sure of keeping your privacy;
- use your imagination to work out what conditions are most stimulating for writing a diary;
- make a decision about how much time and energy you are prepared to put into writing the diary;
- be realistic in your expectations. If your diary does not work out, realize that you may be asking too much of it at that moment. Perhaps you will be able to go back to it later for another try.

Self-Help
Resi Malecki and Monique Pennings

Patient organizations

Since the 1970s, all kinds of health care initiatives have been taken by patients themselves. These are aimed, in various ways, at stimulating patients to take greater responsibility for themselves, to communicate with one another, to offer assistance and information, and to improve the position of the patient or consumer. Many such initiatives have resulted in the formation of patient organizations, which usually consist of people with similar illnesses or problems. They are all in the same boat, and can use the knowledge acquired from their own experience to offer help and support to fellow-sufferers. This can often make it very much easier to learn to live with a particular illness or difficulty. Professional care often falls short in this respect; the health care services tend to place most emphasis on medical and biological factors, with the attention focused on illness rather than on the person affected by it. In other words, the help offered fails to relate to the experience and perception of the client.

The impetus for the formation of patient groups is often a dissatisfaction with professional services, or with the lack of provision of services. It is also true that the last 20 years or so have seen considerable growth in democratization and emancipation: increasingly, people have assumed and demanded more responsibility for their own health and illness. No longer will they rely solely on the expertise of specialized helpers.

The various patient organizations in existence today have, of course, their own specific objectives, and their activities vary accordingly. However, they all have certain important goals in common: putting people in touch with each other, facilitating mutual support, disseminating information, and promoting the interests of members.

Resonance (Weerklank)

Five years ago, a nationwide organization called Resonance was set up in the Netherlands. It devotes itself to the interests of those who hear voices, regardless of whether or not this is associated with psychiatric illness. Today, there are around a thousand members, many of whom are the friends and family of those who hear voices, as well as other interested parties such as providers of health care - a very mixed membership.

Resonance embraces a rather more complex and diverse range of attitudes and beliefs than other groups concerned with more obviously somatic disorders. Some members, for example, regard the hearing of voices as something enriching, while others believe it to be symptomatic of illness; some of those who hear voices themselves find the experience extremely difficult, whereas others are completely at ease with it. Such discrepancies amongst the membership make Resonance a lively association. Clearly, though, there has to be a significant common bond to unite all these disparate elements: the taboo that still surrounds the phenomenon of hearing voices remains a problem for everyone, whatever their individual approach and experience. This means that all the members of Resonance have to remain tolerant of one another, open to one another's ideas and experiences; it is accepted that everyone has his or her own perspective on the phenomenon, and that each individual must therefore find his or her own appropriate coping strategy.

Resonance strives to promote the acceptance and emancipation of people who hear voices; to work against the sense of isolation which so often compounds their difficulties, and to help them to cope effectively with their experiences. The association undertakes all kinds of activities towards these goals. It organizes a network of mutual contact and support via a telephone link, and offers self-help groups for any interested members. It disseminates information and guidance on the phenomenon of hearing voices by means of a quarterly magazine, through television, radio and press interviews, and by the publication of leaflets and brochures; information is also distributed in psychiatric hospitals and community mental health centres. In order to strengthen the bonds between its members, the foundation organizes social events where they can meet up with one another. Resonance is currently involved in setting up a new network to offer help to voice-hearers, and participates in all kinds of commissions and consultative bodies to promote their interests within the health care services.

Self-help groups can make an important contribution to the process of learning to cope with voices. This section is therefore devoted to a detailed discussion of such groups, based largely on the experiences of Resi Malecki, one of this section's co-authors. Resi has been offering guidance to self-help groups for over three years, with the benefit of expertise and understanding acquired from her own experience.

Self-help groups

My name is Resi Malecki. I initially trained as a discussion leader with an organization devoted to principles of self-help for both physiological and psychological illnesses, and now lead three self-help groups in the south of the Netherlands. From my experiences in this work, I have learned that there are a number of important elements to be considered in the creation and running of any discussion group. In this section, I would like to examine some of those that seem to me to be most significant.

Goals

When starting any group, it is important to be clear about your reasons and about what you hope to achieve with such a group. My own objectives were, and are:

- to be heard, recognized and acknowledged;
- to share experiences with others in similar circumstances, and so clarify the meaning of the voices;
- to reduce the fear surrounding the hearing of voices;
- to find ways of living comfortably with the experience;
- to involve family and friends with voice-hearers and their problems.

Reasons for participation

It is also important for members to be clear about their goals in taking part in self-help groups. These may vary, but generally speaking, participation tends to be for such reasons as:

- for reassurance;
- to break down isolation;
- to be able to talk about the voices;
- to find companionship with others who understand the experience;
- to learn from others;
- to find support;
- to learn how to cope with the voices;
- to learn about oneself with the help of others;
- to learn about the wide variety of individual experiences;
- to learn how to discuss the issues with family and friends.

Openness

Some discussion groups are exclusively for those who themselves hear voices. In the group I run in Limburg, however, I have chosen to allow friends and family members to join in as well. This is an open group; in other words, anyone can join at any stage, and the group is ongoing. The size of the membership varies: there is a hard core of long-term regulars, with occasional newcomers, and other members dropping out from time to time. Within the group, there is a great diversity of perspectives and experiences on the part of voice-hearers. In spite of this, I find that people readily identify with one another, and overall the results of this approach have been very positive.

Meeting procedures

There are various elements to be considered in conducting group meetings. In my own meetings, if any newcomers are present, everyone introduces themselves and says something about their past and present experience of hearing voices: 'When and how did it begin? What was the situation at the time? How has it developed? In what ways has it improved or deteriorated? Is any medication being used? Has any help been asked for or received? What is the situation at the moment?'

The needs and expectations of newcomers must also be covered, and this means that when there are considerable numbers of new members present, this period of sharing is kept short. In this case, the members with the longest history of attendance give a broad overview of recent months. One advantage of this is that it gives them the opportunity to let off steam and raise any issues that may be bothering them. Time is always set aside for reflecting on the group situation and examining how things are going at the present time, so that people have the opportunity to express in greater detail any frustrations or difficulties, and to say what might help to put them at ease within the group.

Themes
Some examples of issues that may arise:
- medicines and their side-effects;
- hearing voices and work;
- hearing voices and daily social life;
- hearing voices and intimate relationships;
- hearing voices and leisure pursuits;
- hearing voices and concentration;
- hearing voices as an obstacle to advancement;
- the personal experience of hearing voices;
- living with someone who hears voices.

Homework
It is not possible for everything to be covered within the group setting. Members will often also do exercises at home, based on assignments which have been given out; these are then discussed in the group. Examples of such homework assignments are:
- find quotations in books, poems and songs which are special to you and which you find inspiring or helpful;
- an evaluation exercise: express your experience of participating in the group by means of a project such as drawing;
- review a book or film;
- identify your own positive attributes;
- tension and relaxation: what they signify for you, and how they feel.

Concluding
Meetings normally close with a little time being devoted to:
- Planning: collective decisions about subjects for discussion at the next meeting. This entails making choices and setting priorities.
- Evaluation: what people gained from the discussion: how they feel about what took place.

Important skills for discussion leaders
In my experience as a discussion leader over two-and-a-half years I have seen improvements in a number of the skills which I learned during training. The most important of these are:
- skilful listening;
- facilitating discussion, for example by asking the right questions;
- establishing whether one has understood someone else correctly;
- observing the group process objectively;
- examining feelings as necessary;
- setting or determining limits;
- paying attention to non-verbal signals within the group;
- evaluating the group situation.

These are skills which are useful in all types of discussion groups. In the case of a group specifically concerned with the hearing of voices, I believe it is also necessary for the discussion leader to be someone who hears (or has heard) voices him or herself and has learned to accept and live with that experience. It is equally important, of course, to have a thorough and wide-ranging knowledge of the phenomenon of hearing voices as a whole. In particular, one should be familiar with the available literature on the subject, whether written from within the realms of orthodox health care or from the standpoint of those offering alternatives. It is essential to be fully acquainted both with the experiences of fellow-sufferers and with the perspectives of those offering assistance. One should also be willing to attend open days and conferences associated with the hearing of voices. In a nutshell, one's knowledge of hearing voices must extend well beyond one's own experience.

Additional responsibilities
There is a good deal more involved in being an expert discussion leader than simply leading discussions, crucial though this is. In my own experience, the following tasks are also important:
- organizing the group: this may include finding premises in which to meet;
- recruiting group members;

- preparing for meetings: compiling the agenda; choosing topics for discussion when these have not been fully determined at the previous meeting;
- leading discussion during the meeting itself; keeping an eye on the time, structuring the proceedings, etc.;
- stimulating and developing discussion;
- introducing the various means of coping with hearing voices; exploring the different possibilities with the group members;
- inviting feedback and examining how well particular coping strategies have worked out;
- observing the group process;
- gathering information about the phenomenon of hearing voices, and sharing this with the group;
- putting people at ease and (with the agreement of the people concerned) communicate very severe tensions to their therapists;
- offering a safe arena: for example, by not allowing the discussion of subjects which heighten anxiety, eg suicide;
- keeping records of the discussions;
- maintaining contact with other discussion leaders and/or the rest of the organization concerned.

All in all, my own experiences with self-help groups have greatly helped me in my efforts to accept the hearing of voices. As a result, I have learned to cope with this other reality much more comfortably, and this has led to a harmonious relationship with my voices.

Don't let yourself be overwhelmed. Pay close attention to the promptings of both your head and your heart!

Focusing
Gill Haddock and Richard Bentall

Research has suggested that there is a wide range of psychological approaches which may be helpful to people suffering from auditory hallucinations. A thorough review of these various approaches by Slade and Bentall (1988) has shown that they tend to fall into three main categories: distraction, focusing, and anxiety management techniques. Distraction techniques include listening to personal stereos, reading, performing mental puzzles, engaging in certain social activities - in short, any kind of behaviour which serves to take the hearer's mind off the voices. Focusing, on the other hand, involves paying closer attention to the voices themselves, for example by monitoring them and writing down what they say.

All of these methods appear to be capable of helping people to cope better with their voices, but the mechanisms by which they work remain unclear. We believe that distraction techniques (which are based on the belief that if the voices are avoided for long enough they are likely to disappear completely), although they may well be effective in the short-term, fail to address the underlying content of the voices and are therefore unlikely to offer any enduring resolution of the hallucinator's difficulties. Research suggests that auditory hallucinations generally have some special significance or meaning for the voice-hearer; in this light, only those techniques which explicitly address the meaning of the voices are likely to enable the hearer to take ownership of them as being a part of him or herself.

With all this in mind, we have developed a focusing treatment, whereby the patient is helped to explore the content, development and meaning of his or her voices within the context of a therapeutic relationship. This is achieved by means of a series of graded exercises designed to make the process as unthreatening as possible. Early exercises involve the patient listening to and describing the physical characteristics of the voices, including their loudness, location, tone and gender. Later on, the patient is asked to report exactly what the voices say as they are heard, and to pay particular attention to any associated thoughts or ideas which might indicate their personal significance. The overall aim of the approach, with the help of detailed discussion, is to enable the individual to cope better with the voices, identify their true origin, and gain a measure of personal control over them. If ownership of the voices is distressing to the person, it is important to explore their significance in much the same way that cognitive therapists work with negative thoughts. The following brief case study (taken from our research project into the treatment of hallucinations, which was funded by the UK Medical Research Council) illustrates the general strategies involved.

Mr A.

Mr A. was a 44-year old man who had suffered from auditory hallucinations for more than ten years. He was employed, and lived in a hostel run by the Salvation Army. Despite many years of neuroleptic medication, the intensity and frequency of his voices had remained virtually unchanged; when I first saw him, he was hearing them every day. They were experienced as originating outside his head, and could occur under any circumstances. He described the content of the voices, which were in the third person, as often being hostile and threatening (eg 'We're going to do him in. He's no good'). One particularly frequent voice was that of a close friend, and he occasionally heard others coming from the television set.

Mr A. was treated with distraction techniques over six sessions, but these only served to worsen both the hallucinations and the accompanying anxiety. Consequently, a focusing approach was tried along the lines detailed above. This revealed that the actual content of Mr A's voices was often fairly innocent, and not necessarily directed at him (for example, 'He's useless' could be a comment about someone else); however, his own thoughts and responses convinced Mr A. that the voices were talking about him. This was especially likely to occur under certain circumstances. For example, the bedrooms in his hostel were far from sound-proof, and he could often hear noises from his immediate neighbour, who mumbled and talked in his sleep; Mr A. interpreted these sounds as his close friend talking about him. In this instance, he appeared to be labelling his own thoughts and beliefs as voices, and superimposing them on to an actual auditory event. It seemed quite possible that the voices emanating from the television were the result of a similar process. Mr A. always watched television in the evening, while lying on his bed and he would often fall asleep with the television switched on; it was therefore likely that at least some of his experiences were hypnagogic or hypnopompic. As he came to realize that his voices were caused by his own thought processes, Mr A. began to feel that he could learn to identify and control them by focusing on them. He has now succeeded in accepting all his hallucinatory experiences in these terms, although he knows that he cannot always expect complete control over his thoughts (indeed, who can?).

Gradually, the frequency with which Mr A. reports his experiences in terms of voices has dwindled to almost zero, although under stress he occasionally has moments in which he wonders about the causes of some of his perceptions. It is not surprising that a distraction approach was unsuccessful with Mr A.: in the end, progress was made only by paying careful attention both to his perceived, externally-generated voices and to the beliefs which provided the conditions for the existence of his so-called voices.

References

Bentall, R. P. (1990) The Illusion of Reality: a review and integration of psychological research into psychotic hallucinations; Psychological Bulletin, no. 107, pp.82-95

Slade, P. D. (1993) Models of Hallucination: from theory to practice; in David, A. S. and Cutting, J. (Eds.) The Neuropsychology of Schizophrenia; Earlbaum, London

Slade, P. D. and Bentall, R. P. (1988) Sensory Deception: towards a scientific analysis of hallucinations; Croom Helm, London

Acknowledgement

The research into the treatment of hallucinations which is described in this chapter was supported by a grant from the Medical Research Council.

Anxiety Management Techniques
Jack Jenner

General principles

Unfortunately, there are no golden rules about how to deal with voices or how to respond to others who hear them. There are, however, some general principles that may be of help if given proper attention. As dealt with in this section, we will call these:

- attitude;
- entering into the other world;
- relabelling;
- motivating;
- monitoring;
- exposure.

Attitude

The very definition of these perceptions as supernatural almost guarantees that those who are subject to them will find themselves isolated. The taboo surrounding these experiences, hallucinations, or whatever we choose to call them, discourages open discussion. The creation of an atmosphere and setting capable of dissolving this barrier - however difficult this may be - is therefore essential to any attempt to offer understanding and support.

Entering into the other world

However deluded we might consider the hearers of voices to be, the experiences are clearly a firm reality for the hearers themselves. Consequently, we would be well advised to assume, in our dealings with the phenomenon, that this reality does indeed exist. This demands a readiness to accept the hearer's rightful ownership of their experiences, and to be fully open to the process of learning about the nature of their reality and their suffering. Those of us who have no personal experience of hearing voices can only form indirect judgements: we must rely on the hearers themselves for our information.

People in distress may try to make others partly responsible for their situation; in the case of voice-hearers, this tendency is increased when those around them label them as abnormal and therefore somehow no longer responsible for their behaviour. In our own experience, we have found that most voice-hearers are, in fact, quite capable of taking responsibility for their actions. Indeed, it is our impression that those who are encouraged to do so as far as they are able tend to cope better with their voices.

Some examples

Several times a week, 30-year old Mrs Pelupessy hears her doorbell ringing in the middle of the night. No one else has ever heard this sound, but it frightens her, and she always insists that her partner goes to see who is there. He never sees anybody, but she complains that he cannot have looked properly, and sends him back to make sure. The therapist confronts her with the fruitlessness of this procedure, and asks her to go downstairs herself the next time she hears the sound. She is told that her partner may accompany her if she is too frightened to go alone, but he is advised not to agree to go without her. She tries this, and the noises disappear within one week.

Anneloes, a 16-year old girl, hears the voice of an unknown lover, and keeps demanding that her parents search the area for this boy. When they refuse to do so, she accuses them of not loving her, and becomes aggressive. The therapist points out her responsibilities: because she is the only one who hears the boy, she should accept it as her problem and take the lead in any searching. She is asked to consider whether she might be mistaken, but is told that whenever she is convinced that she hears her secret lover and feels an urgent need to search for him, she may do so. With the help of some medication which she agrees to take, she recovers within a fortnight.

Relabelling

Sometimes self-esteem may be so low, and negative thoughts so severe and predominant, that the ground may have to be prepared for the use of positive relabelling techniques (see example). Before taking this course, it is essential to make absolutely certain that the proposed relabelling is acceptable to everyone involved (ie both the hearer of voices and his or her family): all concerned are invited to modify their behaviour in order to help with the acceptance and amplification of the relabelling.

Example

Mrs Wing was a severely depressed woman who heard voices accusing her of being a burden to her family. She did not respond to any supportive remarks or attempts at empathy, and could find nothing positive to say about herself; all efforts to encourage self-esteem only served to intensify her feelings of self-recrimination. In preparation for relabelling, she was asked whether she had any bad intentions, and - as hoped - denied that she did. This denial then enabled her to accept the relabelling, 'I have no bad intentions'. In the same way, she agreed to a list of several other 'I have no...' and 'I am not...' statements.

Statements like these can be incorporated into a behaviour-therapeutic intervention called counterstimulation. Each relabelling is written on a special card. Whenever the patient hears a negative voice, he or she shuffles the cards and reads loudly the positive statement about him or herself that is written on it.

Motivation

Feelings of helplessness and hopelessness may lead to inertia and apathy, and anyone falling prey to such a state needs fresh motivation for any action. One significant way of offering direct and appropriate motivation is by providing concrete information about the hearing of voices: its occurrence, its various forms, the different theories to account for it, and possible avenues for its management and treatment.

Any attempt at motivation requires the setting of goals; when these are not clear, it is all too easy for the situation to be confused by conflicting advice. One possible way of generating motivation is to clarify the aims of treatment by sub-dividing the voices into the categories of positive and negative; this immediately sets the clear agenda of activating the positive voices and minimizing the impact of the negative.

It is worth noting that when a person is very anxious or paranoid, he or she may tend to feel threatened by statements or instructions. In these cases, it is preferable to supply motivation by less direct means - for example, by asking questions rather than making statements. Such questions should be sufficiently sensitive to avoid any likelihood of avoidance.

Example

In the case of monitoring (see next paragraph), which is known to be successful in reducing the frequency of voice experiences, it is better not to ask whether or not the person would like to engage in the monitoring exercise; this allows them the immediate option of choosing not to do so, which may be detrimental to their well-being. This situation can be avoided by concentrating instead on negotiations about when to begin monitoring, how to timetable it, whether the practice is feasible for all aspects of the hearer's voice experiences, and so on. It will be noticed that in this kind of approach the choice is no longer between yes or no, but simply between more or less. For example, in the case of a woman who heard voices only in certain of the rooms in her house, we asked her to decide which was the best room in which to begin the monitoring.

Monitoring and detailed questioning

Many voice-hearers, and most hallucinating patients in general, appreciate being asked in detail about their experiences. Indeed, the hearers of voices appear to be quite eager to talk about their perceptions, provided the questioner avoids anything that might feel like interrogation, and provided they feel reassured that the normal rules for communication are being applied (ie opening the discussion with questions likely to stimulate comfortable response, and continuing with further questions to elucidate anything that remains unclear). Voice-hearers often report that being asked for a detailed account of their experiences makes them feel that they are being taken seriously; this, in turn, makes them feel very much more willing to co-operate with others concerned in the monitoring of the nature, frequency, and duration of the voices, the circumstances under which they occur, their own reactions to them, and those of other people (Cohen & Berk, 1985; Jenner, 1988).

This kind of monitoring by the hearer and, ideally, by others as well, can provide information that is essential to the selection of the most appropriate therapeutic intervention. Concurrent self-monitoring (ie as and when the voices are perceived) is of particular importance; in fact, this is the only variety that has been found to be effective in reducing the frequency of hallucinatory experiences (Glaister, 1985). Delayed, retrospective monitoring appears to be ineffective, and may even exacerbate the symptoms (Reybee & Kinch, 1973; Moser, 1974; Cohen & Berk, 1985; Jenner, 1988, 1991; Jenner & Feyen, 1991). The sub-division of voices into nasty, neutral and friendly categories can provide a useful framework, and may have a motivating effect that improves the efficacy of the monitoring process, as well as facilitating the acceptance of other types of intervention (Jenner, 1988).

Monitoring can be an extremely useful source of important information; equally valuable, however, is the assistance it may offer in the voice-hearer's efforts to regain some sense of mastery and control.

Example

John is 24 years old, and has heard voices for the last eight years. These voices were so terrifying for him that even in hospital he would bang his head, smash things, and threaten staff and other patients. One of his voices would order him to injure himself by throwing himself through a glass door, jumping out of the window, etc. These problems persisted in spite of several psychiatric hospital admissions (one of which was compulsory) and various therapeutic approaches. Not surprisingly, people were afraid of him, including the medical professionals.

After detailed questioning about the nature and frequency of his voices, his own reactions to them, and the reactions of others, John was asked to monitor these factors throughout the following week. It transpired that the voices appeared at sunset; accordingly, he was told to take whatever precautions he could against possible damage half an hour before sunset, and to take out his aggression on a cushion instead of on himself, other people, or the furniture. The nursing staff were given instructions to remind him when the time came, in case he forgot what he was supposed to do.

Within a week, John's destructive behaviour had reduced dramatically, and since then there has been not one of his previous outbursts. It is open to debate whether this was solely and entirely due to therapeutic intervention, but there is no doubt that a radical change took place.

Monitoring techniques

Even seriously psychotic patients appear to be able to undertake monitoring procedures, provided the instructions to be followed are tailored according to the circumstances. For example, it is hardly practical to expect a person who hears voices for most of the day to monitor them in detail; on the other hand, he or she can certainly start monitoring the voice-free periods. Even those who are unable to read or write can monitor their periods with and without voices by using a chess clock.

The form and timing of self-monitoring procedures are of crucial importance; as already noted, only concurrent monitoring is really effective. If the interval between experience and monitoring is too long, the monitoring may itself result in increased hallucinations (Cohen & Berk, 1985).

Some voice-hearers may object to the idea of monitoring, out of a fear that they might lose any positive, advisory voices. Personally, I am firmly convinced that it is for the hearer to decide whether he or she wants to get rid of the voices, and if so, which ones. Any premature attempt to persuade an individual to surrender voices that may be considered helpful runs the risk of having the therapeutic contact broken. Given a guarantee that this will not be pressed upon them, however, most patients have no objection to monitoring.

The reported positive results of monitoring not only aid therapeutic bonding, but also encourage cognitive processes. Both the monitoring itself and the associated detailed questioning oblige people to examine, evaluate and reconsider - subjectively, but within a guiding structure - the significance they attach to important events and experiences (see the section on Focusing in chapter 10).

Self-monitoring may be seen as a cognitive intervention that requires the focusing of attention, and thus indirectly forces a confrontation with reality. In this way, the monitoring process entails intensified exposure to the experiences concerned, and it may therefore be necessary to include appropriate anxiety management techniques in the therapy.

Exposure

The effectiveness of techniques involving exposure and satiation in the treatment of various anxiety disorders has been convincingly documented (Emmelkamp et al., 1989). When the therapist prescribes the symptom and encourages the voice-hearer to summon the voices deliberately, this may be understood as exposure. In this approach, the patient is requested to summon his or her voices consciously at agreed times, and to try to intensify them whenever they occur (Haley, 1963). Successful reduction and even elimination of visual and auditory hallucinations have been reported as the results of such summoning exercises (Haley, 1963; Jenner & Henneberg, 1982; Jenner, 1988; Jenner & Feyen, 1991).

The patient's first experiment in summoning voices should always be conducted in the therapist's presence, because his or her reactions may be crucial in reassuring both patient and relatives. When voices are successfully summoned, this is explained as a first sign of personal control; should the attempt be unsuccessful, it is suggested instead that this may prove to be a way of deliberately creating voice-free periods. Either way, exercises in summoning are capable of inducing positive feelings of control.

Support for relatives

Information, instruction, and support are crucial elements of family care. It has been demonstrated that reducing the levels of aggression, criticism and over-concern in the families of depressed and schizophrenic patients can make a significant contribution to the lowering of relapse rates (Liberman et al., 1980; Leff & Vaughn, 1985). Specialized help offered to relatives should include information about the disease, problem-focused advice, and the teaching of skills to manage stressful situations (see the section on Family Interaction in chapter 9).

We should not underestimate the difficulty of the tasks facing relatives of voice-hearers. They are likely to suffer extremely painful and contradictory emotions: although full of compassion and sorrow at the sight of someone they love haunted by voices and filled with despair, they must also struggle with feelings of rage and helplessness when the voices result in aggression, self-neglect, or alienation. They may find their attitudes fluctuating wildly between acceptance and rebellion. Every glimmer of hope quickly begins to fade, and feelings of guilt often multiply rapidly; these are particularly pernicious, and everything possible must be done to neutralize them. It cannot be said too often that relatives are in great need of support, understanding, and reassurance that they are not to blame.

Even therapists, with their professional skill to combine compassion and empathy with a distancing objectivity, have difficulty in responding helpfully and appropriately to psychotic phenomena; how, then, can we possibly expect relatives to behave consistently in the midst of all these agonizing emotions and thoughts? Is this a realistic or even a human demand? In the absence of any easier solution, one can only answer 'Yes'. The combination of compassion and reason appears to be the most helpful response to those who hear voices, and they, after all, are our first concern.

Voice Dialogue
Jurrien Koolbergen, therapist; A. P., client

The techniques of focusing and anxiety management have been shown to be particularly helpful in the effort to give voice-hearers greater control over their experiences in the here and now. The approaches associated with anxiety management are, above all, designed to reaffirm the hearer's personal power of speech in the presence of voices. Focusing, on the other hand, seeks to generate greater insight into the nature of the perceptions concerned and thus modify or transform their interpretation.

There is another important stage in this process of improved control, involving the enlargement of self-knowledge, particularly knowledge of one's own consciousness and its workings. In this regard, a method known as Voice Dialogue has recently been developed. We wanted to examine the benefits of this technique and determine whether the dialogues it purported to explore with voices might be more widely helpful. During 1991/92, we made contact with several voice-hearers and therapists who were willing to experiment with this therapeutic approach.

The method

Voice Dialogue is a system of training in self-knowledge and consciousness-alteration, based on a mind model developed by Dr Hal Stone and Dr Sidra Winkelman, both psychologists. The dialogue in question is conducted with the internal voice or voices stemming from our divided personalities; these may have their own will, emotional life, realm of thought, and distinctive voice. All of us are aware, when we stop to consider it, that a kind of conversation is continually taking place inside us as a matter of course. The everyday conscious mind, which we know as the ego, and which regulates our daily affairs and decision-making, is normally relatively undisturbed by this; sometimes, however, the ego may come to be so strongly identified with one particular part of the personality that the voices representing other important parts of ourselves cannot find expression. The Voice Dialogue method (which was not originally developed as a therapy, but which clearly has great potential as such) enables a question-and-answer dialogue to be conducted between the discussion leader - known as a facilitator - and the various sub-divisions of the client's personality.

In humanistic and transpersonal psychology, the concept of the split personality is well-known, but the term is generally used in a symbolic sense to describe aggregates of role-patterns. Stone and Winkelman, on the other hand, have been convinced by many years of experience that these split personalities are actually present in people, each sub-personality having its own full complement of psychological attributes. Stone and Winkelman have drawn on their experience to devise the model of consciousness on which Voice Dialogue is based.

This model is associated with what has come to be known as transformation psychology, a school of thought whose origins can be traced back to the 1960s. As a reaction to classical psychoanalysis on the one hand and behaviourism on the other, the so-called third avenue of humanistic psychology gained considerable ground in the 1960s, with Maslow as one of its leading proponents. In humanistic psychology, consciousness - for many years a neglected subject - was once again brought under full scrutiny at the fore of investigation, as was the oneness of mind and body. In particular, this trend emphasized growth and self-realization, and as a result of this new emphasis, many therapies directed at experiencing body-energy came into being.

Consciousness, however, is stratified, and so there are various levels of consciousness that may be experienced. Accordingly, this model also takes account of transcendental or spiritual experience, reflecting the influence of Eastern traditions such as yoga, in which one is said to emit consciousness as energy.

In the 1980s, transformation psychology developed in California, and offered a new synthesis of earlier trends with the aim of integrating both earthly and spiritual energies in the human consciousness. 'Embracing Heaven and Earth' - the telling title of Stone's first book - is at the very heart of transformation consciousness. In defining consciousness, Stone says:

Your perceptions are of the various 'Is' within yourself, which experience their own energies.

For him, consciousness is not only a matter of knowing, but is combined with a physical experience.

The experiment

The following is an excerpt from a paper given by a therapist and her client to a conference on hearing voices which was held in March 1992 in the city of Den Bosch (Netherlands). This consists of a report documenting ten therapeutic sessions whose objectives were very similar to the aims of Voice Dialogue:
- the voice-hearer must learn to know his or her 'Is' or voices, and participate in their energy (consciousness model);
- there must be transformation of those voices or 'Is' which hinder well-being or growth;
- the ego - the executive function - must become more conscious, enabling the individual to become a freer agent and have a wider range of choices.

Client

Because I have arrived at quite a sound foundation for my life, I felt strong enough to undergo this process. I had friends to fall back on, a job which gave my life structure, and the confidence that, with Mrs Koolbergen, I was in safe hands. All this gave me the reassurance that was essential to me - that a psychosis would not be precipitated. As will be seen, my need for this reassurance was to come to the surface again during the therapy itself.

Therapist

Before starting the first session, the client and I agree that we will always begin the sessions by summoning the controller-protector, one of the most important sub-personalities in Voice Dialogue, and end them in the same way. We also agree that the controller-protector may intervene at any time during a session if anything is not to his or her liking. This will, in fact, happen several times.

Client

Because my youth did not always go as well as it might, my controller has inadequate energy, and needs to develop more powerfully and effectively. A controller is an energy which oversees everything, and permits or disallows other energies. He controls the whole being. If the controller fails to develop sufficient insight, then another energy develops in compensation: this is a masculine energy which stands for structure and regulation. From time to time, this masculine energy will take over the controller's function when the latter is not functioning well. This ensures that there is still effective protection against any other energies that might enter my spirit and manifest themselves as voices. These energies often originate from other people (split personalities).

Therapist

From the very first session, the client seems surprised at the energies of the various sub-personalities that intervene. The controller, however, finds it very difficult to allow some of the more negative voices to finish what they have to say; he explains that to allow them to continue is to give them too much attention. Later on in the sessions, intermediaries will come upon the scene to express the negative feelings of the original voices, but the rest of the time the negative voices speak for themselves. The client distinguishes clearly between negative voices originating within herself and those which come from outside. (In the terms of Voice Dialogue, those of the first type may derive from the inner critic, while those of the second may represent a totally disowned self, a cast-off personality, although in Voice Dialogue we can never exclude the possibility that any such voice actually comes from outside.)

Client

During one session, we also spoke with the fragmented personalities of other people, which had split themselves off as a result of being pushed aside or denied. This helped me to recognize that my voices did not come solely from inside myself, but also from outside. This was also responsible for lot of conflict between my social workers and myself.

Therapist

In the second session, the client describes how some higher energies help her to resist the negative voices. She views these energies as a sort of spirit guide, and her controller now welcomes their appearances during our sessions. They show a good deal of wisdom, and often manifest themselves in later sessions to explain or correct things. Amongst other things, they say they cannot always help the client because she herself must become strong.

There is evidence of some kind of polarity - in this case, between lower and higher energies - the controller asks for an opening to be made for a third voice, which then usually occurs spontaneously. This is usually a very cheerful energy, which says how glad it is to be able to appear once in a while.

In the third session, the voice also speaks of fear, particularly that of precipitating a fresh psychosis. Here, the controller directly addresses my own controller to ascertain the safety of the situation, and also says that the negative voice from outside the client has been terribly difficult during that week. I propose that we allow the negative voice to be fully present during the sessions provided it lies dormant during the rest of the week. I explain once again that it is better for an energy such as him to receive all the attention he seeks. (One of the principles of Voice Dialogue is to stretch an energy in such a way that the tension goes out of it.)

Client

Things often went well in the sessions, but the moment I sat at home alone, things were very different. A lot of the time it was a real struggle to remain by myself, in spite of the agreement I had made with my various energies that each of them would help whenever there was too much weakening. For example, when the feeling energy was having a difficult time of it and not functioning well, the energy of justice took over its function and protected the feeling energy. This process of co-operation was important for proper protection.

The divided energies from outside myself had a habit of coming in without warning, and could drain me of strength. From the moment my protection - and conscious self-protection - improved, a fight began in earnest. My own, conscious contribution to my protection was achieved by deliberately closing off my aura, which was something I learned to do in a course that I took with a paranormally gifted woman. An aura is an energy field around you which can, with concentration, be opened and closed at will. I do this by thinking, for example, of a wall around me, or by projecting a grid between myself and another person. The more I do this, the more effective it becomes.

Through being conscious of all the energies, I also obtained a better overview of what was going on, especially of when something was near me. I would feel a pressure building up inside me, and would get rather confused and dizzy, with my consciousness disappearing to some extent. At times like this I would consciously make use of my protection; previously, I had never been able to do this on my own for very long.

At the beginning of this new phase of strong protection, it was a great struggle to make it completely clear that when I said 'No', I really meant it - the energies did everything they could to put my resistance to the test. By sticking to my guns, though, and with my controller and other energies sending positive thoughts, I was successful. As a result, the divided energies could no longer just arbitrarily enter through the gap and stay as long as they liked, and eventually they detached themselves. Often I would hear them say, 'Not the light, let's leave' (these were two energies which combined together). Looking back, it was like living on a knife-edge; there were times when I felt confident of being able to carry on, but there were others times when my confidence failed me. In the end, though, I was the winner, and could stand my ground against the energies. My 'No' was finally 'No'.

Therapist

In the fourth session, the controller reports that the negative voice has indeed slept, as agreed, but fitfully. The controller is in full agreement that this voice should be given no elbow-room, and instead allow a loving voice - as the client calls it - to speak up. This dwells on issues like affection and desertion, and on what she needs and lacks.

In the fifth session, the first transformation takes place. A voice that has previously been negative and disdainful appears, and maintains that he is sadly misunderstood. By the end of the discussion, he is made to feel that he is understood, and that the validity of his opinions is accepted. He christens himself the Righteous One.

In the sixth session, the Righteous One returns to offer himself as the champion of the client's feeling energy, as well as of others. He even says that he himself is vulnerable, and that he has always felt himself to be a victim, as a result of the controller not being assertive enough.

The second negative voice of the inner critic also presents himself, and says he now feels less vengeful; he will behave more subtly and with more humour from now on. This is the start of a second transformation.

In the seventh session, the client says in the preliminary discussion that she feels better, less solitary and more together. She can also read again. Both negative inner voices have become positive, and the negative voice from outside is now somewhat in the background. The paranormal energy, however, still manifests herself; according to the client, this represents a splitting-off of her feeling energy. This is problematic, because this energy wanders all around incessantly, collecting information. Fortunately, though, her controller is more in control now.

In the eighth session - which is delayed for a week while I am ill - we suddenly find ourselves in a deadlock: the client wants to stop the sessions. We use this one to explore her various motives, and she admits that she is afraid of the sessions ending. She can just about cope, but there is a lot happening and she is worried about what will happen if we suddenly stop this work. She is also experiencing a feeling of desertion (which is familiar to her). On the other hand, she has consulted others and been advised to stop, now that things are more or less under control. But the negative voice from outside, although manageable during the sessions, still makes life difficult for her at home, and this is a cause of concern to her. Consciousness, she says, is painful.

Once she is assured that the sessions will continue for a while after the initial ten have been completed, in order to round things off properly, she chooses to carry on.

In the ninth session, things become clearer about the negative energy emanating from outside. According to the client, this has become very much worse, and continues to try to influence her in a negative way: he is associated with hatred, mistakes, guilt feelings and punishment, and spreads confusion when she refuses to give in to him.

In the tenth session, the controller appears and says that this past week has also been dominated by confusion that he is unable to master.

The ten sessions are now up. It is obvious that the negative voice from outside, which is experienced by the client as either dictatorial or confusing, is still in force and has not yet disappeared or been transformed.

Therapist's conclusions

From this series of sessions, I tentatively conclude that experiments like this have real meaning, but that there are probably real risks involved. Consequently:

- in addition to being a trained Voice Dialogue trainer, the therapist must also be clinically trained;
- the client must be provided with good professional support in his or her home situation;
- the experiment must have a time-limit within which matters can be suitably rounded off.

Client's conclusions

As I can now say 'No' clearly, I am better able to impose limits in my own life. I want to set clear boundaries for the people around me; in the past, I always avoided this, because I could not handle the aggression which I felt arising whenever I tried to set limits. This made me mentally and physically ill and quite wretched. Because I have learned to close myself off properly, I can now cope well. As a result of these new limits, some so-called friends have fallen away.

Another positive change is that I am now better at resolving and assimilating old blockages and traumas, and this means I am less confused and can see more clearly where I stand in my life. I am still involved with Voice Dialogue to this day, and hope to go even further on my journey of discovery in the world of voices. Thank you for your attention.

Therapist's postscript
At the end of the ten sessions, the client and I had agreed to conduct a number of additional sessions until she reached an equilibrium. In these we concentrated on the controller, the vulnerable energy (the victim), and the negative voice from outside. Our aim was to enable the client to handle her troubles better, and also to bring about a change in the negative voice.

In the first three sessions, the controller thundered violently at the negative energy, commanding it to be gone. This was unsuccessful, and the negative voice kept on bothering the client. Together we tried to find all sorts of creative outlets for him, such as writing and painting, but the client seemed afraid of the negative implications of this.

After the third session, the client suddenly came up with a tactic of her own invention: whenever the negative energy/voice appeared, she listened to him and gave him free rein, and then sucked him dry. This seemed to do the trick; according to the client, the energy then collapsed and was defenceless. The success of this approach enabled her to feel strong enough, after the sixth session, to carry on unaided.

The elimination of a stubborn voice/energy may demand the use of a special ritual, rather like those associated with mourning; in this case, it happened spontaneously. At the time of writing, there is no follow-up to report, but for me this was an eye-opening experience.

Rehabilitation
Marius Romme

Hearing voices is not a purely personal phenomenon: it is intimately bound up with the hearer's social environment. His or her place in this environment is often negatively affected by the experience, and this means that due attention must be paid to the process of rehabilitation. This and other social interventions are essential to provide the proper milieu in which the strategies and activities discussed in this book can flourish. The aim of rehabilitation is to ensure the best possible circumstances for the individual's development, thus allowing the

therapies employed to bear fruit. The essential ingredients in this process are:
- quality relationships (for example, with the social worker);
- quality information;
- receptivity to emotions;
- social autonomy;
- trusting relationships (significant others).

Quality relationships

As we have already observed, the hearers of voices are understandably averse to interpretations which deny their experiences and perceptions. It is important to them that others listen to them with genuine interest and concern, rather than patronizingly or purely for the purpose of acquiring data. The relationship must be dependable, and founded on equality.

To illustrate the centrality of these qualities to a good therapeutic relationship, I would like to quote an ex-patient (see Twelfth Contributor's story in chapter 8 for his full account):

Only once in 15 years of psychiatric intervention, and at the age of 36, was I able to find someone who was willing to listen. This proved a turning point for me, and from this I was able to break out of being a victim and start owning my experience. This nurse actually found time to listen to my experiences and feelings. She always made me feel welcome, and would make arrangements so we would not be disturbed. She would switch off her bleeper and take her phone off the hook, and sometimes, as there were people outside her room, she would close the blinds. These actions made me feel at ease. She would sit to one side of me instead of across a desk. She told me that what we said was confidential, but that there were some exceptions, so I could decide what to reveal. Slowly, as trust grew between us, I was able to tell her about the abuse, but also about the voices. Sometimes when I was describing what happened to me, she would tell me that it was hurting her and she needed a break. At last, I had found someone who recognized the pain I was feeling. She helped me realize that my voices were a part of me, and had a purpose and validity. Over a six-month period, I was able to develop a basic strategy for coping. The most important thing she did was that she was honest - honest in her motivations and in her responses to what I told her.

I would like to say that maybe other mental health/social work professionals could learn something from her approach:

- be honest about your motivation and the reasons for your intervention;

- *establish ground rules at the start;*
- *provide a safe environment, and keep it safe;*
- *don't force the agenda - provide people with a breathing space so they can decide what to bring and what not to bring;*
- *be honest about your own feelings - this is not rejection, but a sign that you are also alive;*
- *let the person decide what the goals should be and say if they want changes.*

Quality information

In order to understand and help someone, and to know what that person wants, it is essential for both parties to be fully informed. It is therefore a good idea to begin with a comprehensive inventory of the number of voices, their gender, age and characteristics, to whom they belong, how they are organized, what influence they have on the hearer, what they say, how the hearer reacts to this, what has happened since they were first heard, and so on. This gives both the social worker and the voice-hearer something to think about, and this process of reflection is a vital precursor to the formation of an approach to the voices.

It takes considerable thought on both sides to arrive at an agreement about the nature and objectives of their relationship in this approach, but this does not preclude the setting of short-term goals, which are generally particularly concerned with anxiety management. Reducing anxiety and gaining even a small degree of control obviously makes thinking considerably easier. Other aids to facilitate thinking may also be used, eg writing assignments, the keeping of a diary, and focusing exercises. (For more information about all these techniques, see the relevant sections earlier in this chapter.)

This process of thought and reflection is designed, slowly but surely, to improve the quality of insight into the significance of the voices in the hearer's life. It is therefore important to identify the situations, emotions and persons associated with the occurrence or intensification of voices - the so-called triggers. Triggers represent the circumstances which encapsulate the voices. The voices seem to react to something recognizable: they may recall a traumatic experience (flashbacks), interfere in a situation (assignments) or protect the hearer (prohibitions). Triggers can often be difficult to identify. Many hearers have found it a great help to compose a life-history in which the voices are cast as the leading characters (an ego-document).

It is particularly important, in these explorations, to recognize metaphoric or symbolic meaning. Consider, for example, the case of a voice that speaks like a robot. A robot is suggestive of strength without emotion, a force that is difficult to resist or overcome, and may therefore be the symbol of a person without fear. The robot becomes a metaphor for dealing with emotions; if it is a frightening figure to the hearer, it may also be a metaphor for coping with fear. In such cases, it is vital that the fear of fear be focused upon in the discussions, and the hearer must then be taught to cope with this fear. Another example might be the voice of a small child: this may signify being treated like a child, or suggest a traumatic childhood. In the first instance, the voices would be likely to assign childish tasks, while in the second, the voice might be expected to be characterized as being a specific age correlating to a particularly difficult experience in the hearer's own childhood.

Metaphors are often such that their meaning is stumbled upon only by chance: however concretely and forcefully they are rendered, they may not be readily identifiable. There is no dictionary of metaphors to help with this difficulty, but there are plenty of well-documented examples to be found in various books, such as those on multiple personalities. Focusing can also be of great help on the journey of discovery through the landscapes of metaphor and trigger.

Receptivity to emotions

In their dealings with the hearers of voices, family, friends and helpers alike must be receptive, and prepared to acknowledge their own emotions and the ways in which they go about coping with them. This receptivity entails a sensitivity to the following issues:

Empathy

This involves listening with appropriate emotion, to show that the fear of the voices is felt and appreciated, but that this is no reason to run away. This is not to say that the helper should encourage anxiety but nor should he or she avoid the display of any emotion when extremely unpleasant experiences are recounted. Appropriate human reactions on the helper's part allow the voice-hearer to admit more easily to the severity of the emotions involved, and to feel that his or her turmoil is quite understandable under the circumstances.

When the voices are very threatening, the helper should still try to elicit a description of the experience. Talking things over can help establish which aspects of the phenomenon are grounded in reality and which are imaginary; remaining silent can only serve to reinforce the idea that the problem is entirely the hearer's problem. Proper discussion can also enable the hearer to gain insight into the power structure of the voices; this power exists only to the extent that the hearer attributes it to the voices, however persuasively he or she may insist that it is unlimited.

Confrontation

Voices can serve to protect the hearer against certain emotions inspiring avoidance and flight; under these circumstances, it is clearly not possible for them to learn to cope with such emotions. A helper must therefore appreciate that confrontation with these emotions may be essential to progress, and must not be side-stepped, even if this seems to run the risk of precipitating a violent reaction. There should, of course, be proper provision of emergency measures in case of such a crisis. For example, a female student first started to hear voices at the age of 23. During the previous year she had undergone hazing, an initiation ceremony for first-year students. (In the Netherlands, some student organizations have a custom of seeking to shock new students over sexual matters during the induction period.) She had been thrown into confusion by the confrontations involved in this ritual, and had avoided sexuality ever since. Even after several years of help, including a couple of years of out-patient treatment with us, she continued with this evasion.

Ever since the onset of this problem, she had consistently embraced the role of patient, and saw this as her future. She could not see herself finding a partner, having children or holding down a job. This was such a severe handicap that we confronted her with the lifestyle she had chosen, and with what we felt to be the underlying problem: her fear of her own sexuality. This confrontation triggered absolute uproar from the voices; the woman became psychotic, and fled to her parents home, as though she might somehow find protection there from her own emotions. This spontaneous reaction confirmed our suspicions of a sexual problem.

A violent reaction like this calls for special support and guidance. Clearly, these confrontations should not be undertaken without meticulous preparation, but it is vitally important that helpers should not collude with their patient in evading a problem out of fear of psychosis. Indeed, a psychotic reaction may prove to be extremely instructive for both patient and helper.

Acknowledgement

Voices may refer directly to situations and experiences, past or present, which inspire shame, fear or horror; they may, for example, be associated with aggressive sexual abuse which is too painful to recall. (In such cases, it may be particularly tempting to sanction the denial or repression of the memory, given the unpredictability of individual reactions to the dredging up of painful material, but as we have observed, this is unwise.)

Unfortunately, painful events do not always reside in the past: sometimes they persist into the present, and then they are even more difficult to inquire into. In the process of exploring these, the helper will occasionally find him or herself reluctantly involved in uncharted territory, and must therefore be prepared for any eventuality in daring to feel the voice-hearer's emotions as well as his or her own reactions to these.

It can be difficult not to flinch from this challenge, but full acknowledgement of the hearer's experience is all-important. When a situation is glossed over, the threatening emotions will disappear from consciousness, but will continue to be verbalized by heavily-charged voices.

We know, for example, a mother whose son had hanged himself. After his death, the son regularly called out to her, asking her to join him. In this situation, if the help offered did not fully acknowledge the content of the voice's message, there might have been great danger of an eventual suicide attempt by the mother. Consequently, we explored the nature of this message before tackling the mourning process.

Social autonomy

Hearing voices is a very penetrating experience, and it demands considerable strength and stamina for the hearers to retain control over their conduct. This is scarcely helped by the fact that society often shows them little understanding or tolerance, so that they are all too prone to isolation. The maintenance or development of personal power requires proper social autonomy: in other words, the granting of a place within society that will help to foster identity and independence. Amongst other things, this entails the full provision of social services such as independent housing, some kind of occupation, and a degree of financial independence. These are the elements that enable individuals to structure their daily lives and build relationships, and are the foundations of social identity. The voice-hearers who tell their stories in chapter 8 were all successful in meeting these conditions: they received help and support from friends, family and helpers, but ultimately they took responsibility for themselves.

In the process of developing a social identity, there may be unexpected problems, as with one voice-hearer whom I had known for many years. When this woman first came to me, she lived in her own house (with two large dogs), but in a neighbourhood whose social norms and values were alien to her. I explained this problem to her family, and with their help the woman moved to an area more appropriate to her age and social background. This move proved enormously helpful in stimulating her development and sense of self.

Another obstacle to the acquisition of social autonomy may be seen in those who remain living in the parental home for too long. This is as true for voice-hearers as it is for any other adolescent; when one's dependence on others is excessive, it is difficult to learn to make decisions independently, and thus to take personal responsibility and develop one's own identity. The parents of voice-hearers are sometimes heard to observe that their children's lack of any real sense of responsibility is due to an incapacity for independence, but our experience is that they are very often capable of leading quite normal, independent lives, even during so-called psychotic episodes.

The privacy offered by having one's own house or flat can also be an important element in the development of a sense of social autonomy, although it is essential to distinguish clearly between privacy and isolation. As is the case for us all, it is crucial for people who hear voices to have relationships, to maintain contact with others and to engage in social activities. What we are speaking of here is the ability to be master or mistress of one's own living-space without interference from others. It may, however, be wise in the first instance to give priority to those things likely to avoid any danger of isolation: for some, this may mean training in social skills, while others may need to develop an active interest in expressive pursuits such as dance, music, drawing, etc., or to engage in some kind of study.

Given the way our society is organized, any sense of social autonomy is particularly dependent on having some kind of employment; this makes it especially important for the hearers of voices to be able to retain their jobs or find other suitable occupation (see chapter 8 for some good examples. The evidence suggests that the job or activity concerned must allow scope for exercising some responsibility, in accordance with the temperament of the individual. Hearing voices can be debilitating, and often leaves the hearer with only limited energy to create such opportunities for him or herself. As we saw in chapter 8, given the right circumstances, many voice-hearers show themselves to be willing and able to adjust imaginatively to their working conditions when these are flexible and allow room for their creativity.

Trusting relationships

Almost all those voice-hearers who have learned to live with the experience describe how important it was for them to have a friend, partner or family member who listened to them, accepted them, and made them feel safe. What matters here is not the number of these relationships, but the quality: even one such can offer a real sense of security during periods when the voices are especially overwhelming.

Finding appropriate support during difficult phases can be something of an art. Even those voice-hearers who manage to avoid recourse to psychiatric treatment of any kind report that there are times when they are overwhelmed by voices and run the risk of hospital admission and long-term treatment. Those who describe their experiences in chapter 8 have all, in one way or another, protected themselves against coming to the attention of the medical authorities. For example, in London, the organization Lambeth Link offers the facility of a rented flat where voice-hearers can stay a night or a couple of days and be given support by other members of the network who themselves hear voices.

Not everyone, however, is fortunate enough to have such a network at their disposal; in any case, it is perhaps just as important to find ways of feeling safe in one's own milieu. Any campaign of rehabilitation must therefore include adequate information for voice-hearers' families, partners, friends, acquaintances, and anyone else with whom they may have significant contact. Such information-sharing should include the following:

- discussing the fear and prejudice about the voices that may exist within the family or circle of friends;
- obtaining from the family a record of the duration of periods when the voices are overwhelming, in order to establish that so-called psychotic episodes do not actually last that long. Given that extreme emotions may closely resemble psychotic episodes, it is critical to become more aware of the temporary nature of these phases;
- discussing the aims of any possible treatment, to ensure co-operation (see the section on Anxiety Management in chapter 10);
- accepting that everyday reality is not the sole concern, and that the hearer of voices needs the time and space (often literally) for preoccupation with the voices;
- giving confidence to the hearer, and jointly seeking solutions appropriate to his or her experiences. This helps to avoid conflict, and can therefore have a positive effect on the duration of domination by the voices (see the section on Family Interactions and Psychosis in chapter 9);
- after any overwhelming phase, jointly investigating what the voice-hearer has experienced as pleasant or unpleasant reactions from his surroundings, in order for all concerned to learn from the experience (see also Family Interactions and Psychosis in chapter 9);
- determining the helpfulness or otherwise of particular reactions in the improvement of control over conduct, so that any subsequent episode can be dealt with more effectively (see Family Interactions and Psychosis in chapter 9).

It will be clear that the rehabilitative measures discussed here are all based on principles of equality and on the involvement of the voice-hearer's own experiences in the helping process. In this way, any support that may be offered is always designed to avoid encouraging dependence, and to enhance the possibility of a growth in self-awareness and self-determination.

Hearing voices represents an enormous challenge: a challenge which can be regarded either as a threat which renders one powerless or as a teacher capable of empowering one to withstand the trials of life. However, the development of personal power can only take place when the immediate surroundings provide the appropriate stimulation and real opportunities within society at large. The ultimate objective is the full development of a personal identity as one who happens to hear voices.

Medication and Hearing Voices
Adriaan Honig

Introduction
We have felt it appropriate to incorporate this chapter on medication because voice-hearers who turn to psychiatry for help are so often prescribed drugs. The frequency of this response is the natural consequence of most psychiatrists' interpretation of the phenomenon. Hearing voices may be a sign or symptom of a variety of psychiatric illnesses, each of which is also accompanied by other, more or less specific signs. If you go to see a psychiatrist, he or she will question you about these signs, and conclude which illness is most probable in your case. Based on this information, advice will be given on medication. This chapter attempts to put the reader in the psychiatrist's position, in the hope of helping you to understand why, when you say you hear voices, he or she asks particular questions and prescribes particular medications. Our aim is to make the psychiatrist's behaviour and actions more understandable and predictable, and perhaps make some contribution to the development of a more trusting relationship and better treatment.

From a psychiatric point of view, there are two types of problem that may be indicated by the hearing of voices: a psychosis or a neurosis.

In psychosis, hearing voices is often accompanied by confusion or fear - a fear that can be so overwhelming that the hallucinator is either totally petrified or intensely restless. The voices heard may be so forceful that their commands, bizarre or harmful though they may be, have to be obeyed, so that the hearer is completely overpowered.

In neurosis, one generally remains capable of keeping the voices at bay, although sometimes only with considerable effort. One is not especially confused, nor entirely at the mercy of the voices, and the experience does not usually prevent the pursuit of normal daily activities.

We will examine the various types of medication used in both psychosis and neurosis, as well as their side-effects, and offer some suggestions of possible strategies when such medication is advised.

Hearing voices and psychosis

Although psychosis may sometimes persist for a prolonged period of time, it is often a temporary or even transient state. The state of psychosis may be characterized by any of three types of symptom: a disturbance of orderly thinking (confusion); a disturbance of perception (hearing voices); and a disturbance of volition (the power to use one's own will). When a person is psychotic, he or she is so taken over by the voices that they dominate his or her whole life, and everything else has to make way for them. Only the reality of the voices exists; the mundane world - which for others is the only real world - is blurred. The psychotic's world has changed radically, and as a consequence his or her behaviour changes, too. This is a world in which the voices have taken control.

There is no special blood or X-ray investigation to help with the diagnosis of a psychosis; the doctor is almost entirely dependent on the information given by the patient and his or her family and friends. Questions which might be asked when a psychosis is suspected include:

- Have you ever been convinced that you were controlled by some external force which makes you do things or think things not of your own free will?
- Have you ever been convinced that a radio or TV programme was transmitting special messages meant only for you, or that a particular programme was meant only for you?
- Have you ever been convinced that somebody could read your thoughts or take thoughts out of your head?

As yet, there is no consensus on one single cause for psychosis, but whatever else may be the case, it seems likely that there must be a clear initial vulnerability. This may be related to, and triggered by, such things as a genetic predisposition (as in schizophrenia), or by other vulnerability factors (see Figure 1).

Figure 1: Vulnerability to psychosis

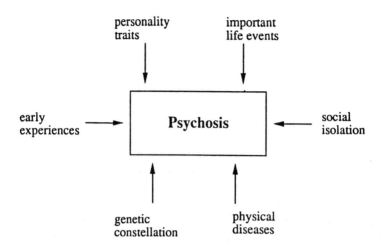

One current explanation of what happens in psychosis is the filter theory. Under normal conditions we are aware of many things which happen inside and around us, but perceive only those impressions and impulses which we regard as important or necessary; we unconsciously filter the daily bombardment of emotionally-loaded information which is directed at us. This capacity to filter information is decreased during a psychosis. Not surprisingly, this disturbance is often accompanied by fear.

One consequence of this broken filter is that the individual is flooded with impulses which make it very difficult to think clearly. In such circumstances, the person is often accused of talking rubbish, of telling a story with no beginning or end, of rambling, and so on. Another sign of a disturbed thinking process may be that the person is unable - perhaps for hours or even days on end - to express or formulate thoughts. He or she may also develop fixed ideas which are not shared by anyone else, and which are held on to in spite of all evidence to the contrary - the so-called delusions. There may also be disturbances in perception (hearing, seeing, smelling and feeling), such as hearing voices. In psychiatry, these phenomena are defined as perceptions which arise in the absence of an external stimulus; for this designation to apply, the voices heard must be perceived as ego-dystonic (ie not arising from inside the hallucinator), clear in quality, and situated in the outside world.

In a person who is vulnerable to psychosis and who subsequently develops a psychosis as the result of some trigger, there may be some dysfunction of the brain. The brain is a bundle of complex nerve cells and nerve tracts; between the nerve tracts there is a continuous exchange of chemicals called neurotransmitters, and the normal balance between some of these is disturbed in psychosis. This may result in hallucinations, disordered thinking and fear. Certain drugs are capable of restoring this balance and so decreasing psychotic symptoms such as hearing voices; these drugs are called neuroleptics or major tranquillizers.

Medication in psychosis

There are more than 30 different neuroleptics. The first, chlorpromazine (Largactil), was discovered 40 years ago and is still widely used in the UK. Neuroleptics are not addictive. They often result in the complete disappearance of psychotic symptoms, although this may sometimes take days or even weeks. In some cases, the only effect of a neuroleptic is an increased distancing from psychotic symptoms, whereby delusions and hallucinations fade but remain present in the background.

Neuroleptics produce a partial or complete restoration of the broken filter. Stimuli are once again filtered, but sometimes with the difference that they are completely or partially stripped of their emotional charge (see Figure 2). The neuroleptic also has a positive effect on fixed and false ideas (delusions), such as the conviction that one is being spied upon, or that someone is taking the thoughts out of one's head or broadcasting those thoughts on radio or TV. The neutralizing effect on emotions may lead to feelings of being too distanced from the outside world, dulled, unable to take any initiative, or even of complete apathy. On the other hand, however, feelings such as these may also be a sign of the very disease for which the neuroleptic has been prescribed. In schizophrenia, for example, apathy and loss of initiative are core (negative) symptoms.

These effects sometimes cause people to stop taking medication altogether, but not all neuroleptics have the same positive or adverse effects: these are variable, mostly reversible, and differ from one person to the next. However, should any of these unpleasant effects be experienced, it is important to try to find a specific neuroleptic in a specific dose which diminishes them as much as possible without reducing the antipsychotic effects.

Figure 2: Effects of neuroleptics

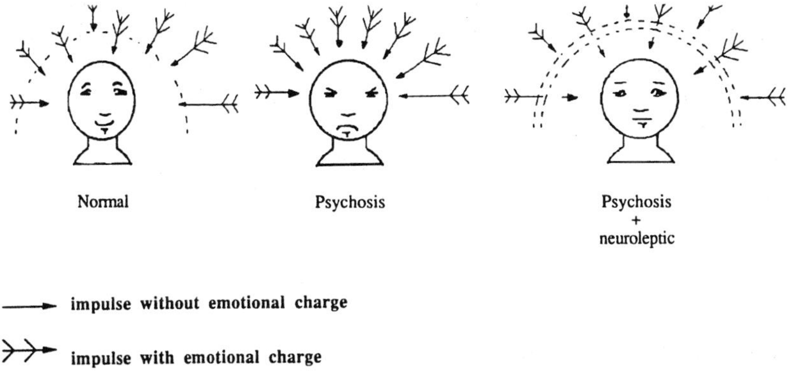

Normal   Psychosis   Psychosis
                                                          +
                                                      neuroleptic

———▶ impulse without emotional charge

≫▶ impulse with emotional charge

Whenever a psychosis remits (lifts), there may be a risk of symptoms recurring, and it is therefore important to learn to recognize the early signs of a renewed episode. These may follow a consistent pattern of disturbed sleep, increased irritability, poor concentration, a tendency to social withdrawal, more intense hearing of voices, or imminent loss of control. Whenever these signs occur, it may be helpful to start taking a neuroleptic again, and possible triggers which might spark off a renewed period of illness may be identified. It is also advisable to discuss with your doctor what medication has been of most help to you in the past. It is not always necessary to take neuroleptics continuously for a prolonged period, although in the case of schizophrenia a maintenance dose of a neuroleptic may be very helpful. In general, the prescription of medication to any individual patient remains custom-made.

Some neuroleptics which are regularly prescribed are:

Trade name		Chemical name	Remarks
Largactil	....	chlorpromazine	...tablet/by injection
Haldol	....	haloperidol	...tablet/long acting by injection
Orap	....	pimozide	...tablet
Modecate	....	fluphenazine decanoate	...long acting by injection
Semap	....	penfluridol	...long acting by tablet
Depixol	....	flupenthixol decanoate	...tablet/long acting by injection

Management of side-effects

Side-effects are the unwanted and unintended effects of drugs, and can be of great distress to a patient. With neuroleptics, these generally diminish after one or two weeks of use. The most frequently-occurring side-effects of neuroleptics are: coarse tremor, stiffening of the limbs, restlessness, fidgeting, rocking of the body, and dizziness. Also, though less frequently: blurred vision, dryness of the mouth, increased appetite, and sexual problems. When side-effects occur, one or a combination of the following strategies may be useful:

- wait and see; side-effects often diminish after the first week of using a particular medication;
- diminish the dose of the neuroleptic, or change to another type;
- add a specific tablet for the side-effects: Kemadrin (procyclidine) or Disipal (orphenadrine).

The tablets mentioned above diminish some side-effects such as stiffening of the limbs and restlessness; others, however, such as blurred vision or dryness of the mouth, may be worsened by these medications. Another disadvantage is that they somewhat diminish the antipsychotic action of the neuroleptic. For these reasons, it is generally wise to take a minimum of tablets for the treatment of side-effects.

If taken continuously over a period of at least six months neuroleptic medication might cause an adverse effect which psychiatrists call tardive dyskinesia. This condition consists of involuntary movements particularly of the tongue and facial muscles but can also involve other parts of the body. The risk of tardive dyskinesia increases if long-term neuroleptic use is combined with medication such as Kemadrin and Disipal (as mentioned above). Unfortunately there is no treatment to reverse this long-term side-effect.

Hearing voices and neurosis

As we have already noted, hallucinators in this second group are normally able to keep at a distance from their voices, and are sometimes even capable of continuing regular daily activities to some extent. By neurosis, we mean a state in which there are signs of psychiatric illness without disturbance of thinking processes or of contact with reality, and in which reality-testing is still in force. Reality-testing means you know that what you hear or think is generated inside yourself, and only heard by yourself: in other words, you question yourself, and not the outside world, on the nature of what you perceive. You may also not be completely overwhelmed by these new perceptions. As explained elsewhere (in the section on The Dissociated Personality in chapter 9), causal factors in this condition are believed to stem from emotional conflicts rather than disturbed brain functioning.

Some psychiatric conditions involving hallucinations are also called dissociative disorders. Dissociation literally means breaking up; in these conditions, the unconscious is splitting off or repressing something (often a severe traumatic incident), so that the accompanying feeling or memory is not perceived by the self. This repression is a natural defence mechanism, but one which may, in time, start to lead its own life, and end up being more damaging than helpful.

Dissociative disorders are often initiated by severe, threatening events in the past, such as car accidents, rape, etc. (see the sections on The Dissociated Personality and Trauma in chapter 9), when the person defends him or herself from an intolerable but inescapable situation by splitting off parts of the self. The part of the self (ego) that is split off may, for instance, be that which is not under threat or being attacked at that moment; once the event itself is over, the split part may re-attach itself to the rest of the ego, or it may continue to lead a separate life (see Figure 3). If the split persists (idée fixe), the separated part may identify itself to the other parts of the ego by means of a voice, which may then recur during times of stress in later life, or in any renewed confrontation with the original frightening event. These situations may be accompanied by the same emotions that were experienced during the actual trauma.

Figure 3: Mechanism of neurosis

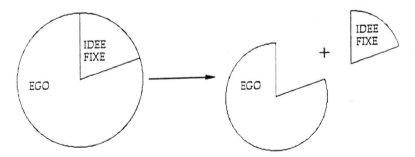

Questions which you might be asked when a dissociative state is thought to be present are:
- Have you ever had the experience of being unable to remember what you have done, for hours or days at a time?
- Have you ever found yourself in a place, not knowing how you got there or what you were supposed to do there?
- Have you ever felt that you were watching yourself from somewhere outside of your body, as if you were seeing yourself from a distance or watching a film of yourself?

Medication and neurosis
Unlike psychosis, neurosis only demands medication of a supportive nature, aimed at reducing the feelings of fear as well as any accompanying physical sensations (shortness of breath, palpitations, etc.). The drugs most commonly used in these circumstances are sedatives, which are generally prescribed only for shorter intervals of time (maximum 14 days continuously) due to the possibility of addiction. Short-acting sedatives are often preferred, because the chemicals in the longer-acting types tend to accumulate in the body and progressively increase the effects of sedation.

Apart from various sorts of benzodiazepines (eg Valium), other forms of medication, such as neuroleptics, are also sometimes prescribed. In these cases, though, these are used not for their (light) antipsychotic properties but for their sedative effect. Their major advantage is that even prolonged use is not thought to cause addiction.

Medications prescribed may include:

Trade name	Chemical name	Type
Serax	oxazepam	sedative
Ativan	lorazepam	sedative
Insidon	opipramol	antidepressant
Melleril	thioridazine	neuroleptic
Neulactil	pericyazine	neuroleptic
Sparine	promazine	neuroleptic

Common adverse effects of sedatives include drowsiness, impaired reactions, flattening of affect, and occasionally paradoxical disinhibition. As in psychosis, the drug of choice depends very much on the individual situation, and requires careful discussion between patient and doctor.

Conclusion
The hearing of voices may occur in both psychoses and neuroses, and it is therefore important for a psychiatrist to determine which is involved before any advice on medication can be given. Neuroleptics are preferred in cases where the hearing of voices is accompanied by other psychiatric symptoms like disturbed thinking and clearly altered behaviour. In neuroses, on the other hand - that is, in the absence of obvious thought disorder or of disturbed reality-testing - sedatives are preferred as a complement to treatment. This classification of voice-hearing into the two categories of psychosis and neurosis is rather simplistic; in practice, as with most systems of classification, there is considerable overlap between the two.

It is important to realize that medication alone is often not enough to alleviate symptoms and allow the resumption of normal life: as a rule, it is only an aid to recovery. In co-operation with the prescribing doctor, a hallucinator may be able to find out what kind of medication is most helpful for relieving symptoms and so enabling other forms of treatment to be more successful.

11. SUMMARY

Marius Romme and Sandra Escher

In our introduction, we outlined the ends we hoped to achieve with this book. It seems appropriate, in this summary, to review the contributions made to each of these aims by the various kinds of information offered by our many contributors. The goals we set ourselves were:

1. To enable people who hear voices to relate their own experiences to those of others.
2. To show that the real problem is not so much the hearing of voices as the inability to cope with the experience.
3. To demonstrate the wide variety of experiences and their origins, and the different possible approaches to coping.
4. To provide therapists and families with information that will help both them and the voice-hearers themselves to cope more effectively with the voices.

1. Exchange of experiences

We asked a number of voice-hearers to describe their experiences. Their stories are presented in chapters 6 and 8.

The accounts appearing in chapter 6 have a great deal in common. These are the experiences of people who have never been psychiatric patients and who, in everyday life, function normally as housewives, teachers, therapists, and so on. These are people with socially active lives: all have succeeded in making contact with other people who were able to understand or recognize their experiences, and this has enabled them to avoid the dangers of isolation. They have managed to integrate the voices with the rest of their lives, and are more inclined to adopt a parapsychological or spiritual perspective.

Unfortunately, not everyone is lucky enough to have such positive experiences. Many voice-hearers have suffered great difficulties and sought psychiatric treatment, and their stories are told in chapter 8. These often paint a picture of extreme isolation over long periods of time. Those concerned have eventually managed to find their way out of this isolation, but only after being lucky enough to come across people who were willing and able to accept them and their voices; this has helped them gradually to take ownership of their perceptions. It is clear that this point had to be reached before they could properly develop their own identities with the help of work and personal relationships which allowed room for their voices. In this way, they found a stable pattern of living in which any downs were compensated for by the ups.

All of those who have learned to cope with their voices have discovered the importance of communicating with others about their experiences. Communication is a way of breaking through the barriers of isolation, and is essential to the process of integrating voices into everyday life. In chapter 5, we have seen graphic illustrations of the advantages to be gained from this, which might be summarized as follows:

- By talking or writing about the voices, you begin to recognize their games and tricks, and also their more positive sides. You learn to identify triggers and the situations in which the voices are more or less active or prominent.
- Fear can lead to avoidance, and avoidance to isolation and dependence. Communication diminishes anxiety and breaks these disruptive vicious circles.
- The exchange of views and information can yield both helpful and unhelpful advice. Generally speaking, the most positive guidance is offered by advice that increases the personal influence of the hearer: for example, self-medication or applying a structure to one's contact with the voices. Attitudes (such as a belief in possession) that tend to accentuate powerlessness are not likely to give good results.
- Talking about medication can be very useful, provided the discussion is based on balanced conclusions drawn from experience, and not exclusively on conviction or prejudice.
- Acceptance of the phenomenon of hearing voices is made considerably easier - for all concerned - by getting together with large numbers of those who are familiar with the experience (for example, at conferences, etc.). This can be very encouraging and normalizing, and often stimulates greater acceptance on the part of hearers and relatives alike. It can also be very rewarding to develop a close individual contact with a fellow voice-hearer; the equality of status can offer the experience of being able to help others, instead of remaining a victim.
- Sharing the experience of hearing voices makes it easier to embrace and integrate them.
- Communicating about one's voices means accepting oneself. As one hearer put it: 'You can't brush aside something that exists in yourself and manifests itself so intensely'.

2. The problem of coping

We have seen that the hearing of voices can be an extremely positive and rewarding experience. When we look back through history, we find many great men and women who heard voices and were usefully guided by them in their lives: Socrates, Moses, Jesus, Muhammad, Eckhart, Teresa von Avila, Joan of Arc, Bruno, Gichtel, Swedenborg, Fechner, Jung, etc. (See chapters 4 and 7) A little historical awareness may make the experience of hearing voices less strange, and perhaps more acceptable within society at large.

We have also found that there are people hearing voices today who are socially adequate and function effectively. (See chapters 2 and 6, and the studies by West, 1948; Posey and Losch, 1983; Slade and Bentall 1985; Tien, 1991; and Eaton, 1991.) These are people who have learned to cope with their voices, and have successfully integrated them in their lives - people who are neither saints nor psychotics, as Myrtle Heery puts it.

Our conviction that the voices themselves are not the real problem is reinforced by the results of a survey of 173 voice-hearers (chapter 2). Fifty eight of these people appeared to have succeeded in finding some way of adequately coping with their voices. The striking common feature was that all had managed to maintain a relationship with their voices in which both sides were on an equal footing. In contrast, those who were unable to cope with their voices tended to regard themselves as inferior to their voices. When we compare the two groups, it becomes apparent that the essence of learning to cope with voices lies in the development of the hearer's personality. If we say 'No' to the voices, we say 'No' to ourselves: to our own desires and emotions, to our past, to what has really happened - to everything that frightens us and makes us feel powerless. If we say 'Yes', we have to accept a lot of unpleasant realities both within and around us, but the process will enable us to continue to grow.

3. Varieties of origin

After listening to the experiences of people who hear voices and reading the many theories about the phenomenon, one is bound to conclude that there is a wide variety of different origins.

We have already mentioned the historical evidence showing that there have been many great women and men who were guided by the voices they heard. Among them are religious leaders, scientists, and politicians. We also know that there have been sailors who started to hear voices when they were alone at sea for long periods of time. Amnesty International reports that the victims of torture, too, often hear voices either during or after their ordeal. We know from the relevant literature and from some of the examples in this book (chapter 9) that all kinds of childhood or later trauma can give rise to voices. Some people have telepathic experiences involving voices, while others associate the phenomenon with mediumship or the presence of a guiding spirit (chapter 6). We know that voices may appear in childhood and persist into adult life. We know, too, that there are a great many patients in psychiatric care who hear voices.

In this summary, we will review the most significant differences between the various explanations for voice-hearing, both within and outside the field of psychiatry. Most striking of all is the difference between the view that voices may be teachers of an inner curriculum and the view that they are a symptom of illness.

In chapter 7, we read of Myrtle Heery's study of 30 people with inner voice experiences. This led her to divide the group into three main categories:

1. those whose voices were interpreted as fragmented parts of the self;
2. those who described their voice experiences as providing guidance through creative dialogue;
3. those who felt their voice experiences to be opening channels towards and beyond a higher self.

This categorization can be applied to the contributors who tell their stories in chapter 6. The seventh contributor, for example, may be considered as a representative of category 1, with the voices arising from a fragmented part of this young man. He describes the voices as searching for something meaningful; in all likelihood, he himself was searching for his own lifestyle, his own identity. The first and third contributors may be seen as examples of category 2, in which voices provide guidance, and the second and fourth as examples of category 3, where channels are opened towards a higher self. On the other hand, most of the contributors to chapter 8 exemplify the first category; those in this group are rather more likely to seek psychiatric help than those belonging to either of the others.

Heery relates these three categories not to psychopathology but to spiritual awakening. She refers to the work of Assagioli, who outlines three types of reaction to spiritual awakening that parallel Heery's own categorization of inner voice experiences. Assagioli observes that:

1. One possible outcome of a peak experience is that it fails to bring about a higher level of organization. In this case, the experience is often painful.

2. A second possibility is that the experience may provide an ideal to follow, a sense of direction that can be put into practice.

3. A third possible outcome is a higher integration of the personality, which permanently transforms the individual's life.

If we associate Heery's findings with Assagioli's ideas, Heery's second and third categories suggest an ongoing inner education, with the voice as teacher, while the first suggests that the voices reflect those things that are perceived as negative.

Frames of reference within psychiatry

The types of distinction drawn by both Heery and Assagioli are very different from those generally used in psychiatry, given the nature of the two approaches involved. In the former, the patient finds help as the result of a learning process, while in the latter, help tends to be given in the form of treatment with neuroleptics, especially when a diagnosis of schizophrenia is made in psychiatric care. This does not stimulate personal development.

In psychiatry, the distinctions made are between the types of disease assumed to be responsible for the hearing of voices. Here, the main categories are:

- schizophrenia (see chapter 9);
- dissociative disorder (chapters 5 and 9);
- manic-depressive psychosis;
- psychosis n.o.s. (not otherwise specified);
- psycho-organic disorder (drugs, epilepsy, etc.).

The consequence of this psychiatric categorization is that a person who hears voices will be treated with medication (see chapter 10), particularly in the case of schizophrenia or manic-depressive psychosis, while a dissociative disorder will be treated with psychotherapy (possibly in combination with medication). The voice-hearers describing their experiences in chapter 8 had all been diagnosed as having schizophrenia. However, there is also evidence of a relationship between early trauma and hearing voices (first and fifth contributors); where this exists, these people might equally be categorized as having a dissociative disorder.

We believe that the connection between hearing voices and the diagnosis of schizophrenia should be made with great care. The distinction between a dissociative disorder and schizophrenia, or the possibility of their co-existence, is often overlooked, and many mistakes have been made (see Kluft, and first and fifth contributors). Any diagnosis of schizophrenia should therefore always include measures to identify any dissociative phenomena. A second good reason for exercising this care is the possible combination of schizophrenic symptoms and the kind of peak experience described by Assagioli. Our knowledge of this territory is very limited; perhaps we might learn more if psychiatry, parapsychology and transpersonal psychology were to share their research efforts and results more freely.

Psychiatry does not always confine the phenomenon of hearing voices to the diagnosis of schizophrenia; there are a number of other frames of reference, as described in chapter 9. Each of these represents a different facet of interpretation which, in turn, is associated with a particular emphasis in its approach to therapy. Yet it is striking that patients themselves do not conform to these systematic divisions: all the different theoretical aspects may be seen in a single case.

Brian Davey illustrates this in his section on Psychosis in chapter 9, where he talks about interpreting background noises as voices talking about him. This idea might be considered to belong to the domain of cognitive psychology. Davey also says that when a child is ignored emotionally and abused by the greater power of adults, he or she will develop a sort of

numbed extreme emotional detachment, a sort of zombification. Psychiatrists call this 'poverty of affect' when this lack of feeling response is relived in later life.

These are some of the most common emotional states experienced in psychosis. In clinical psychiatry one would interpret hearing voices and 'poverty of affect' as symptoms of schizophrenia, without relating them to the life history of the person. The relationship which Davey suggests between life history and emotional reactions in later life is precisely the kind of concern emphasized by the psychodynamic frame of reference. Davey goes on to say that these emotional states are evoked by re-creation in later life, in situations which combine fear and a sense of helplessness. The perspective of social psychiatry concentrates on exactly these issues in seeking to describe the roles of relationships and threatening situations, both of which might be symbolized by the voices. When the emotions evoked are sufficiently intense, they trigger psychotic regression.

Frames of reference outside psychiatry

Most people who hear voices - even those who can cope well with their experiences - remain convinced that the voices come from outside themselves. For this reason, we have given due consideration to those frames of reference directly related to this conviction. These are described in chapter 7, whose contributors interpret the voices they hear as evidence of communication with energies outside our world of sensory perception.

Two of these authors describe their voice experiences from a metaphysical point of view, associating the voices with the spirits of the dead. Others adopt a spiritual perspective which regards the voices as having a mystical nature, or as being related to what spiritual psychotherapy calls a higher self, or as a link with our collective unconscious.

In this summary, we have brought together many different strands of thought in an effort to make sense of the phenomenon of hearing voices. Given the wide variety both of personal experiences and of explanatory theories, there are some pertinent questions we might ask ourselves when faced with voice-hearers seeking help and support:

- To what extent do the voices indicate a sensitivity to other people's emotions or to situations elsewhere (eg during the Gulf war)?
- To what extent do they relate to a stage of spiritual growth, demonstrated in terms of peak experiences?
- To what extent do they reflect a destabilized identity resulting from either trauma or incomplete development?
- To what extent do they reflect recent or past traumas?
- To what extent do they reflect current emotional problems?
- To what extent do they reflect unfavourable current relationships or living circumstances?
- To what extent do they reflect interference with energies of a metaphysical nature?
- To what extent do they reflect illness, physiological or psychological?

Before we can answer any of these questions, we must have a frame of reference. Perhaps the most significant difference between the models available within and outside psychiatry is this: within psychiatry, treatment begins from an assumption about the origin of the voices. Once this is established, one can attempt to interpret the voices. Outside psychiatry, on the other hand, treatment takes as its point of departure the subjective experience of the person who hears the voices. On this basis, one then proceeds to develop an explanation connected as closely as possible to that experience.

Removing barriers

Therapists are faced with certain important difficulties when seeking to help those who hear voices. There is a considerable distance to be bridged between the voice-hearer's subjective experience and the rationalizing approach of many forms of therapy. In the present context, it is perhaps only feasible for us to become aware of the barriers between the therapist's objective connotations and the patient's subjective experience. I believe the following need to be carefully considered:

Barrier 1: Differences in perception.
The fact that two people are discussing voices in a therapeutic context does not necessarily mean that there is equality of commitment on both sides. In extreme cases, the therapist may be inclined to view the voice-hearer's experiences as non-existent, or to consign them to the realm of fantasy. If this inclination is recognized, the voice-hearer may be afraid to talk about his or her experiences. In this kind of situation, all communication about the voices will come to an abrupt halt.

Barrier 2: Differences in concepts.
Therapists and voice-hearers have different, often mutually exclusive conceptual frameworks for understanding the meaning of voices. The therapist may simply choose a specific clinical diagnosis, while the voice-hearer may attribute them, for example, to the existence of demons. Given these divergent points of view, considerable communication is required for the therapist and the patient to understand each other. It is of little value to try to force a particular explanation upon someone; it should be recognized that other frames of reference may offer additional explanations (see chapter 9), and are in any case likely to be sought out by the patient regardless of the therapist's personal insistence. Any frame of reference serves to order thought, and tends to encourage the desire to seek out a wider variety of explanations. Instead of sticking doggedly to one particular framework which may so far have been ineffective, it may prove far more fruitful to consider a number of other possible explanations.

Barrier 3: Different ideas about treatment.
The therapist and the voice-hearer may have difficulty co-operating in the light of unilateral treatment that restricts itself to the prescription of neuroleptics. The voice-hearer may feel misunderstood or unacknowledged, given that few, if any, of his or her perceptions and experiences have been the subject of discussion. Another possibility is that the medication prescribed does not produce the desired results; there may, for example, be too many disturbing side-effects. Situations like this may arise when psychiatric interpretations are too specific or inflexible. Unfortunately, this can result in too little attention being paid to other important issues such as perception, coping behaviour, and social functioning.

Barrier 4: Unawareness of personal history.

If insufficient attention is paid to the voice-hearer's life history, and particularly to any traumas that may have been experienced, this may result in excessive emphasis on the phenomenon of hearing voices. There are two reasons for this:

– Psychiatric diagnoses are made largely on the basis of the phenomena present at the time of the assessment.
– Traumas from early childhood (before the age of six or seven) may have been completely erased from the memory, so that the individual is incapable of spontaneously recalling them. In this case, the therapist must carefully help with the process of recalling such events.

Given these factors, it is quite possible for a psychiatric diagnosis to be based exclusively on current symptoms, without taking into account any traumatic experiences which may be responsible for dissociative phenomena (see chapter 9).

Barrier 5: Unawareness of the relationship between voices and everyday life.

People who hear voices are not always aware of the close relationship between their attitude to the voices and the way they deal with people and problems in day-to-day life. Instead, hearing voices is experienced as an isolated phenomenon, and all energy is devoted to this particular struggle. It would, however, be more profitable to begin by learning to cope better with the people and problems encountered in everyday life, and then to see what the voices still have to say.

4. Provision of information

Our fourth aim was to provide therapists and families with information that would help everyone concerned in the process of learning to cope with the voices. The most important element in this process is improving and organizing the relationships between the voices, the voice-hearers, and the people with whom they are involved. There are, then, three kinds of relationship at issue:

– the relationship between the voice-hearer and the voices;
– in the case of several voices, the relationships among the voices themselves;
– the relationships between the voice-hearer and those with whom they have daily contact.

In this summary, we will review some important information that may be especially helpful in the improvement of these relationships. In particular, we will examine the association between three phases, as described in chapter 2, and coping strategies (chapters 6 and 8) and interventions (esp. chapter 10). These phases are:

- Phase 1: startling: the sudden onset of the voices, which is usually described as frightening, or at least strange, and which inspires confusion;
- Phase 2: organization: the process of communicating with and about the voices, and of structuring the contact with them, as well as trying out different coping strategies;
- Phase 3: stabilization: the period during which some kind of balance is found and consolidated, both with regard to the voices and to society. The voices are given a proper place in the person's life, and he or she can find an effective social role, as illustrated by the examples in chapter 8.

The startling phase

During the startling phase, therapy focuses primarily on anxiety management techniques (chapter 10), although medication can also be quite helpful in reducing the initial anxiety and confusion (chapter 10). However, it is important to note that any such therapy must be based on the full recognition and acceptance of the actual experience, even though one may question the extent of the voices' power. The next step is to seek possible ways of gaining some control over the voices. To this end, it is important for therapists and others to foster a sense of security (see examples 5 and 6 in chapter 8) by showing, among other things, emotional involvement (chapter 10), and by taking careful note of events and their timings. This is accomplished by such techniques as monitoring or focusing (chapters 10 and 5). Contact with other voice-hearers during this phase can provide valuable reassurance that one is not alone. In due course, one will try to bring some fundamental order to the daily routine, so that there is time both for the voices and for other things. In all of this, it is vital for the family to be kept fully informed (see chapters 7, 9 and 10), for they have an important role to play in offering support rather than criticism.

The organization phase

Once the initial anxiety and confusion have clearly been reduced, or even when they have only been temporarily suspended, it is possible to concentrate on organizing the voices and the relationship with them. During this phase, detailed attention is paid to such issues as: analysis of the possible significance of the voices, with regard to both the past and the present (chapter 9); exploration of the life history (chapter 9); the meaning of the voices in daily life (chapters 9 and 10); the influence of the family's attitude to the voices (chapter 9); any indications of parapsychological propensities or peak experiences (chapter 7); accompanying symptoms of dissociation or of emotional repression (chapter 9), and/or any symptoms suggesting a delayed development of the self (chapter 7) or a disturbed grasp of the boundaries between self and others (chapter 9).

A great deal of time will also be devoted to such matters as the particular circumstances under which the voices are heard, what they have to say, the physical qualities of the experience, the nature of any triggers and accompanying perceptions. All these questions are dealt with by applying the techniques of focusing (chapter 10).

The next step is to try to introduce a variety of perspectives on the phenomenon in order to rise above the rather limited point of view that tends to be imposed by therapists, voice-hearers and their families alike (chapters 7 and 9).

Finally, attention will be paid to the social position of the person hearing voices, his or her degree of dependence, the necessary social provisions, and the available opportunities to develop and present a full identity as someone who hears voices (chapter 10).

The stabilization phase

In this phase, the focus is primarily on expanding knowledge and developing the personality with various types of psychotherapeutic help. These may include Voice Dialogue, Pathwork, spiritual psychotherapy, and insight into coping with emotions. Important contributions are also likely to be made by social assistance in the realms of employment, education, and independent living. Once again, support from the family or partner is crucial to the process of helping the voice-hearer to develop a sense of control and secure a proper position in society (chapter 10).

Conclusion

By now, it will have become apparent to the reader that the case histories, theories and therapeutic techniques described in this book have been carefully and deliberately selected with specific goals in mind. Our selection of case histories was compiled partly for the express purpose of demonstrating that hearing voices is also experienced by people who have never found cause to seek psychiatric help (chapter 6). Our other main aim was to show that voice-hearers who have sought psychiatric help have succeeded in transcending the role of patient, and have gained their own social identity. Our selection of explanatory theories and perspectives was determined partly by the choices or preferences of voice-hearers themselves, and partly by the spectrum of variations in use within the field of psychiatry. We were also eager to show that resignation and fatalism are not the only available responses to hearing voices. Finally, all the therapeutic techniques discussed in this book have been tested by people who hear voices.

We would like to close with the words of Dr Verhoeff, Chief Inspector of Mental Health Care in the Netherlands. At the very first conference ever held for people who hear voices (Utrecht, 1987), Dr Verhoeff said:

Insight into adequate ways of coping with hallucinations can be an important instrument, both in treatment and in the responses of therapists.

12. CONTRIBUTORS

P. Baker, Development Worker, Alliance for Community Care, Manchester, UK

R. P. Bentall, BSc, PhD, M. Clin. Psychology, MA, FBPScS, Senior Lecturer, Department of Clinical Psychology, University of Liverpool, Liverpool, UK

H. J. H. M. van Binsbergen, psychic, Roermond, Netherlands

D. J. Bosga, MA, Parapsychology, Director, Parapsychological Institute, Utrecht, Netherlands

A. Brackx, Publishing Director, MIND (National Association for Mental Health), London, UK

G. M. de Bruijn, PhD Psychology, Amsterdam, Netherlands

M. Croon, member of The Path since 1978, Amsterdam, Netherlands

B. Davey, Development Worker, the Voluntary Factor Mental Health Development Project; Nottingham Advocacy Group Ltd., Nottingham, UK

P. Elias, Dutch to English translator of most of the Dutch contributions to 'Accepting Voices'

A. Escher, science journalist, Community Mental Health Care Centre and Department of Social Psychiatry, University of Limburg, Maastricht, Netherlands

I. J. M. Elfferich, MA Psychology, gerontologist, Rotterdam, Netherlands

B. J. Ensink, PhD Psychology, Psychological Institute, University of Amsterdam, Amsterdam, Netherlands

W. van der Graaf, Dutch to English translator of the section Carl Jung on Extrasensory Perception in 'Accepting Voices'

G. Haddock, BA, M. Clin. Psychology, Department of Clinical Psychology, University of Liverpool, UK

P. Hage, voice-hearer by experience, Goirle, Netherlands

Prof. O. van der Hart, PhD Psychology, Community Mental Health Centre, Amsterdam, and Department of Psychiatry, Free University of Amsterdam, Netherlands

M. W. Heery, PhD Psychology, private practice, Petaluma, California, USA

R. J. van Helsdingen, MD, PhD, Emeritus Psychiatrist, Hilversum, Netherlands

A. Honig, MD, PhD, MRC.Psych., consultant psychiatrist, Community Mental Health Centre, Maastricht, and Department of Social Psychiatry, University of Limburg, Maastricht, Netherlands

B. Hutchinson, technical editor of the English edition of 'Accepting Voices'

Prof. F. A. Jenner, MD, PhD, FRC.Psych., psychiatrist, Emeritus Head of the Department of Psychiatry, University of Sheffield, Sheffield, UK

J. A. Jenner, MD, PhD, psychiatrist, Senior Lecturer, University of Groningen, Head of the Psychiatric Outpatient Department, Academic Hospital, Groningen, Netherlands

Mrs J. Koolbergen, MA Psychology, Institute of Transpersonal Psychology, Amsterdam, Netherlands

J. van Laarhoven, MD, consultant psychiatrist, Elisabeth Hospital, Tilburg, Netherlands

A. van Marrelo, PhD Theology, Head of the Psychiatric Rehabilitation Service, Community Mental Health Centre, Maastricht, Netherlands

Mrs R. Malecki, voice-hearer by experience, and Chair of the self-help groups of the Resonance Foundation, Geleen, Netherlands

M. Pennings, MA Health Education, Department of Social Psychiatry, University of Limburg, and Community Health Care Centre, Maastricht

T. van der Stap, PhD Theology, Maastricht, Netherlands

Prof. N. Tarrier, PhD Psychology

Prof. M. A. J. Romme, MD, PhD, Professor of Social Psychiatry, Deartment of Social Psychiatry, University of Limburg, and Consultant Psychiatrist, Community Mental Health Centre, Maastricht, Netherlands

We would also like to thank all those voice-hearers not named here for their valuable contributions to chapters 6 and 8. We respect their wish to remain anonymous.

WM204 ROM X